Voyager Expanded Learning

PASSPORT READING
JOURNEYS™ III

STUDENT ANTHOLOGY

ISBN 978-1-4168-1612-6

Printed in the United States of America   09 10 11 12 13 14 WEB 9 8 7 6 5 4 3 2 1

Table of Contents

Expedition 1

Expedition 2

Expedition 3

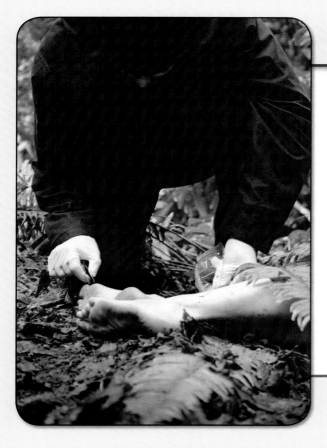

Expedition 4

Expedition 5

Expedition 6

Expedition 7

Expedition 8

Expedition 9

Expedition 10

Expedition 11

Expedition 12

Expedition 13

Expedition 14

Who Am I?

- What makes you who you are?
- Do genetics determine who you are, or do your surroundings?
- What about you is unchangeable?

You Are What *Your Genes* Make You— Or *Are* You?

Danny Melendez hoped to be taller than girls in his class. Janie Martin wanted straight, blond hair. Amir Makabi hoped he would not be bald at age 30 like his father had been. But, Danny, Janie, and Amir had genes that said otherwise.

We have tiny "blueprints" in our bodies' cells called chromosomes. Each chromosome has thousands of bits of protein called genes. These genes control how our bodies grow and develop. Half of our chromosomes come from

our mothers, and the other half from our fathers. They determine many aspects of our **physical** appearance, including the color of our eyes, whether our hair is straight or curly, how tall we will grow, and the color of our skin.

A branch of biology called genetics focuses on this process. Geneticists study how genes work. In addition to traits such as height, hair type, and eye color, genes influence other **attributes**, such as strength and intelligence. A person's

What makes people so different?

genes can even determine if he or she is particularly susceptible to, or likely to get, a disease.

Your **ethnic** heritage, much like your genes, can influence your looks. Each ethnic group has genetic features that influence hair, skin, and eye color. Many families are a blend of different ethnic groups, which may cause offspring to reflect the genetic traits of more than one group.

Genetic research tells us that genes play a role in your physical appearance and what diseases you may be more likely to develop, but things like intelligence, physical strength, and personality are more dependent on how you live and how you use the talents and strengths you have. Your genes can influence your abilities and talents, but your environment and opportunities can enhance your genetic traits. In other words, genetics matters far less than how people choose to live and use their basic talents.

You cannot change some attributes of your genetic makeup. Your height and skin tone are basically unchangeable. However, you can do a lot to affect other parts of your genetic inheritance. You can choose to make the most of the genes that have been passed down to you. With hard work and perseverance, you can continually try to develop your mind and body in ways you desire. **End**

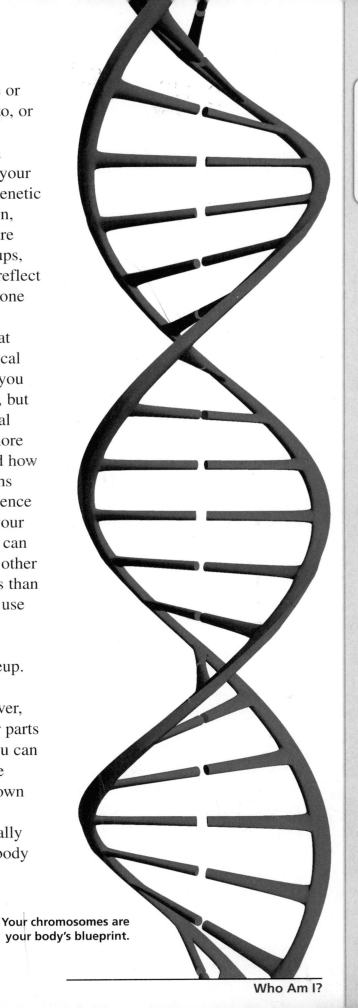

Your chromosomes are your body's blueprint.

ethnic (adj) *to do with a group of people sharing the same national origins, language, or culture*

Nature Versus Nurture—A Story of Genetics

Vocabulary

exact (adj) *perfectly correct*

". . . and thus, because blue eyes are a recessive trait, two blue-eyed people do not typically have a brown-eyed child," concluded Mr. Riazi. What? Surely, he got that wrong. That can't be true. My parents both have blue eyes, and I have brown eyes. I thought about my family. My parents have blue eyes, my two brothers have blue eyes, and my baby sister has blue eyes. I am the only one with brown eyes. I wondered how that happened.

The bell rang, and I stayed in my seat thinking. I looked at the textbook and read the part about weak recessive traits and strong dominant traits. As I read, I came across other things that made me wonder how my parents ever had me. They have straight hair, but I have curly hair. My skin is much darker than their skin. I couldn't move. I was paralyzed with fear. *What if my parents aren't really my parents?* I thought. *Is that possible?*

Mr. Riazi approached my desk. "Is genetics an **exact** science?" I asked. He responded by showing me pictures of people who look nothing like their parents. There were two African Americans, with a son who had white skin, red hair, light eyes, and freckles. There was a short couple whose children were all

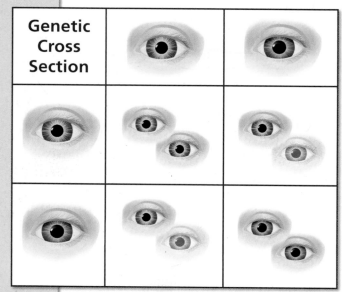

Genetic Cross Section		

short **except** one—who was more than 6 feet tall.

"Nothing in this world is exact," he said.

"I have been listening to your discussion on genetics, and I have read the information in the book. It makes me wonder if my parents are my real parents," I said. "I think it is **probable** that I am adopted."

"It's something you should ask them about. But, do you act like them?"

"Yes."

"Do you like the same things as they do?"

"Yes."

"Do you love them?"

"Yes."

"Then they are your parents—in every way that matters."

"Yes, but you mentioned that sometimes people are susceptible to diseases based on their genetic makeup. Don't I need to know where I came from?"

Mr. Riazi told me he thought it would be a good idea to talk to my parents about my concerns. He said that if I am adopted, it would be good to know my birth parents' health issues and what probabilities I have of contracting a disease.

After basketball practice, I went straight home. I was on a mission. My special task was to find out where I came from. Was I adopted? If so, why did my birth parents put me up for adoption? Why did my parents adopt me when they were able to have kids? Who am I? **End**

Daughter and mother

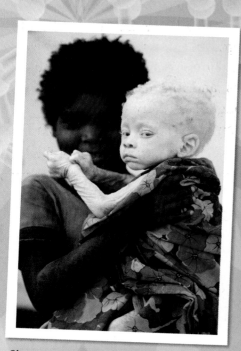

Sister and brother

Vocabulary

except (prep) *apart from; not included in the general rule*

probable (adj) *likely to happen or be true*

The Truth About Birth Order

President Barack Obama
Oldest Child

News Reporter Barbara Walters
Middle Child

Comedian Whoopi Goldberg
Youngest Child

Are you a bossy person who likes to be the leader, or are you always following others' commands? Do you try to keep the peace and make others happy? Or, are you the clown who makes others laugh hysterically? Your personality may be linked to birth order. Researchers have been looking for **patterns** in people of the same birth order to see how birth order influences personality.

Many observers think an only child gets used to being the center of attention. Only children may get spoiled and overprotected. They tend to lose their temper when they do not get their way. On the other hand, they may feel inept, or foolish, because they see adults do things more easily.

Oldest children with no older siblings as role models are likely to be more self-reliant, or able to do things without help from others. Because they frequently deal with younger siblings, they are natural leaders and often take positions of **authority** and responsibility. More than half of the U.S. presidents were oldest children, and many who weren't the oldest were first-born sons. Twenty-one of the first 25 American astronauts were oldest children. All of the original seven Project Mercury astronauts were first-born children. When blended families add siblings, that changes the birth order. For example, President Obama went from being an only child to an oldest child.

Youngest children are often creative rebels who resist authority. Parents sometimes call them "the babies" of the family—even when they grow up. They may feel like babies because their elders may not take them seriously. They often are described as wonderful storytellers and very persistent, or unwilling to give up. Many youngest children pursue creative careers, like comedy or acting. Eddie Murphy, Jim Carrey, and Whoopi Goldberg are youngest children.

Middle children have to deal with older *and* younger siblings and may feel stuck in the middle. Having been in the middle and often making peace between the siblings, they are likely to grow up to be excellent negotiators. They tend to be very tactful in their speaking, so they rarely offend or hurt people. These are very useful qualities in adult life. Some middle children who have become successful adults include Donald Trump and Barbara Walters.

Do any of these **profiles** sound familiar to you? Does your personality fit the pattern for your birth order? For some people, the personality types are very accurate. Still others have defied the research and become the opposite of what researchers expect them to be.

All theories are likely to have exceptions. Scientists may get it wrong. But, if you want to know whether you fit the profiles, the best way to find out is to ask someone who knows you well. Maybe you would make a great leader, artist, or negotiator, but just don't know it. **End**

Vocabulary

profiles (n) *brief accounts of people's lives*

The Company You Keep

Vocabulary

phase (n) *a stage in growth or development*

identity (n) *who you are*

mutual (adj) *shared or joint*

When Clarice Spellings was 12, her favorite activity was going to the mall. She and her friends would shop and talk about movies and music. Clarice's mall hobby lasted until one day in physical education class, when she had to race around the school track. Suddenly, Clarice discovered that she could run quickly, and she began doing something different in her spare time. She started a new **phase** in her life.

"I still do my schoolwork," says Clarice, now 16. "But now, I identify myself as an athlete. I'm on the track team. My specialty event is the 100-meter dash. Although we have meets only in the spring, running is a year-round activity for me. I'm always training and working out. I used to eat tons of junk food, but not anymore. These days, I eat right and get plenty of rest. I think I actually have a good chance of getting a college scholarship—maybe even a free ride. I see a few of my old friends occasionally, but we sort of speak different languages and care about different things now. My close friends are my athlete friends."

Clarice found an **identity** for herself through running, and she developed an exciting awareness of what she could achieve. Her current circle of friends has bonds, or connections, of **mutual** interest. They share a love of competition and self-improvement.

Jeff Castillo, 18, had serious discipline problems a few years ago and did not control his behavior in or out of school. Thinking

back, he shakes his head. "I am not proud of that phase of my life," he says. "My mom used to say my friends were a bad influence, but I think I was the bad influence. If I hadn't turned things around . . . , who knows what would have happened?"

Jeff had been a "tagger" who spray painted his personal signature on every available wall. One day, a woman caught him tagging the wall of her art gallery.

"Ilene told me I should be doing my stuff on canvas and framing it. She said I was an excellent artist and should be selling my work in her gallery," Jeff says. **1** "She dragged me inside and gave me old canvases and supplies to use. I was never good at studying, but I liked painting. I discovered there were other guys around who liked doing what I did. Just like that, I wasn't a vandal who destroyed people's property anymore. I had a different identity. I was an artist, spending time with other artists who had a mutual understanding and respect for one another's work."

Many people had regarded that part of Jeff's life as destructive. However, his new peers provided him with a different yardstick with which to measure himself.

There are times when all it takes for people to see themselves in a positive light is finding a group that has a similar perspective. That can make all the difference. **End**

1 Context Clues

Using context clues, what does the word *gallery* mean?

Genes:
Assets or Obstacles?

Sally is a scientist. Her mother was a scientist, and her mother's father was a scientist. Was Sally born to be a scientist? Or, did she **explore** other careers and choose this profession on her own? Are we genetically programmed to do certain things well?

Michael Phelps was born to be a swimmer. He is tall with long limbs and large hands and feet. The world record-holding swimmer is an example of having the **appropriate** genes to pursue his dreams. His physical attributes led him toward swimming. His drive and work ethic made him an Olympic gold medal winner. However, not everyone is so lucky.

Many people want to do things they are not genetically programmed to do. Can a 7-foot-tall man become a gymnast? Can a deaf man become a pianist? Can a shy woman become a stand-up comedian? Can a quadriplegic man become a painter? Can a woman of modest means overcome that limitation and become a millionaire? Can a small, nonthreatening man become a menacing defensive lineman for the NFL?

Thirteen-year-old Daniel Torres holding a football while posing in front of fellow uniformed football teammates at Thomas A. Edison Middle School

What if you are born without the appropriate attributes to achieve your goals? What if your body isn't designed to be a swimmer? Many aspects of your heritage are changeable—intelligence, personality, and even your physical makeup. You can make changes or alterations to the color of your hair or the color of your eyes. You may have **eliminated** your need for glasses with surgery or contacts. You can tan your skin, remove body hair, and straighten your teeth. There is much about you that isn't set in stone. But, some things, like your height, cannot be changed. They become either assets, faults, or exceptions.

Spud Webb, a former NBA player, is an example of overcoming not only his genes but also his circumstances. Webb grew up without many advantages. His family was poor, and opportunities for him were minimal. He loved basketball and practiced whenever he had a chance. His vibrant dream of playing in the NBA brightened his days. He thought basketball might be his way to eliminate poverty in his life and explore the world. But, poverty wasn't the only thing holding him back. There was one drastic problem—his height. Most NBA players of the time were more than 6 feet tall, but Webb was only 5 feet 5 inches tall. Webb knew this was a severe limitation, so he worked tirelessly on his skills. He became an offensive and defensive threat on the court. As a senior in high school, he averaged 26 points a

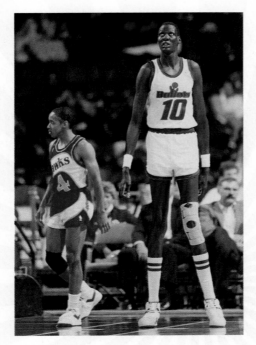

game, opening the door to college basketball. By working on his skills and jumping ability, this 5 foot 5 inch player was drafted into the NBA. **1**

Michael Phelps used his physical attributes as an asset. Spud Webb made his physical attributes an exception. Neither saw them as a fault or used them as an excuse. They both worked hard and were determined to achieve their goals. Some might say that Phelps had an advantage over Webb. It could be said that Phelps won the genetic lottery, but Webb did not. But, they both had the drive and will to succeed and realize their dreams.

So, what do you think? What are the most important things in determining your future: genes or the will to make things happen for you? What about the people around you? How much do your surroundings influence your future? What is your role in your future? **End**

Vocabulary

eliminated (v) *left out or got rid of*

1 Make Connections

Do you know someone who has worked hard to overcome a genetic trait and eventually accomplished his or her goal?

When Identical Twins
Grow Up Apart,
How Identical Are They?

Are identical twins really *identical*? At first glance, they do not seem to have any differences, at least not any visible differences. Because their physical traits often appear the same, when twins are **united**, most observers cannot tell them apart. But, what happens when identical twins are separated at birth? How different do you think they become?

Researchers have studied pairs of identical twins who were reunited after being separated since infancy. Often they were adopted as babies by families with different values and lifestyles. Still, even with different upbringings, they **manifest** many similar traits.

For example, a set of identical British twins had no connection for 40 years before being reunited. Both women had dyed their hair auburn, preferred cold coffee, and would push up their noses with their palms, a practice they each called

Ultrasound scan of twins at 4 months

"squidging." For their meeting, they chose to wear the same color of clothes. Each had two sons and a daughter. There was only a one-point difference in their IQs, and they both had the same health problems. The manifestation of these similarities was probably not a coincidence. They were most likely products of shared genes.

Other sets of identical twins follow the same pattern. When they first met as adults, a pair of male twins found they used the same type of shaving lotion, toothpaste, and hair product. They went back home after their time together and sent each other birthday presents. Each sent the other the exact same gift.

After long separations, many reunited pairs of twins demonstrate similar attitudes and mannerisms, or ways of doing things. Though they have not **interacted** as young children, they feel close ties. Two brothers had opened fitness clubs and cared a great deal about good physical health. A set of sisters had edited their high school newspapers and gone to film school. This kind of similarity, or parallel, happens in case after case.

However, there are always distinctions. One twin may be outgoing and social, while the other is quiet and shy. They may not share all the same likes and dislikes. This, of course, might be because of nurture, or how one is raised, rather than nature. Even after years apart, it seems likely, though, that identical twins will have many striking similarities to each other.

On the other hand, even when identical twins grow up interacting with each other, there are differences. Their personalities can be quite distinct. And, in case you were wondering, no, they do *not* have the same fingerprints. **1** In other words, no two people are ever exactly alike. **End**

1 Ask Questions

As you read, some things might be unclear. Ask yourself questions about the text to help you understand what you are reading. For example: How can identical twins have the same DNA, but not have the same fingerprints?

The Road Not Taken

By Robert Frost

Two roads **diverged** in a yellow wood,
And sorry I could not travel both
And be one traveler, long I stood
And looked down one as far as I could
To where it bent in the undergrowth;

Then took the other, as just as fair
And having **perhaps** the better claim,
Because it was grassy and wanted wear;
Though as for that, the passing there
Had worn them really about the same,

And both that morning equally lay
In leaves no step had trodden black.
Oh, I kept the first for another day!
Yet knowing how way leads on to way,
I doubted if I should ever come back.

I shall be telling this with a sigh
Somewhere ages and ages hence:
Two roads diverged in a wood, and I,
I took the one less traveled by,
And that has made all the difference.

Vocabulary

diverged (v)
branched out; split apart

perhaps (adv) *maybe or possibly*

R U Online?

- What are some benefits of the Internet?
- What are some of the problems with using the Internet as a way of communicating with people around the world?
- How has the Internet changed the way people interact with one another?

Friends or Foes?

Vocabulary

founders (n)
people who start or establish something

correspond (v) *write to someone*

risk (n) *the chance of losing, failing, or getting hurt; danger*

---

1 Context Clues
What does the word *virtual* mean? What clues help you discover the meaning?

---

2 Make Connections
How do you and your friends use networking sites?

Michelle recently joined a networking site. When she logged on, she found that a lot of her friends and classmates were already a part of this virtual community. They could use this seemingly real community to instantly catch up with one another during the weekend instead of waiting until Monday morning at school. **1** Through this online social network, people can "get together," communicate with others, share photographs, and meet new people. When Michelle got her hair cut one day after school, her friends didn't have to wait to see it at school the next day. They got to see it right away because she posted a photo of her new haircut as soon as she got home.

The **founders** of one online networking site that connects people from all over the world said they wanted to make it easy for friends to catch up and hang out with each other online. Michelle was able to do this and meet new people on the site. Soon, she had friends all across the country. She said she likes to meet new people and **correspond** with them online. **2**

However, Michelle found there was a downside to this new form of communication. A guest speaker came to her school to talk about the **risk** of online networking. As she listened to him, she never imagined she would soon learn firsthand that the dangers are very real.

Michelle
104 photos in album

173 Friends
113 in Network
Member since 09/06/07

Michelle

Here For	Friends
Gender	Female
Age	16
Location	Rochester
Interests	Dancing Skateboarding Shopping
High School	Carver High
Favorite Music	Lupe Fiasco Fall Out Boy
Favorite TV	Degrassi Heroes

Michelle's Friends

Caleb

Keeli

Sadie

Angel

What Can I Do Now?

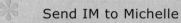

✳   Send IM to Michelle

✳   Add Michelle as a friend

✳   Invite Michelle to group

✳   Ignore Michelle

Vocabulary

expanding (adj)
*growing bigger
or wider*

enrich (v) *make
better by adding
something*

3 Make Connections

What safe practices do you follow while using networking sites?

Before the end of the week, Michelle learned that some of the new friends in her **expanding** social network were not who they said they were. Michelle began corresponding with a young woman her age who had the same favorite band and liked horror films. One day Michelle's new friend said she wanted to buy something online but didn't have a credit card. So, she asked Michelle for her credit card number and promised to mail her a check to pay her back. Fortunately, Michelle had heard about this Internet scam from the guest speaker and knew she couldn't trust her new "friend." Michelle spent a few days chatting with a young man who said he was her age and loved the same music she did. A few days later, she tried to find him in an online yearbook search and learned he was much older. He wasn't a student at all; he was an adult with his own house and business. She told her parents in case they needed to alert the police and make them aware of the older man.

"I was lucky to figure this out before we became any closer," Michelle recalled. "There are a lot of creepy people out there. There is a risk they can turn into stalkers, or worse."

Michelle realized there were rewarding aspects, or features, of virtual communities. However, she learned to keep herself safe from people who might be lying about who they are. She also learned she should never give out personal information or take the risk of meeting her new friends in person. However, if she ever did decide to meet an online friend in person, she should tell her parents, bring along several trusted friends, and meet in a public place. **3**

"Online networking is cool. It can really **enrich** your relationships and expand your circle of friends," she said. "You need to be really careful though. Enriching your life isn't as important as your personal safety." **End**

DotComGuy:
A Life Alone on the Internet

His name was Mitch Maddox, but he legally changed his name to DotComGuy. He decided not to leave his house for a full year. To begin his experiment, he moved into an empty house in Dallas, Texas. He brought nothing with him. UPS delivered his computer less than an hour after he walked into the empty house.

Why did he **terminate** his face-to-face interactions with the outside world? What was his **motive**? It was the year 2000, and Mitch was a 26-year-old systems manager. He wanted to **impose** this confinement upon himself to prove something. He would prove that he could **manage** with only a computer to access the outside world. He said he was motivated to show the world how all-embracing electronic **commerce**, or e-commerce, had become.

In January 2000, DotComGuy began his project by setting up his home with his laptop. For an entire year, he imposed the following rule upon himself: He would use only his computer to get everything he needed. He ordered absolutely everything he needed online. He purchased furniture and dishes for his home, books to read, and even all his groceries online. **1** He communicated with people who

Vocabulary

terminate (v) *bring to an end; stop*

motive (n) *reason that makes a person do something*

impose (v) *set as something that has to be paid, obeyed, or fulfilled*

manage (v) *succeed in getting something done*

commerce (n) *the buying and selling of goods; trade*

1 Visualize

Imagine your house without anything in it. What would you need to buy online so you could live in it for one year?

DotComGuy used his computer and Webcams to communicate with the outside world.

wrote to him on his Web site. People everywhere could watch him on their computers because he installed cameras all over his house. He turned them off only when he went to sleep or to the bathroom. Friends and family would stop by, and he gave interviews for the media. He even had a personal trainer who visited regularly, but DotComGuy never left his house.

Why did he choose to impose these restrictions on himself? DotComGuy said he did it "to show people the extreme possibilities of the Internet." He said he also wanted people "to go watch my experiences, learn from them, and also discuss e-commerce." **2**

After the year ended, he returned to the outside world, not much the worse for wear. He posted a farewell message on his Web site that read, "It's been a great year everyone. Now it is time for DotComGuy to re-enter society." When he reflected back on the year, he admitted he'd been bored now and then. But, he claimed he never felt desperate or unhappy or trapped. On the other hand, after he terminated his project, he returned to his old life, took his original name back, and has not repeated the experiment.

As Mitch proved, you certainly can manage to live without going to the store. E-commerce has made that possible. But, is it a good idea? The Internet allows people to make new friends around the world and keep in touch with distant family members. However, for many users,

2 Make Connections

If you performed DotComGuy's experiment, what would you miss the most?

DotComGuy even installed cameras in his bathroom.

DotComGuy ordered everything for living in his home on the computer and had it delivered to his house.

it may be replacing important day-to-day human interactions.

Today, computers are an important part of everyday life. Many people spend time each day in front of their monitors. They e-mail, shop, play games, listen to music, and chat with friends. But, they do it alone. Instead of face-to-face contact, people are isolating themselves from the world by spending their time with their computers. **3** Terminating face-to-face contact with others may become a huge problem.

Mental health professionals and observers have noted this growing trend with alarm. Computer addicts distance themselves from their families, their friends, and the world at large. Because computer addicts all behave in similar ways, some

3 Context Clues
What clues in this sentence help you determine the meaning of *isolating*?

psychologists think that computer addiction should be a recognized syndrome, and many studies have been written about it. Computer addicts are less and less motivated to spend time with family and friends. Their computers become their most important companions.

Computer addiction can be a **vicious** cycle; the less contact computer addicts have with flesh-and-blood human beings, the more difficult such contact becomes for them. Their social skills weaken, and any fears they have concerning the outside world get bigger and less manageable. Experts claim that excessive Internet use can lead to depression, isolation, and failure at work or school.

The key to solving this growing problem is finding the right balance and learning how to manage your time. However, there are a growing number of computer addicts that represent the dark side of the constantly changing computer world. Many feel this dark side merits serious examination and is worthy of concern. Human beings are by nature social animals. Just because it's possible to exist without regular human contact does not mean it's a good idea. **4 End**

4 Ask Questions

After reading this passage, what questions would you like to ask DotComGuy?

Web Designer

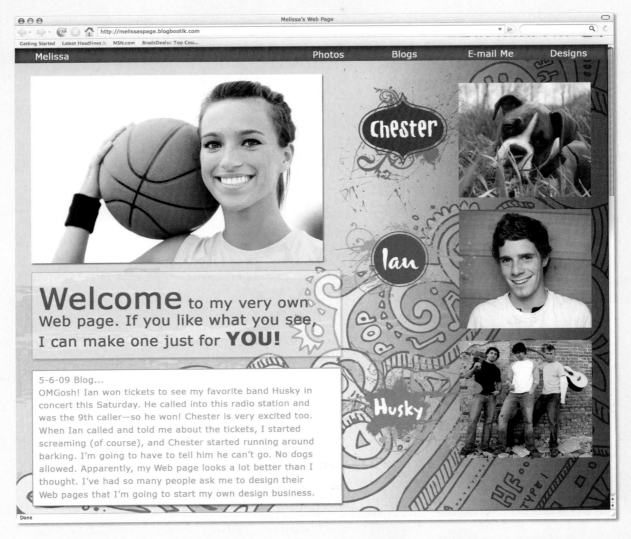

Everyone at school is talking about Melissa Tait's Web page. She has great photos, music, and links—but everyone has those. Her page really stands out because of the design. She put together a mixture of colors, fonts, photos, and boxes to create an amazing look. Now many of her friends are asking for help. They want their pages to look as enticing too.

After designing a few more pages, Melissa began to think. She enjoyed doing the design, and she often had original page design ideas that worked well. Melissa decided to see whether she could turn this hobby into a career. She began to research the possibility of becoming a Web designer.

Web designers are responsible for a wide range of tasks. They create and arrange a Web site. They are usually responsible for the layout of the pages. Web designers have to be able to combine fonts, type size, color, images, and sometimes even sound to create their final product. Sometimes Web designers write computer programs to make the Web page more interesting. They also work to make sure the Web site functions properly. Finally, they are responsible for making sure the pages work on a variety of browsers.

Melissa learned that most designers have college degrees in computer science, art, or marketing. However, others are self-taught. Some people start off like Melissa, playing around at home with a personal Web page, and find they have a passion for this type of work. Many designers then explore their skills further by doing volunteer work for nonprofit organizations. With some hands-on experience, they are then able to turn their talent into a well-paid career. Estimated average salaries for Web designers in 2008 ranged from $40,000 to $80,000 a year.

However, Web designers need to have much more than a good design eye. They need to have a flexible personality to be able to work with many different kinds of clients. They also need to be able to take constructive criticism in stride and not allow their feelings to be hurt. During a project, they frequently receive client requests for changes and alterations. These requests need to be accepted and implemented quickly. Another key element to becoming a successful designer is the ability to meet deadlines and work well under pressure. Finally, most Web designers learn to write computer programs.

There is a need for Web designers in most every industry. Since almost all businesses have a Web site, they all use designers. This allows designers to pursue many different passions. For example, a Web designer who loves cars may be able to combine the best of both worlds and design Web pages for a car company.

Today, Web design is a growing field. There are many opportunities for growth and advancement. Employment for talented designers is expected to grow at a steady rate for the next 10 years. As demand continues to grow, more jobs will be created. Almost every business Web site needs to be constantly updated. These changes keep information current and make sure people return to visit the site.

Melissa thinks this may be the perfect job. She now dreams of heading off to work each morning to design Web pages. Melissa is sure she would enjoy this career path.

"It would be a great way to earn a paycheck," she said. "I would love to see my ideas come to life online and to work with other designers to create Web pages. Maybe I could even influence other Web designers!"

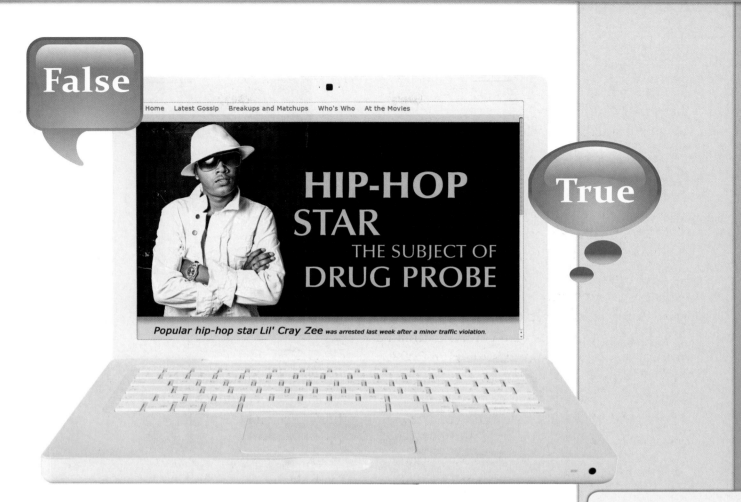

Popular hip-hop star **Lil' Cray Zee** was arrested last week after a minor traffic violation.

Truth, Lies, and the Internet

Vocabulary

spectrum (n) *a continuous sequence or range*

Michael recently heard some kids talking during class about the arrest of one of his favorite musicians. Michael logged onto his computer to find out what had happened. A quick online search supplied him with the following results:

1. Hip-Hop Star the Subject of Drug Probe
2. Self-Indulgent Lifestyle Finally Catches Up to Hip-Hop Star
3. Scandal Sheets Smear Hip-Hop Star with Lies!

Michael was confused by the headlines. How could there be so many interpretations of the same event? How could he figure out which stories to trust? **1**

Thanks to the Internet, there is a broad **spectrum** of information at your fingertips. But, what you read is not always true. Anyone can write and publish a blog or a Web page.

1 Context Clues
What does the word *interpretations* mean? Which clues from the text helped you determine the meaning?

Vocabulary

viewpoint (n) *a way of thinking about something; attitude; point of view*

influence (v) *have power over something or someone*

emphasize (v) *give special attention to; put stress upon*

react (v) *act in response to something*

opinionated (adj) *sticking to one's thoughts, feelings, or beliefs in an excessive way*

2 Ask Questions

A good question you might ask right now is: "How can you know if the information is correct or true?" Keep reading to see if this question is answered.

Because of this, facts may get twisted to tell a certain story. Many news organizations report the news fairly and accurately. However, sources like blogs report the news as their writers see it and not necessarily as it happened.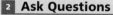

A newspaper cites sources to show where the information came from, but a blog frequently reflects a subjective **viewpoint**. Being subjective means that you base your opinion on your own feelings and thoughts rather than facts. A writer's feelings can **influence** which facts he or she chooses to **emphasize**. Feelings also influence which facts the writer decides to omit or downplay in the article.

So, how can you get a sense of the spectrum of viewpoints that lie behind the news you read before you **react** to it? Probably the best way to begin is to identify the viewpoint of the writer or the Web site. Most people who publish information want to influence readers to adopt their viewpoint. As a result, they will often pick and choose facts and data to make their case.

For example, try a search of Dr. Martin Luther King, Jr. It will bring up more than nine million results. The results reflect a wide spectrum of information. There are many sites with accurate, historical information, but there are also quite a few articles written by **opinionated** authors. Some of these

SCANDAL SHEETS SMEAR HIP-HOP STAR WITH LIES!

sites admire King's work for equal rights. These sites emphasize his nonviolent, positive leadership that helped change people's lives for the better. Others choose to show King in a negative light. They emphasize his relationships with communists, people who hold political ideas that the government should control all social and economic activities of a country. They even accuse him of plagiarism. Plagiarism is copying someone's written work and saying that you wrote it yourself.

Another popular example of sometimes unreliable information is Wikipedia. The online encyclopedia has become a popular reference source. This site is often a great place to start a research project. However, it may supply information that is not accurate. Wikipedia articles can be written by anyone, even you. Other readers can edit your article and add to the collection online. Wikipedia does post a warning at the top of some pages to alert readers that an article may be missing citations, making it hard to determine where the facts were obtained. **3** However, Wikipedia authors don't need to have any qualifications to write or post an article. Some people or groups use this site to emphasize their own

3 Context Clues

What are *citations*? Which words in the sentences help you determine the meaning?

Others, like those that end in .com or .net, are often commercial and are not restricted. Therefore, the information may or may not be accurate. Finally, .org Web sites are linked to a specific organization, which may be lobbying for a certain goal. Knowing the position of the writer before reading the article may help you decide whether the reporting is opinionated or factual.

Armed with all of this information, Michael looked back through his search results. He read each headline again. He guessed that the first story was probably the most objective. The second appeared to be a story written by someone who has a poor opinion of the celebrity. The third headline seemed to be written by someone who is a fan of this star. Michael decided to read all three because he is a big fan. Because he knew that some of the search results were biased, he was able to filter the information as he read and then react to the story. **4** **End**

opinions and influence readers.

Before you react to the information as the truth, you might want to check another source. Find another article on the same topic that is based on factual information. The facts may offer a different viewpoint.

Another clue to the position of the writer may be in the Web address of the site. Web sites that end in .edu are used by educational institutions, like colleges and universities. Those that end in .gov are maintained by the U.S. government. Both of these sources are generally reliable.

4 **Ask Questions**
Think about what you read. Ask yourself if you could describe to a friend how to recognize whether something is fact or opinion.

Online Shopping
Versus Brick-and-Mortar Stores

For a long time, people have bought items without going to the store. Mail-order catalogs like Sears Roebuck have been around for more than 100 years. Catalog shopping is still common today. However, the rise in popularity of the personal computer has changed the shopping world. Today, more and more people are doing their shopping online. But, has Internet shopping improved the experience for shoppers? How has this affected the business done in so-called "brick-and-mortar" stores?

Benefits of Online Shopping

Today, many people love to shop with online retailers, or sellers. One of the main benefits is convenience. Shoppers can "visit" many different stores quickly. This allows them to compare styles and brands instantly. Online shoppers can also quickly **determine** which stores have the best prices. An Internet **merchant** is often able to offer better prices than traditional stores. Internet merchants can **avoid** some of the costs of traditional stores, like paying a sales staff. Online operations like Amazon.com carry a wide **selection** of products. They also offer price and shipping discounts. As a result, a **majority** of shoppers often find them to be convenient one-stop shops. Shopping at home is also appealing to some. It is great for people who like to avoid crowded parking lots and stores, especially during the holiday season. Online stores never close. People can log on, shop, and place their **order**

Sears, Roebuck and Co.
SATISFACTION GUARANTEED OR YOUR MONEY BACK
Spring and Summer 1942
PHILADELPHIA

Some people prefer the quiet solitude of shopping online to the chaos of shopping at a store.

anytime they like. Additionally, the rising price of gasoline can also entice people to shop at home. This allows them to save money on fuel. Others report online shopping is ideal when buying gifts that need to be shipped. By ordering online, gifts are purchased and mailed in one step. This saves the buyer a trip to the post office.

These benefits have lured some shoppers away from traditional stores. Unfortunately, the volume of business done by online sites has happened at the expense of brick-and-mortar stores. That is, it takes away from their business. **1**

Traditional Shopping Has Benefits

Not everyone is ready to make the switch to online merchants. A

1 Ask Questions

Review what you read by asking yourself, "What are the benefits mentioned of online shopping?"

majority of people prefer shopping in traditional brick-and-mortar stores. Shoppers like to touch and try on some types of products, like clothing and shoes. That is how they determine which ones they like. Shopping online for these types of items can be difficult. There may be no guarantee, or promise, the product will look like the image on the screen. Some people report that returning or exchanging items purchased online is a lot of trouble.

Another downside to online shopping is inaccurate information. Many Web sites offer a wide selection of items. However, some sites don't include enough information about a product. Without clear pictures, a size chart, or accurate measurements, shoppers are often frustrated. Other Web sites are slow to update their sites to reflect product availability or shipping times.

Many people simply prefer the experience of

shopping in a traditional store. Some view a shopping trip as a social event. It is a great way to catch up with family and friends. For others, online shopping can feel like work. They spend all day at work and do not want to shop in front of their computers. For some products, like books, many shoppers like to browse and read different parts of a book before they purchase the item. Therefore, they prefer the in-store experience. **2**

Best of Both Worlds

As their popularity grows, online retailers are taking business away from brick-and-mortar stores. In order to keep up, many traditional merchants are creating and updating their Web sites. Studies have

Increased online shopping could take away business from brick-and-mortar stores.

2 **Ask Questions**
Review what you read by asking yourself, "What are the benefits mentioned of traditional shopping?"

Online stores ship orders from large warehouses like this one.

3 **Context Clues**

What does the word *coexist* mean? Use what you know about the root word *exist* and context clues to determine the meaning.

shown that many people use their computer to do research. For major purchases, like a car, they look online. They determine what they want online. Finally, they make the purchase at a traditional store.

Additionally, many brick-and-mortar stores are working harder to improve their stores. They are improving lighting, store layouts, and customer service. Some stores are working to provide online shopping along with their brick-and-mortar stores. They are carrying a limited assortment of products in their stores and offering a wider selection online. Others are offering in-store pickup for orders placed online. Larger stores and chains have developed their own e-shopping sites to combat the exclusively online operations.

Both online and traditional stores continue to refine their operations. They are always trying to find new ways to lure shoppers.

It's unlikely that the rise of e-shopping will mean the end of the brick-and-mortar store. The two forms of commerce will find ways to coexist. **3** Perhaps they will even boost each other's business. **End**

MALIBU BMX

> accessories
> apparel
> boots
> goggles
> helmets
> protective gear

8479 Pacific Hwy
Malibu

10 to 6 m,t,w,th | 12 to 9 f,s

check us out online
malibubmx.com

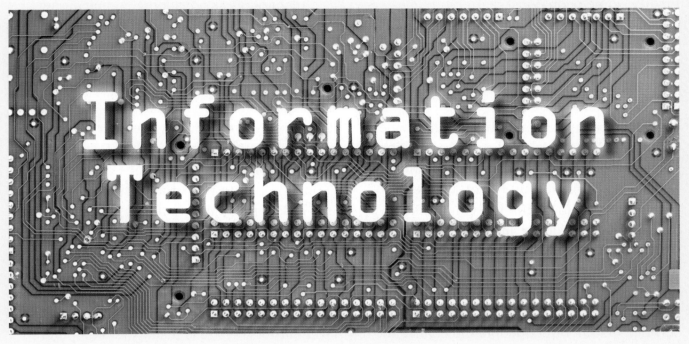

Information Technology

Webmaster. Graphic designer. Writer. Systems manager. Technical support specialist. Advertising agent. Product manager. Each of these job titles represents a career available to those wishing to work in the Information Technology (IT) field.

Information Technology is defined as the development, installation, and implementation of computer systems, hardware, and software. In other words, it includes any job related to computers. A majority of businesses depend on computers to manage their staff, communicate internally, and compute their payroll. They also rely on technology to keep in touch with their clients and the rest of the outside world. As a result, IT professionals are often responsible for keeping their companies running.

You may think you want no part of this field, that only computer geeks could be happy in an IT job. But, you probably use and enjoy more benefits of IT than you realize. From sending e-mail and text messages to playing video games, technology touches our lives in many ways. There is a wide selection of jobs to consider. Some people are involved with building the hardware. Others develop the programs that make businesses operate properly. Some IT career options involve designing Web sites, setting up computer networks, or managing software systems, to name just a few. Information Technology is an all-encompassing field.

There are many different ways in which to enter this field. Many people attend college and pursue degrees in computer science or computer engineering. Others decide to get

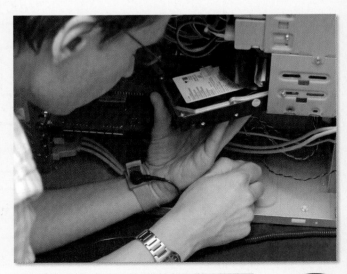

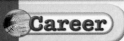
vocational training at a technical college. Finally, some people just learn by doing. Others start by creating their own Web site or by developing a program for others to use. Or, some people begin with an entry-level position and work to gain knowledge and experience on the job.

One attractive element of IT is the wide variety of jobs available. There are positions at all levels, from data entry positions to the chief information officer of a large corporation. If you think you might like to explore an IT career, an entry-level job or internship may be the best way to get a taste of the industry. By working alongside professionals, you can easily learn the day-to-day details of life in the IT world. It is no surprise that IT offers people the chance to work in almost any industry, from accounting to television production. Everyone needs computers and wants them running efficiently.

Technology is advancing and changing. With the rise in popularity of the Internet, more and more jobs are being created. As a result, IT jobs are also thriving. There is a strong demand for qualified IT people. Many IT positions are expected to grow at a faster-than-average pace during the next 10 years. There are good benefits in the IT world. Salaries for these types of jobs can range from $35,000 to more than $100,000 a year.

Today, more and more people turn to Digg, YouTube, and Google to get their news and entertainment. The Internet has been a strong influence on businesses. As a result, the IT industry continues to grow. People with a passion for computers can become Webmasters, systems managers, computer programmers, or any number of other occupations in the IT field.

Sounds of Life

- How has music guided people in the past?

- Where does the music you listen to come from?

- What impact has music had on America's history?

- What is the future of music?

MUSIC WITH A MESSAGE

"Who shot me?
But you punks didn't finish
Now you're 'bout to feel the wrath of a menace . . ."

The lyrics are from the song "Hit 'Em Up" by Tupac Shakur, a West Coast rapper who was shot to death in 1996. The song speaks clearly to his rivals on the East Coast. In the 1990s, a feud, or quarrel, began between East Coast and West Coast rappers. East Coast rapper Tim Dog released a single insulting West Coast rap artists. His song was soon answered. The reply came in the song lyrics of rappers on the West Coast. The feud escalated. During the next few years, as the quarrel grew stronger, rap lyrics were filled with messages and warnings to the rival artists on the opposite coast. Deaths were even associated with the feud.

Messages have always been embedded within musical lyrics. 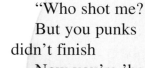 In the 1800s, slaves used songs like "The Drinking Gourd" to reveal hidden messages and **express** their emotions. Rap music is one genre, or style of music, that also frequently contains messages. Rappers have used their music to communicate with one another. They also have used their lyrics to **protest** government injustices and motivate the public to react to current events.

The hip-hop group the Beastie Boys released their single "In a World Gone Mad" in 2003. The song, which protested the Iraq War, expressed the group's **disapproval** of current **politics** in the United States. In the chorus, they sang about how violence and hate prevent people from thinking properly.

Rapper Jadakiss also used his songs to **convey** his political opinions. He **captured** his disdain for President George W. Bush in his single "Why?" In the song, he blamed the president for failing to prevent the destruction of the Twin Towers in New York City on September 11, 2001. Perhaps he hoped his song would encourage others to voice their own disapproval of the president.

Hurricane Katrina devastated the Gulf Coast in 2005. After the storm, many musical artists expressed their feelings in their songs. Many were angered by the government's slow response to those who needed assistance. They used their music to convey this message to the public and to political officials. In his single "Mother Nature,"

rapper Papoose captures some of the frustration. In the song, he highlights the horrible conditions of life in New Orleans. He asks, "How can I rap about my life and claim honor? When people out in New Orleans don't have water." Many other artists used their songs to draw attention to the problems as well as raise money to help those in need after the storm.

In addition to entertaining their fans, many musicians use their work to express their opinions about current politics and to motivate their listeners to take action. Just as slaves communicated with song, Americans today use music to capture their feelings and speak to one another. **2**

2 Make Connections
Can you think of other songs that have a message? What do the songs ask you to do or to think about?

Follow the Drinking Gourd

When the sun comes back,
and the first quail calls,
Follow the drinking gourd.
The old man is a-waiting for to carry you to freedom
If you follow the drinking gourd.

Follow the drinking gourd,
Follow the drinking gourd.
For the old man is a-waiting for to carry you to freedom
If you follow the drinking gourd.

The riverbank will make a mighty good road,
The dead trees show you the way.
Left foot, peg foot, traveling on,
Follow the drinking gourd. **3**

Follow the drinking gourd,
Follow the drinking gourd.
For the old man is a-waiting for to carry you to freedom
If you follow the drinking gourd.

The river ends between two hills,
Follow the drinking gourd.
There's another river on the other side,
Follow the drinking gourd.

Follow the drinking gourd,
Follow the drinking gourd.
For the old man is a-waiting for to carry you to freedom
If you follow the drinking gourd.

Where the great big river meets the little river
Follow the drinking gourd.
The old man is a-waiting for to carry you to freedom
If you follow the drinking gourd. **End**

3 Visualize
Picture the scene in your mind. What do you see on the ground and in the sky?

Evolution of Music

**Singer and actor
Elvis Presley**

Vocabulary

indeed (adv) *certainly*

On his way home last night, Juan heard a great new rap song on the radio. **1** This morning, he turned on his computer and downloaded the song so he could listen to it on the way to school. At breakfast, he told his mother about the new tune. "Times have changed **indeed**!" she remarked. Juan wasn't quite sure what she meant. With a research paper due soon, he decided to find out by exploring some of the history of American music. He had no idea homework could be so interesting.

Juan soon learned that Elvis Presley recorded "A Little Less Conversation" for a 1968 movie. But, in 2002, the song was remixed and became a number one hit in 20 countries. The remix of this popular Elvis tune was also used in

1 Make Connections
Listening to the radio is a way to hear new music. How do you find new music?

universal (adj) *found everywhere; shared by everyone and everything*

prominent (adj) *important or famous*

population (n) *all the people living in a certain place*

diverse (adj) *varied or assorted*

roots (n) *the source, origin, or cause of something; where it came from*

Little Richard rocks and rolls on his piano.

movies, advertisements, television shows, and presidential campaigns. It was even the theme song of the 2007 NBA All-Star Game. Juan began to see how **universal** rock 'n' roll is and wanted to learn more. This is what he found out.

The Birth of Rock 'n' Roll

Rock 'n' roll began in the United States in the 1950s. Since then, American music has never been the same. Rock 'n' roll grew from the blending of rhythm and blues with country and western music. Loud instruments and heavily stressed, or emphasized, beats defined the music and gave it universal appeal. The sounds of rock 'n' roll quickly swept the nation. Two **prominent** artists in the early years of rock 'n' roll were Little Richard and Elvis Presley.

The first weekly *Billboard* chart was released in 1955. This chart is based on the sales of songs and albums. *Billboard* magazine creates the chart to estimate, or make a

rough guess of, the popularity of an artist or group and assign a position from 1 to 100. Soon, the American **population** watched these charts to see where their favorite songs ranked. Today, there are about 20 different charts. Some categories include jazz, dance, hip-hop, and Top 40.

The Music of the 1960s and 1970s

American music represents the country's **diverse** population. Regional music continued to develop distinct sounds. Many of its genres reflected the ethnicity of the artists. The music also reflected American culture and lifestyle. Motown emerged in Detroit in 1959. This style of music has its **roots** in gospel music. This distinct style of singing was combined with rhythm and blues instrumentation. Motown was also one of the first genres of pop music that featured female groups.

By 1977, disco was the new

craze. Enthusiastic Americans were dancing to songs such as "Stayin' Alive" and "The Hustle." **2** While people danced under disco strobe lights, another new sound was emerging. The hip-hop sound was developed by DJs in New York City. It quickly became popular with African American and Hispanic listeners. Rap, with its strong rhythmic beats and spoken lyrics, also became a prominent sound in the music world. Indeed, these two genres quickly developed a large following.

More Changes in the Music World

In the early 1980s, music videos made their way into American homes with the introduction of MTV. Soon, videos became almost as important as lyrics and music in determining the popularity of a song. **3**

Popular music in the 1990s came

2 **Context Clues**
What clues from the second sentence help you understand the meaning of *craze*?

3 **Make Connections**
Do you watch music videos? Do they affect your attitude toward songs?

Actor John Travolta dances with Karen Lynn Gorney in a disco scene from the 1977 movie *Saturday Night Fever* directed by John Badham.

The Rock and Roll Hall of Fame and Museum in Cleveland, Ohio, is the preeminent home for the celebration and study of rock 'n' roll music.

from a variety of different types of musicians. In the 90s, grunge entered the popular music scene. With its roots in 1970s hard rock, grunge put Seattle's music scene on the map. Alternative punk, metal/hardcore, and techno music also became popular during this decade.

In 1995, the Rock and Roll Hall of Fame and Museum opened in Cleveland, Ohio. The museum features a huge collection of artifacts from prominent musicians of the past. The exhibits showcase the roots of rock and new sounds on the music charts.

Today, music from all eras of history is available. Many popular clubs feature music from only one decade, such as the 1970s. Others play a single genre, such as hip-hop. The next popular sound is just around the corner, as garage bands and vocalists work out their latest arrangements. Many people turn to the Internet to explore new sounds, and they download their favorite music. **4**

As Juan finished his research, he thought about his mother's comment. The popularity of different types of music has come and gone over the years, but one thing remains the same: The American population loves to listen and dance to music. Music has a universal appeal. While it helps some people express their individuality, it unites others. It entertains and inspires. Above all, it does indeed reflect the diversity of the American people. **End**

4 **Main Idea**

What is the stated main idea in this paragraph? What details support it?

DISC JOCKEY

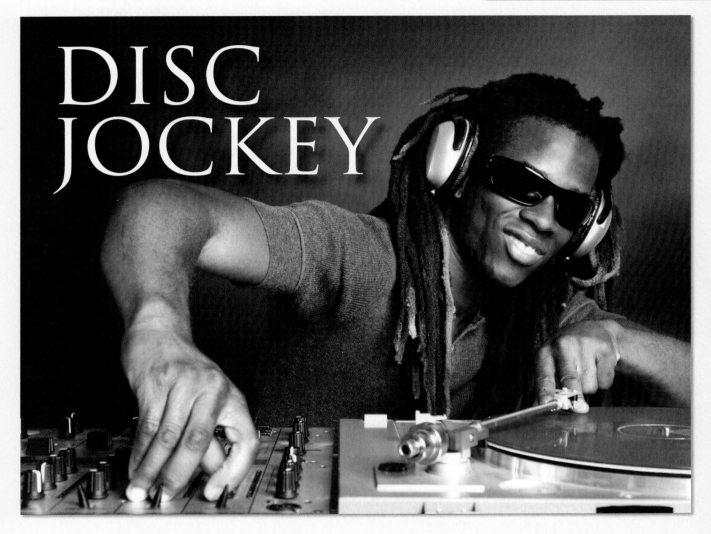

Rusty has invitations to every party at school. Everyone knows that without him choosing the music, the party won't be nearly as fun. When he isn't getting his friends out on the dance floor, he spends a lot of time organizing his music on his computer. Sometimes, he evens mixes his own music. He dreams of one day being paid to do this.

Well, he might not be dreaming at all. With a little luck and some work, he just might be able to support himself by doing what he loves. A DJ, or disc jockey, is someone who plays musical recordings. He or she can work in a variety of different places, from parties to wedding receptions to radio stations.

Anyone with a passion for music and the willingness to learn can become a DJ. Most DJs do indeed have an extensive knowledge of music. Some focus on one genre. Others know a lot about a wide range of music. Additionally, they are excellent listeners. Many can easily identify different components of songs just by listening to them.

However, being a DJ involves much more than a passion for music. DJs must be able to express themselves clearly. They announce the artists and titles of the songs they play. Many radio personalities also read the news, interview guests, and do commercials or promotions for their station. They frequently do guest appearances at locations around

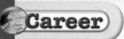
town. They may help celebrate the opening of a new business. Others might entertain guests at a party or a charity auction.

But, having knowledge about music and speaking well are just part of the job. DJs must be able to use a wide range of sound equipment. One key technique to master is the ability to make seamless transitions between songs. Additionally, DJs need to

understand how to handle equipment such as microphones, speakers, cables, and amplifiers.

One of the most important qualities for a DJ is connecting with the audience. DJs have to get a feel for what kind of music their listeners crave. That often changes. A DJ has to vary the music to keep people excited and responsive. DJs often are required to multitask. They must watch the clock as songs play and be able to prepare for the next song or commercial. Party and wedding reception DJs also must be able to field requests from guests while playing music.

By nature, most DJs are chatty and have outgoing personalities. Some say that one of the greatest challenges of their jobs is the time spent alone. They often are isolated in

a DJ booth. Many radio station DJs have to work overnight or early in the morning when the station is fairly empty. Adjusting to the solitude is just part of the job.

Although higher education is always helpful, you do not need a college degree to become a successful DJ. Many people take speech, drama, and language arts classes in high school to help perfect their speech and delivery. Some choose to pursue broadcasting degrees in college.

On-the-job experience, however, is necessary to become a successful DJ. Internships at radio stations are a great way to learn the ropes. Working at a college radio station is another excellent way to learn the day-to-day tasks and get some on-air experience. A third way to gain hands-on experience is to assist a professional DJ at a party or a wedding.

The pay scale for DJs generally is reflective of where you live, the company you work for, and how much experience you have. The starting annual salary for the average radio DJ is about $25,000. Experienced radio personalities can earn more than $70,000 a year. The average annual salary for a club DJ is about $16,000 a year. However, many club DJs are paid hourly. Their rate also depends on their location and experience. Hourly rates can range from $8 to more than $50.

So, if Rusty is willing to put in some time and learn the ropes, he certainly could become a professional DJ. There are a vast number of opportunities for him to become a success on the air. Soon, he may be able to share his passion for music with listeners everywhere.

Music without Instruments

Glenn Weyant uses a cello bow and a cardboard tube to play a section of the wall in Arizona that separates the United States from Mexico.

Glenn Weyant has always been a musician at heart. Like many aspiring artists, he achieved his goal and recorded a song. But, his **instruments** were anything but ordinary. In a project called The Anta Project, Weyant played a three-mile-long section of a steel wall that separates the United States from Mexico. Using chopsticks, egg beaters, and a cello bow to make music, Weyant recorded his song.

He even used the sound of the wind vibrating the fence and the noise from the U.S. Department of Homeland Security helicopters to add depth to his music. **1**

Weyant's project and his **unique techniques** have received a lot of media attention. "All of us has [*sic*] an inner artist, an inner musician," he said. "Playing found objects allows us to bypass obstacles to expressing that musicianship. It gets

1 Ask Questions
Be sure you understand what you read by asking questions. For example, what objects did Weyant use to make music?

to the core of the connections that exist between people and music."

Today, many people take a **vast** array of ordinary objects and combine sounds to make music. This new format is becoming quite popular. The Portland Bike Ensemble performs live music by playing actual bicycles. The Oregon-based group turns the vehicles upside down and attaches microphones to them that **convert** the bikes into an orchestra. They then pluck the spokes like a harp

and turn cranks to keep the beat. They even touch their microphones to spinning wheels to create new sounds. This technique creates a unique sound that delights audiences.

Matmos is another group that uses a vast **range** of everyday sounds in their music. They recorded the sounds of liposuction and other forms of surgery. By converting the sounds into beats and melodies, they created an entire album from this recording. The duo is featured on a Björk album. A solo on one of the tracks is made from a

deck of cards being shuffled. Björk said, "All their noises are recorded around the home." These everyday sounds really add depth to the music.

Recording artists are also exploring new techniques that can be used to make music. For example, mashups have become very popular. A mashup is a song that combines the vocals from one song with the music from another. On Girl Talk's 2008 album *Feed the Animals*, there are 14 tracks of mashups from more than 300 artists. This album is made up almost entirely of samples from music by other artists. Listeners can hear everything from Pachelbel, a 17th century German composer and organist, to Vampire Weekend, an indie rock band. These songs are then mashed with a wide range of hip-hop hooks.

"United State of Pop" by DJ Earworm is another example of this style. This song is a conversion of the top 25 billboard hits of 2007 into one hit song—the ultimate mashup. **2**

Other musical artists are bringing everyday sounds into their albums in different ways. The sounds from Nintendo games play a prominent role in many tracks on Beck's *Guero* album. Critics say the Nintendo sounds lend a techno feel to the songs.

STOMP is a Broadway musical that also captured this trend. In the show, the performers use anything

2 Summarize

What are some examples of mashups?

but ordinary instruments to create the soundtrack. There is no dialogue, or conversation, at all in *STOMP*. The actors use a vast selection of everyday objects to create upbeat, cheerful percussion music. The clapping, stomping, bashing, swishing, and clashing of water, brooms, lighters, and trash cans combine to produce the soundtrack for this stage show. **3**

The Blue Man Group is another theatrical experience that uses a range of unusual musical instruments. In the late 1980s, the Blue Man Group was a street performance group in Chicago. Today, they perform in theaters all over the world. Over the years, the group designed many unique instruments from everyday items. For example, they play the PVC, an instrument made from PVC pipe. They also use airpoles. Airpoles are flexible, hollow fiberglass rods.

3 Make Connections
STOMP does not use dialogue. What other performers don't use spoken words in their art?

4 **Visualize**

Look over what you have read. Picture in your mind what a *STOMP* or Blue Man Group performance might look like.

When moved through the air they make a "swoosh" sound. Finally, they even "play" a group member's dog. They call this instrument the "dogulum." The dog is stroked until he is content. The group records the noises he makes once satisfied, and uses them in their songs. **4**

Countless other famous and not-so-famous musical acts are integrating, or blending, everyday noises and objects into their performances. So, the next time you hear water dripping in the sink or trains passing each other on the tracks, listen closely. You may just have front row seats at the best concert in town. **End**

THE SCIENCE of SOUND

Vocabulary

amplifies (v) *makes louder or stronger*

volume (n) *loudness*

renders (v) *makes or causes to become*

particles (n) *extremely small pieces of something*

The crowd screams as the home team scores a basket. Thump. Thump. Thump. The basketball echoes as it is dribbled up the court. The loudspeaker system **amplifies** the announcer's voice as he relays the score. In the next row, a couple talks about their plans after the game. A vendor selling programs walks through the section and calls, "Programs!" The guy in row L gets caught up in the excitement of the last quarter and shares his counsel, or advice, with the coach.

At the basketball game, there are many different types of sounds—some loud and some soft. All of these sounds interact with one another. So, depending on your location, the sounds may be different from the ones a friend across the arena hears. The pitch and **volume** of the sound varies based on your location.

What Is Sound?

Guitar strings vibrate, or move quickly back and forth, to produce music. In the same way, when we speak, our vocal cords vibrate, creating the sound of our voices. Sound is a vibration that travels through matter. The matter can be a solid, liquid, or gas. When an object vibrates, it **renders** movement in the air **particles**. As the particles

Sounds of Life

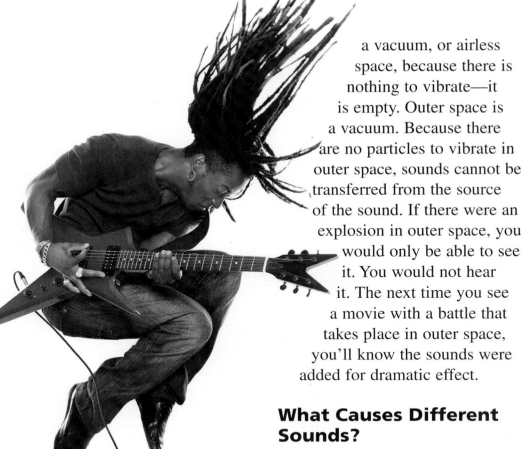

Vocabulary

factors (n) *things that help produce a result*

a vacuum, or airless space, because there is nothing to vibrate—it is empty. Outer space is a vacuum. Because there are no particles to vibrate in outer space, sounds cannot be transferred from the source of the sound. If there were an explosion in outer space, you would only be able to see it. You would not hear it. The next time you see a movie with a battle that takes place in outer space, you'll know the sounds were added for dramatic effect.

What Causes Different Sounds?

Why are there so many different sounds? The frequency, amplitude, and wavelength of the sound waves are **factors** that combine to determine which sound you hear. Sound waves travel 340 meters, or about three football fields, per second through air. In water, sound travels more than four times as quickly, at a rate of 1,500 meters per second.

The frequency is the number of waves that pass a given point per second. Another way to describe the frequency is to describe how quickly the particles vibrate. The faster the waves move, the higher the pitch of the sound. The pitch is how the note or noise sounds compared to other notes or noises. A foghorn renders a low-pitched sound. A dog whistle renders a high-pitched sound.

bump into one another, they create sound waves. If you are within range, your ears will pick up these vibrations. You hear them as sounds. The closer you are to the root of the sound, the louder the volume will be. **1**

Sound cannot travel through

1 Summarize

What is sound?

An explosion in space can be seen, but not heard. Why?

Wavelength is another factor that affects the pitch. The wavelength is the distance from the top of one wave to the top of the next. Another way to describe it is the distance between matching points on a wave. The slower the frequency, the longer the wavelength will be. Therefore, the longer the wavelength, the lower

pitched the sound. **2**

Another factor that determines the sound you hear is the amplitude. The amplitude is the amount of energy in a sound wave. The volume of a sound is determined by the amplitude. The height of the wave is used to measure this. The taller the wave, the louder the

2 Text Features

Look at the diagram below. It says that the waveforms have the same frequency. Which waveform has the lower pitched sound?

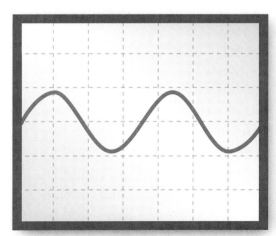 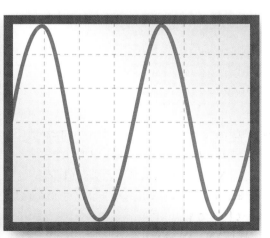

The waveform on the left has a smaller amplitude, but the same number of peaks in a given time (frequency). The only difference between the sounds is that the first one is quieter because it has less energy.

3 Ask Questions

What questions would you ask yourself about frequency, wavelength, and amplitude before you describe the science of sound to a friend?

4 Make Connections

Do you know anyone who uses the mosquito ringtone?

sound. An amplifier is a device specifically designed to make a sound louder. It does so by increasing the amplitude of a signal. Many electronics products, from computers to televisions, have devices in them that amplify the sound. **3**

Communicating with Sound Waves

Although they don't have vocal cords or words, dolphins have communicated with one another for centuries using sound waves. A mother dolphin often whistles to her baby for several days after giving birth. This allows the calf to identify his mother simply by the pitch of her whistle. Dolphins also use sound waves to navigate their way through the dark waters, as well as hunt and communicate.

Recent studies show that teenagers can hear higher pitches of notes than adults. Some businesses have installed devices that emit a high-pitched sound to keep teens from loitering. The inventor says most people who are older than 30 cannot hear this sound. Some teens have figured out how to benefit from this ability. They have created a new ringtone, the mosquito. Now, they can receive text message notifications on their cell phones without adults knowing. **4**

Sounds are everywhere. They allow us to communicate with each other and take in our surroundings. Sounds also provide us with entertainment and help us learn. So, the next time you hear a soothing sound that brings a smile to your face—or a horrible screech that makes you crazy, stop and think about how the sound was created. **End**

Behind-the-Scenes Music Careers

Everyone knows what it takes to become a singer or musician. But, what if your passion for music doesn't come with a talent for singing or playing an instrument? Can you still earn a living in the music industry? Absolutely! There are a wide variety of job opportunities for those wanting to work behind the scenes in the music world. Here is a look at a few of them.

Recording Engineers

Recording engineers install, test, repair, set up, and operate the electronic equipment used to record songs. They must be able to use a wide range of equipment. They also must have the necessary skills to record, edit, and mix musical recordings. There are no specific educational requirements for becoming a recording engineer. However, most recording engineers have some formal education from a technical school or four-year college. Technical skills and on-the-job experience are the two most critical needs for engineers. Many engineers gain valuable hands-on experience as interns at recording studios. The average engineer earns about $36,000 a year.

Record Producers

Record producers work with the talent, session musicians, and the recording engineer to produce the recordings. They make sure projects are done on time and within budget. The producer's job includes planning every detail of a recording project. He or she supervises the recording session and helps the artists achieve a certain sound. Most producers start as sound engineers or music editors. After gaining experience in the recording studio, they move up to become producers. Many producers have degrees in music production from a college or technical school. Some earn a master's degree. The salary range for producers is wide. Starting salaries can be around $20,000 a year. Successful producers can earn more than $1 million annually. Additionally, some artists pay their producers royalties if their song or album becomes a commercial success.

Music Journalists

For those who like to write as well as listen to music, being a music journalist or critic might be the perfect job. Music critics listen to new music and review it for the public. They also write about performers and music trends. Some review concerts. Many music journalists also interview musicians. They write for newspapers, magazines, Web sites, and even television. In addition to writing well, critics must give fair and honest reviews of the music. They must be able to express themselves clearly. Journalists must be able to work independently and meet critical deadlines. To get started, most critics earn a bachelor's degree in English or journalism. Many critics begin as freelance writers. They take small jobs or submit their reviews to local papers or Web sites. Average starting salaries for this position range from $25,000 to $36,000 a year. Experienced critics can earn more than $60,000 annually.

Radio Plugger

A radio plugger promotes music to radio stations. Hired by record labels, pluggers get music of the artists they work for played on the air. They work to get songs put on radio stations' playlists. Pluggers may also set up on-air interviews or concerts for the artists. Radio pluggers generally work job to job. Frequently they negotiate a fee for working a particular album or tour. They generally do not have a regular salary. But, experienced pluggers can be well paid. To get started, many people will work for free or for a reduced rate. By doing so, they gain valuable experience. They also begin to establish contacts at radio stations.

Artist Manager

An artist manager, or agent, supervises the business side of the band or singer. An agent books gigs and finds work for the artist. Additionally, the job includes promotion and negotiating contracts. Excellent communication and people skills are two of the most important qualities of an agent. Most managers are paid a percentage of an artist's income. Generally, they earn between 20 percent and 30 percent of an artist's salary. Many people begin as interns at a management or entertainment company. Others meet and quickly bond with an artist. They then decide to work together and enter the entertainment world as a team.

So, even if you do not have the vocal talent to become America's next pop star, you can still earn a living in the music industry. You can channel your interest and passion for music into one of these exciting behind-the-scenes music careers.

Criminology

- How have advances in science made it more difficult to get away with a crime?

- Has criminology reduced the number of crimes that are committed? Why or why not?

- Why do some crimes still go unsolved?

AX MURDERER

or Beloved Daughter?

> Lizzie Borden took an ax
> And gave her mother forty whacks.
> When she saw what she had done,
> She gave her father forty-one.

Vocabulary

bear (v) *put up with something*

suspicion (n) *thought or feeling that something is wrong or bad*

1 Make Connections
Have you ever been so bothered by something you saw or heard that you couldn't think straight?

All that most people know about me is that awful rhyme. But, there is more to my story. I was the one who found my father's body lying in a pool of blood. The slashed face, sliced and bleeding, looked up at me like a stranger in my father's clothing. It was more than I could **bear**. I screamed in horror at the sight. Bridget, our maid, was the first to come to my aid. I didn't even think to look for anyone else. **1**

They found Mrs. Borden, my stepmother, dead too. She and my father had been brutally, violently murdered with an ax. The police at first thought Bridget might have done it. I was shocked when their **suspicion** shifted from her to me. How could I, a 32-year-old Sunday school teacher and respected church member, have possibly done something so vicious, so cruel?

The police thought my motive was money. My father was wealthy. Mrs. Borden was a gold digger who wanted his money. The police believed that I killed them so his money would go to me—not her.

Father was good to me. Why would I kill him?

No one was home the day of the murders except Bridget and me. So that left only us as witnesses. We had to **submit** to endless hours of questioning until I couldn't bear to hear another question. Bridget tried to **defend** herself by saying she was

Vocabulary

submit (v) *agree to obey something*

defend (v) *protect something or someone from harm*

Lizzie Borden Murder Trial

Lizzie Borden
murder suspect

Andrew Borden
Lizzie's father

Abby Borden
Lizzie's stepmother

Emma Borden
Lizzie's sister

Bridget Sullivan
maid

Borden home

Abby Borden's body
in bedroom

Andrew Borden's body
in living room

Ax
murder weapon

napping during the murders, so the police let her go. I told police I was in the barn when my father was killed. Investigators said there were no footprints in the dust on the barn floor, so I must be lying.

A drugstore clerk falsely reported that I came in looking for poison a few days earlier. **2** Police used this to determine that I poisoned my parents like helpless rats, then chopped them up like lumber. There was no poison found in either of their stomachs. Still, I was officially accused of double homicide. Did the police think I was somehow able to **transport** myself from the barn to the house, up the stairs to kill my stepmother, down the stairs to kill my father, to the bathroom to wash up, to the basement to dispose of the weapon, and back again without being seen or heard by neighbors?

There was no blood on my clothes, my face, or my hands. They found a half-burnt hatchet handle with no blood on it in the fireplace that they claimed was the weapon I tried to burn. A few days after the murder, a neighbor saw me burning a dress that had paint on it. She thought it was suspicious and told police. They used that against me in court, claiming I must have been burning my bloodstained clothing. **3**

Thankfully, the jury understood. They found me, Lizzie Borden, **innocent**. My sister and I inherited everything, receiving all of Father's money. I lived the rest of my life quietly in a mansion. **End**

CSI AT THE LIZZIE BORDEN CRIME SCENE

Andrew Borden's skull

Murder weapon

Crime scene investigation (CSI) and the science of forensics have made it possible to solve crimes that 100 years ago would have gone unsolved, like the case of Lizzie Borden. If a CSI team from today could be transported through time and space and arrive on the scene at the same time those turn-of-the-century investigators did, the case of Lizzie Borden might not be so mysterious. **1**

Steps of the CSI

The first thing CSI team members would have done is to secure the scene so they could take fingerprints. This would **reveal** for certain whether someone besides Lizzie, Bridget, and Mr. and Mrs. Borden had been in the house.

Modern-day investigators would not determine the time of death by relying on touch to measure the temperature of a body as they did in the Borden case. Instead, they would use an internal thermometer and take

Vocabulary

reveal (v) *make known*

1 Make Connections
Think about what you read in the last passage about Lizzie Borden as you read what the CSI might do at the site.

Investigators secure the scene so they can make a careful analysis of the crime.

An investigator analyzes items found at a crime scene.

temperatures over a period of time. Even so, they could determine the time of death only within a few hours of the murder.

There was much debate about the dress that Lizzie wore that day. Was it indeed the light blue dress she later burned, or was it a dark blue dress? CSI would have recorded the scene by taking photographs and videos of everyone there, including Lizzie in her dress. The video also would have shown how Lizzie reacted to the scene. Were her emotions **genuine**, or was she a clever actress? **2**

Today, a CSI team would use blood spatter **analysis** to reveal many clues to the mystery. The CSI team would collect bloodstain data at the scene, and a blood spatter expert would interpret the blood patterns. The results would reveal the positions of the victims, of objects in the room at the time of death, and of the assailant, or attacker. The analysis would also help the investigators establish the type of weapon used and the number of blows. The trajectory, or path, of blood spatter would help estimate the height of the assailant and

the movements of the victim and assailant after blood was shed. **3**

Finally, the modern-day crime scene investigators would use high-intensity light to search for blood at the crime scene. **Diluted** blood leaves a brownish stain where someone has tried to clean it. The team would use modern techniques to detect blood that seeped into cracks in the floorboards or behind baseboards. If the investigators discovered what looked like blood on the floor that someone attempted to clean up, the floorboards would be removed and taken to the crime lab for further testing. **4**

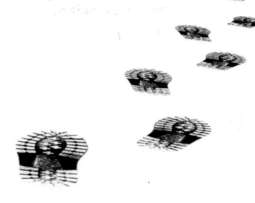

2 Ask Questions

Think about what you just read. Ask yourself, "Why are photographs and video of a crime scene helpful?"

3 Visualize

Think about how the trajectory would help estimate the height of the assailant. Draw a picture, if necessary.

4 Summarize

What are the steps a CSI team might take to investigate a crime scene?

Chemical Reactions

Many techniques used today in criminal investigations involve a chemical test of the evidence found at a crime scene. Tests performed by the investigators often result in a chemical reaction from one chemical mixing with another. During a chemical reaction, tiny invisible particles or molecules of one substance react with molecules from another substance. The molecules of each substance undergo a change. This change is a chemical reaction that produces totally different chemicals. Chemical reactions are common and occur around you and inside your body each day. Digesting the food you eat is a common type of chemical reaction. So is iron changing to rust and gasoline burning in a car engine.

Luminol

Today, crime investigators use a chemical reaction to detect blood at a crime scene. In this chemical reaction, investigators use a special chemical called luminol to identify blood particles that may be invisible to the naked eye. Before luminol will work, it has to undergo a

chemical reaction with blood. When luminol reacts chemically with blood, it changes and produces a substance that has a greenish blue glow. Locating a trail of blood using luminol could help reveal the escape route of a murderer who is either bleeding or carrying a bloody weapon. Luminol could even reveal the presence of blood on a suspected murder weapon. **5**

How Luminol Works

Luminol is a powder made up of nitrogen, hydrogen, oxygen, and carbon molecules. Criminalists will mix luminol powder with hydrogen peroxide, distilled water, and washing soda to form a liquid that is poured into a spray bottle. The liquid is then sprayed on a surface thought to contain traces of blood. If blood is present, it will react with the luminol and start to glow in the dark.

Before the luminol can glow, a chemical reaction must take place. To make a chemical reaction, the liquid luminol needs a **catalyst**, or something to cause the molecules from the luminol to start reacting

5 Summarize

Name some ways luminol is helpful with crime scene investigation.

A bloody handprint glows in the dark after luminol is sprayed on it.

the form of light particles called photons. It is this same chemical reaction that causes fireflies and light sticks to glow in the dark. In a dark room, luminol will make a bloody footprint or fingerprint glow.

Drawbacks of Luminol

Luminol, however, is not the CSI's first choice for detecting blood. If a bloodstain is so diluted that it can only be made visible with luminol, the chemical also will destroy the sample so no further testing can be done with the blood. For example, DNA tests could not be performed to confirm whose blood it is because the luminol would destroy the DNA. Also, luminol can react with other iron molecules, copper molecules, and even urine, giving a false positive reaction. But, as a final step, when used with a high-intensity light, luminol is ideal to **enhance** bloody fingerprints and shoeprints. **End**

with the molecules in the blood. The catalyst needed is iron. Hemoglobin, an oxygen-carrying protein in blood, contains iron. Molecules of luminol react with the iron contained in hemoglobin. When criminalists spray the luminol mixture on the surface of an object where there is blood, they will see a green glow from the chemical reaction.

The chemical reaction that takes place is called an oxidation reaction. In the oxidation reaction, the luminol loses nitrogen and hydrogen atoms and gains oxygen atoms. (See the diagram.) The result is a completely new compound called *3-aminophthalate.* **6** This new compound glows in the dark because it releases extra energy in

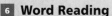
6 Word Reading
Sometimes it may not be necessary to pronounce a word correctly to understand the text. Do the best you can quickly, then keep reading.

H_2O_2 + hydrogen peroxide, luminol $\xrightarrow{\text{base catalyst}}$ 3–aminophthalate + light

This diagram shows how molecules are exchanged during the oxidation reaction that happens when hydrogen peroxide and luminol react with a base catalyst (iron found in hemoglobin).

Expedition 4

Courtroom Professionals

Many people work in the United States legal system to ensure that all Americans receive a fundamental right when charged with a crime: to be judged by a jury of their peers. Most people expect the professionals in a courtroom trial to be the judge, the defendant's attorney, and the prosecution. Many others are also important to the trial. Two such positions are the bailiff and the court reporter.

Bailiff

The bailiff prepares the courtroom for use, making sure necessary items are in place for the trial. These include everything from paper and pencils to pitchers of water. The bailiff protects the people in the courtroom and in the courthouse. He or she might wear a uniform and carry a gun. He or she makes sure everyone follows the judge's orders and follows the rules. If someone causes a disturbance in the courtroom, the bailiff can

One of the bailiff's duties is swearing in witnesses.

make that person leave. The bailiff takes care of the jurors' needs when they are deliberating, or deciding, the verdict. He or she makes sure no one has contact with the jurors. The bailiff also receives the verdict

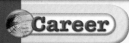

from the jury and presents it to the court clerk for reading.

People who apply for the position of bailiff must be U.S. citizens, at least 21 years old with a high school diploma or GED certificate. They must be in good physical condition, and their weight should be proportionate to their height. Several pre-employment tests, aptitude screenings, and psychological examinations, as well as a background investigation, may be required. As a trusted officer of the court, bailiffs are expected to have a good reputation and moral character. Depending on the state or county, new hires will successfully complete a basic corrections officer's program, which may be up to five weeks long. As of 2008, a bailiff's salary ranged from $30,000 to $40,000 a year.

Court Reporter

Every trial has a court reporter who uses a special machine to record every word said during the trial. The machine has 22 special keys that allow the court reporter, also called a stenographer, to capture what everyone says by pressing key combinations. Today's machines then translate the keys into words. Years ago, the stenographer would have to transcribe the typed shorthand by retyping it in words. The court reporter may also use abbreviations. It's similar to text messaging except the stenographer can type up to 240 words per minute. That is much faster than most people type.

Anyone who has graduated from high school and completed an accredited court reporting school program can become a court reporter. It takes some time to develop this skill, and some court reporting college programs can be 2,700 class hours. During that time, a skilled stenographer may record almost 39 million words! It takes the average student two to three years to complete the program. Court reporter salaries range from $30,000 to $40,000 a year according to 2008 statistics. Some stenographers are freelance, charging an hourly rate as companies hire them. Courtrooms are not the only place you will find stenographers. Some companies use them to record meetings.

from

The Red-Headed League

Part 1

by Sir Arthur Conan Doyle

Sherlock Holmes and his assistant and good friend, Dr. Watson, are seated in the drawing room of Mr. Holmes's residence on Baker Street in London, England, in June 1890. They listen as a large, red-headed gentleman relates his unusual problem. **1**

Vocabulary

presume (v) *take for granted; assume*

1 Make Connections
Have you ever seen a mystery movie or TV show? Think about how this story compares with mysteries you've watched.

"Well, it is just as I have been telling you, Mr. Holmes," said Mr. Wilson, mopping his forehead. "I have a small pawnbroker's business. It's not very large, and recently it has just made me enough money to pay the bills. I used to be able to keep two assistants, but now I only keep one. He is willing to work for half pay so he can learn the business. His name is Vincent Spaulding. I know very well that he could better himself and earn twice what I am able to give him. But, after all, if he is satisfied, why should I put ideas in his head?"

"Why, indeed? You seem most fortunate to have him," replied Holmes.

"Oh, he has his faults, too," said Mr. Wilson. "He is always snapping photographs and then diving down into the cellar like a rabbit into its hole to develop his pictures."

"He is still with you, I **presume**?"

"Yes, sir. It was Vincent who showed me the ad just eight weeks ago today."

Vocabulary

wedged (v) *forced your way into or through*

2 Summarize

This is part of a larger story. Stop every so often to summarize what you have read. What do you know so far?

"Here's another vacancy on the League of the Red-Headed Men, says he. It's worth quite a little fortune to any man who gets it."

"Why, what is it, then, an opening?" I asked.

"You've never heard of the League of the Red-Headed Men?" he asked. "The League was founded by an American millionaire. He was himself red-headed. When he died, he left his fortune to provide easy jobs to men whose hair is of that color. It is splendid pay and very little to do." **2**

"Vincent Spaulding seemed to know so much about it. So we shut the business up and started off for the address.

"I hope I never see such a sight again, Mr. Holmes. Every man who had a shade of red in his hair had tramped into the city to answer the advertisement. Fleet Street was choked with red-headed folk, and Pope's Court looked like a sea of oranges. We **wedged** in as well as we could and soon found ourselves in the office.

"A small man with a head that was even redder than mine said a few words to each candidate, then he always managed to find some fault in these men who seemed qualified for the position. Getting a vacancy did not seem to be such a very easy matter, after all. However, when our turn came the little man closed the door as we entered.

"This is Mr. Jabez Wilson," said my assistant, "and he is willing to fill a vacancy in the League."

"And he is admirably suited for it," the other answered. "He has every requirement." He took a step backward and gazed at my hair. Then suddenly he plunged forward, shook my hand, and congratulated me warmly on my success.

"You will, however, I am sure, excuse me for taking an obvious precaution," he said. With

Vocabulary

deceived (v) *fooled or tricked; misled*

nominal (adj) *trifling; insignificant*

forfeit (v) *have to give up or lose something because of a failure to do something*

that he seized my hair in both his hands, and tugged until I yelled with the pain. "There is water in your eyes," said he as he released me. "I perceive from your tears, that all is as it should be. But we have to be careful, for we have twice been **deceived** by wigs and once by paint." He stepped over to the window and shouted that the vacancy was filled. The folk all trooped away in different directions until there was not a red head to be seen except my own and that of the manager. **3**

3 Visualization

Mr. Wilson has begun telling his story of his experience with Vincent Spaulding. Picture in your mind the scene as it is described.

"My name," said he, "is Mr. Duncan Ross. When shall you be able to start?"

"Well, it is a little awkward, for I have a business already," said I.

"Oh, never mind about that, Mr. Wilson!" said Vincent Spaulding. "I should be able to look after that for you."

"What would be the hours?" I asked.

"Ten to two."

"Now a pawnbroker's business is mostly done on an evening, Mr. Holmes, especially Thursday and Friday evening, which is just before payday; so it would suit me very well to earn a little in the mornings. Besides, I knew that my assistant was a good man, and that he would see to anything that turned up.

"That would suit me very well," said I. "And the pay?"

"Is 4 pounds a week."

"And the work?"

"Is purely **nominal**."

"What do you call purely nominal?"

"Well, you have to be in the office, or at least in the building, the whole time. If you leave, you **forfeit** your whole position forever."

"And the work?"

"Is to copy out the Encyclopedia Britannica. You must find your own ink, pens, and blotting paper, but we provide this table and chair. Will you be ready tomorrow?"

4 **Inference**

Why would Mr. Wilson think this? What in the text helps you make your inferences?

"Certainly," I answered.

"Then, good-bye, Mr. Jabez Wilson, and let me congratulate you once more on the important position which you have been fortunate enough to gain."

"I began to think the whole thing a **fraud**. **4** In the morning I determined to have a look at it anyhow, so I bought a penny bottle of ink, a quill pen, and seven sheets of paper, and I started off for Pope's Court.

"The table was set out ready for me, and Mr. Duncan Ross was there to see that I started my work without any problems. He started me off upon the letter A, and then he left me; but he would drop in from time to time. At two o'clock he told me good-bye and locked the door of the office after me.

"This went on day after day, Mr. Holmes, and on Saturday the manager came in and plunked down four golden coins for my week's work.

"Eight weeks passed like this. I had written about Abbots and Archery and Armour. And then suddenly the whole business came to an end."

"To an end?"

"Yes, sir. And no later than this morning. I went to my work as usual at ten o'clock, but the door was shut and locked, with a sign. Here, you can read for yourself."

He held up a piece of white cardboard.

Sherlock Holmes and I surveyed this announcement until the comical side of the affair completely overcame us. We both burst out into a roar of laughter.

"I cannot see there is anything very funny," cried our client, his red face flushing up to the roots of his flaming head.

> The Red-
> Headed League
> is Dissolved.
> October 9, 1890

"No, no," cried Holmes. "I really wouldn't miss your case for the world. But, there is something just a little funny about it. What steps did you take when you found the card?"

"I called at the offices round, but none of them seemed to know anything about it. The landlord said the red-headed man I knew as Duncan Ross moved out yesterday. He said he had never heard of the Red-Headed League."

"Your case is an exceedingly remarkable one," said Holmes, "and I shall be happy to look into it." **End**

from

The Red-Headed League

Part 2

by Sir Arthur Conan Doyle

Dr. Watson and Sherlock Holmes have been listening to Mr. Wilson, the red-headed pawnbroker, as he tells the story of his unique problem. Holmes now begins to question Mr. Wilson.

Vocabulary

grave (adj)
significantly serious

"From what you have told me I think **grave** issues hang from it, worse than might first appear. **1** This assistant of yours who first called your attention to the advertisement—how long had he been with you?"

"About a month then."

"How did he come?"

"In answer to an advertisement."

"Was he the only applicant?"

"No, I had a dozen."

"Why did you pick him?"

"Because he was handy and would come cheap."

"At half-wages, in fact."

"Yes."

"What is he like, this Vincent Spaulding?"

"Small, stout-built, bulky, no hair on his face, though he's in his thirties. Has a white splash of acid upon his forehead."

Holmes sat up in his chair in excitement. "I thought as much," said he.

1 Make Connections
Connect this text with the passage you read previously.

2 Visualize

Make a mental picture of the scene. What do you see?

"Have you ever observed that his ears are pierced for earrings?"

"Yes, sir. He told me a gypsy had done it for him when he was a lad."

"That will do, Mr. Wilson. I shall be happy to give you an opinion upon the subject in a day or two. Today is Saturday, and I hope that by Monday we may come to a conclusion."

We traveled to Saxe-Coburg Square. A brown board with "JABEZ WILSON" upon a corner house announced the place where our red-headed client carried on his business. Sherlock Holmes walked slowly up the **shabby** street and then down again to the corner, still looking **keenly** at the dingy houses. **2** Finally he returned to the pawnbroker's, and, having thumped vigorously upon the pavement with his walking stick two or three times, he went up to the door and knocked. It was instantly opened by a bright-looking, clean-shaven young fellow.

"I only wished to ask you how you would go from here to the Strand," said Holmes.

"Third right, fourth left," answered the assistant promptly, closing the door.

"Smart fellow, that," observed Holmes as we walked away.

"Evidently," said I, "Mr. Wilson's assistant counts for a good deal in this mystery of the Red-Headed League. I am sure that you inquired your way **merely** so you might see him."

"Not him."

"What then?"

"The knees of his trousers."

"And what did you see on his pants?"

"What I expected to see."

"Why did you beat the pavement?"

"My dear doctor, this is a time for observation, not for talk. We know something of Saxe-Coburg Square. Let us now explore the parts which lie behind it."

We turned round the corner to one of the main streets of the City. The line of fine shops and stately businesses abutted on the other side bordering the faded and **stagnant** square which we had just left.

"Let me see," said Holmes. "There is Mortimer's, the little newspaper shop, the Coburg branch of the City and Suburban Bank, the Vegetarian Restaurant, and McFarlane's carriage building depot. That carries us right on to the other block. **3**

"This business at Coburg Square is serious," Holmes said. "A considerable crime is in contemplation and it has been considered for quite some time. I believe we shall be in time to stop it. I shall want your help tonight."

"At what time?"

"Ten will be early enough."

"I shall be at Baker Street at ten."

"Very well. And, I say, Doctor, there may be some little danger, so kindly put your army revolver in your pocket."

It was a quarter past nine when I made my way to Baker Street. I found

3 **Summarize**
What do you know about the mystery so far?

Holmes in animated conversation, his hand moving about as he talked with two men, one of whom I recognized as Peter Jones, the official police agent. The other man was a stranger to me.

"Ha! Our party is complete," said Holmes, buttoning up his peajacket and taking his heavy hunting crop from the rack. "Watson, I think you know Mr. Jones of Scotland Yard? Let me introduce you to Mr. Merryweather, who is to be our companion in tonight's adventure."

"It is the first Saturday night for seven-and-twenty years that I have not had my card game," said Mr. Merryweather.

"I think you will find," said Sherlock Holmes, "that you will play for a higher stake tonight than you have ever done yet, and the play will be more exciting. For you, Mr. Merryweather, the stake will be some 30,000 pounds; and for you, Jones, it will be the man upon whom you wish to lay your hands." **4**

We rattled through an endless **labyrinth** of gaslit streets until we emerged into Farrington Street.

"This fellow Merryweather is a bank director and personally interested in the matter," my friend remarked.

We had reached the same crowded main street in which we had found ourselves in the morning. Mr. Merryweather stopped to light a lantern and conducted us down a dark, earth-smelling passage into a huge vault, or cellar, which was piled all round with crates and massive boxes. **5 End**

Can you solve the Mystery of the Red-Headed League?

Detectives

The life and career of a TV detective probably look exciting and glamorous. In reality, being a police detective may have some exciting moments, but many "behind the scenes" aspects of the job don't appear on your favorite detective show. Much of the detective's time is spent writing reports. These reports document in detail everything that happened during an investigation or interview. Their record keeping must be accurate and detailed in case it is called into question in a courtroom.

They investigate crimes by gathering facts and collecting evidence. Let's look at what is involved in becoming a detective. It may prove to be an attractive career choice.

Required Education

You can't apply to be a detective like you would apply for a job as a salesclerk. Unless a person has previous military experience, a detective must first be a police officer. Detectives are appointed based on previous work experience and accomplishments as uniformed officers. A police department applicant must be a U.S. citizen at least 20 years old and meet rigorous physical and personal qualifications. Most police departments require that officers have a high school diploma. Some departments even prefer one to two years of college coursework in classes such as law enforcement or administration of justice.

Applicants to the police department need to be in top physical shape, so a background in physical education or organized sports is helpful. Also, knowing a second language can make you a prime candidate for the force. If you intend to join a federal agency, like the FBI, a four-year degree is required.

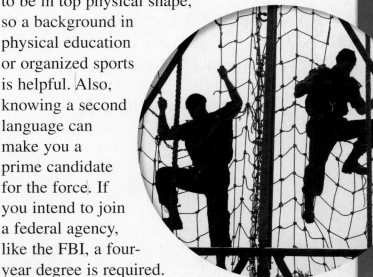

Training to Become a Police Officer

When you have been accepted as a new recruit to the force, you will train in the agency's police academy for 12 to 14 weeks. The academy training includes classroom instruction where you will learn about constitutional law, state laws and local ordinances, civil rights, and accident investigation. Recruits will receive training and supervised experience in patrol, traffic control, emergency response, self-defense, first aid, and use of firearms.

The Work of a Detective

After a few years on the police force, you can be appointed to detective by applying for the position. However, you obtain the rank of detective based on merit, or your accomplishments, as an officer. When you are a detective, you will be assigned cases. You will work on these cases until an arrest and conviction have been made or until the case is dropped.

Detectives are scheduled to work 40 hours a week and are expected to be armed at all times. They usually work a lot of overtime, for which they receive overtime pay. Being a detective is dangerous and stressful. Witnessing death and suffering caused by criminals can affect a detective's personal life.

Salary

In 2008 the national average annual salary for a detective was around $60,000 at state and local levels. The annual detective salary in the federal executive branch was up to $85,000; these positions require a college degree.

Some police departments in large cities hire high school students as police cadets or trainees to do clerical work. These students also attend classes for one to two years until they reach the minimum age requirement to join the force. Many police agencies pay all or part of college tuition if the police officer or detective wants to pursue a higher degree.

If you are interested in criminal justice and want to help your community, becoming a police officer and working your way up to detective may just be the career for you.

An Army of Progress

- How does the modern military differ from the military of the past?

- How has the role of soldiers changed over the years?

- What military inventions have become a part of the lives of American people?

Military Technology

When they were six, Dave and Miguel played with toy guns. Shouting "Pow!" as they pretended to fire, they turned the local park into a battlefield. Their **initial** choice in weaponry made no sound and was very different from an actual pistol. Today, they still battle with each other at the park, but they've traded their toy guns for laser guns. Because of new technology, they now have enhanced controls that accurately **register** hits and misses, track fuel, and make realistic sounds. These **advanced** weapons are much more like the real thing and bring the battle to a whole new level.

Technology has not only improved the boys' game, but also

1916: Pilots from the Royal Air Force prepare to drop bombs by hand over Germany.

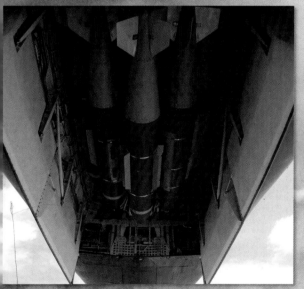

B-1B Lancer with loaded bomb bay

U.S. Army Specialist inside his Humvee checks a map on a computer screen in Tikrit, Iraq.

has improved military weapons. During the Revolutionary War, American soldiers used weapons such as cannons, which could hit targets from about half a mile away. **1** Even if a cannonball made a direct hit, it wouldn't kill that many people. But, at the time, these were the most up-to-date weapons available. Today, they are considered antiques. They have been replaced by machine guns, chemical hand grenades, and nuclear weapons. A modern smart bomb can be aimed at a mark, fired from miles away, and hit the specific target the size of a postage stamp. Today's nuclear weapons can devastate, or destroy, entire cities.

Technology and military research have allowed for the advancement of more powerful and effective weapons. But, military technology has developed much more than weapons. Each day, many of us **depend** on these inventions that came from military developments.

The Internet has its origins in the military. It was initially developed during the Cold War as a way to **exchange** defense information. As a result, people in different locales, or places, were able to quickly share top-secret information. It also allowed information to be stored in various locations around the country. At first, only four computers were connected to this system. Soon, other people learned

1 Make Connections
Because of the ineffectiveness of the weapons of the past, how would battles then have looked different from battles today?

about it and also wanted to be able to exchange information over the network. Then, the military began sharing the network with others. Today, the Internet is used in homes and businesses around the world. **2**

GPS, or Global Positioning System, was developed by the military in the late 1970s. The intent, or purpose, of GPS was to make weapon delivery more precise. To do this, the system uses floating satellites to determine locations on Earth. Because there are enough satellites in orbit for signals on the ground to bounce off several at once, exact locations can be determined in most cases today. GPS is still owned and

operated by the U.S. Department of Defense but is used widely by American **civilians**. GPS units are commonly installed in cars, boats, and cell phones, so people depend on them to find destinations, map their routes, register past trips, or calculate the distance between two locations.

As technology research continues, our military will develop new tools to help defend our country. Today's smart bombs will probably become the antiques of the future. Civilians will continue to benefit from these advances, and these new applications, or uses, may soon become common for many people. **3** **End**

2 Main Idea
Find the main idea sentence in this paragraph. What details support it?

3 Summarize
Describe how military technology has advanced and how those advancements have impacted civilians.

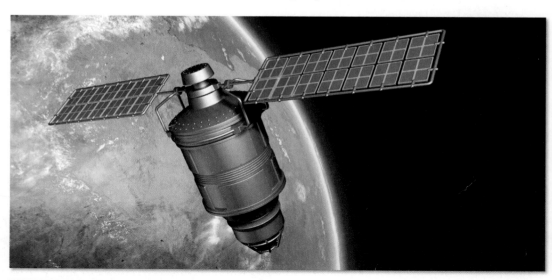

Women ★★★★ in the Military

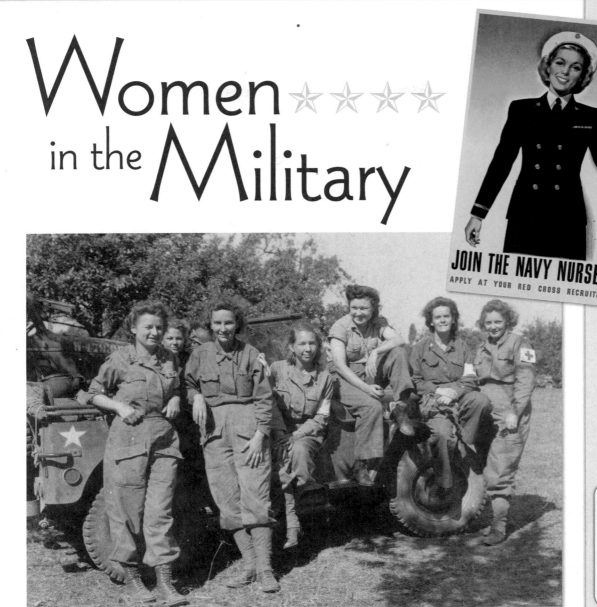

JOIN THE NAVY NURSE CORPS
APPLY AT YOUR RED CROSS RECRUITING STATION

Army nurses in World War II

Dramatic music plays as the commercial begins. An American soldier carrying a heavy pack and a rifle runs toward a helicopter. As the soldier stops and looks up, we suddenly see long brown hair and a woman's smiling face. The army slogan "Army Strong" sprawls across the screen. With this ad campaign, army recruiters are hoping to **encourage** new members to join their forces.

Today, women certainly can be all they can be in the U.S. Armed Forces. Women play **vital** roles as active participants in all four branches of the military. These essential roles include staffing and commanding divisions of the U.S. military. How did women enter this historically male-dominated field?

Women have always been involved in the military. During the Revolutionary War, women played different vital roles than they do today. They worked on battlefronts

Vocabulary

controversy (n)
a discussion or argument over an issue

critical (adj)
especially important

foreign (adj) *having to do with another country*

positions (n) *jobs*

1 Inference
What is the controversy about women working outside the home?

2 Context Clues
Using the surrounding sentences, determine what the word *voluntary* means.

as nurses, cooks, and laundresses. Since then, the role of women in the military has changed dramatically.

During World War II, many new opportunities opened up for women wanting to serve their country. Across America, females were encouraged to help with the war effort. The war was being fought in Europe. Despite the **controversy** over whether women should work outside the home, some American women took up the countless jobs left behind by the fighting men. **1** Many others chose to contribute to, or play a significant part in, the war effort by joining the military. Their voluntary participation in the military was controversial at first. **2** Although they chose to join, many people had trouble accepting the idea of women in uniform. But, America's female military members quickly erased those doubts. They

became a **critical** part of the U.S. forces.

More than 150,000 women served in the Women's Army Corps (WAC). They were the first women besides nurses to serve in the U.S. Army. For the first time, women were sent to basic training camps and deployed, or sent into action. They did not see any frontline combat. However, WACs served as medical technicians, radio operators, and secretaries in the United States and in **foreign** countries. They also worked as training instructors, mechanics, photo interpreters, and parachute riggers. Women in the WAC happily took these **positions**. This freed up men to fight the war in foreign countries.

Soon after the WAC was created, other branches of the armed forces encouraged women to enlist, or join. The WAVES (Women Accepted for

Volunteer Emergency Service) was the female unit of the Navy. These women held many of the same positions as their counterparts in the Army. However, some took on even more responsibility. WAVES were the first women in the U.S. military whose duties were exactly the same as male aircrew members. The number of women volunteering to enlist was amazing. By the end of the war, there were more than 8,000 female officers and close to 80,000 enlisted WAVES.

The first women trained to fly American military aircraft were members of WASP, the Women Airforce Service Pilots. These women were a vital part of the Air Force. There were about 1,000 female pilots who were a part of this branch, and they flew almost every type of military plane. Combined, they flew more than 60 million miles, or 2,500 times around the world, in three years. **3**

Although they may not have known it, they were paving the way for future generations of American women to become members of the armed forces. By the 1970s, each of these separate divisions was disbanded, or broken up, and women became active parts of the Army, Navy, Air Force, and Marines.

Women in the military are becoming more common. Today, about 20 percent of the military is female. They hold a wide variety of positions and are a critical part of the armed forces. Many of them are

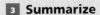

3 Summarize
What were the three military units created for women?

WACs inspecting an airplane

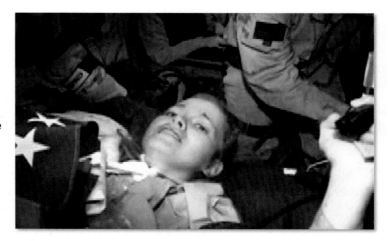

Jessica Lynch was the first female POW to be successfully rescued.

stationed in foreign countries. As more and more females enlist in the military, they continue to break new ground.

In the 1990s, women began to be recognized as military leaders. During this decade, many women were promoted to become commanding officers. The Marine Corps opened pilot positions to women. The Air Force assigned the first woman to command an Intercontinental Ballistic Missile unit.

Female soldier Jessica Lynch made national headlines when she was taken as a prisoner of war (POW) in 2003. She was captured by Iraqi forces when her unit was ambushed. Lynch was rescued about a week later. It was the first time an American female POW had been saved. It was also the first successful rescue of an American POW since World War II.

While some people still see their involvement as controversial, women are in active combat roles on land, at sea, and in the air. Some have graduated in the top of their class at military academies. Others hold high-ranking positions, managing others and making important tactical decisions, critical for each battle's victory. With the many opportunities the military offers its members, women continue to prove that they can be all they can be. **4 End**

4 Ask Questions

Think about what you just read. Was there a part that was confusing? Reread the sections that are still unclear.

U.S. Army Capt. Cindy Stockamp counts with children of Afghanistan.

When most people tried to pilot a helicopter in the video game Battlefield 2: Modern Combat, they would either crash into the nearest building or quickly end up shot down by another player. David was the exception. The controls were complex, but he quickly mastered them. He was able to pilot the helicopter all over the map and lead his team to victory, round after round.

He knew it was just a video game, but while he played, he really felt like he was flying. He loved it! Perhaps a military career as a helicopter pilot might be a perfect fit for David. But, becoming a pilot isn't as easy as playing a video game.

The Army has requirements prospective pilots must meet before beginning their training. Candidates must be U.S. citizens between 18 and 32 years of age. They must be in good physical shape. They also have to meet the Army's height and weight standards. Finally, future pilots must have good vision. They cannot be color-blind nor have vision worse than 20/50 in either eye. After meeting these basic requirements, future pilots must take two tests: the Armed Forces Vocational Aptitude Test and the Flight Aptitude Selection Test. Soldiers must meet minimum scores on each of these tests before they can

move on to the next step in the process.

Becoming a pilot involves a lot of training. Future pilots must be prepared to complete a demanding program. The Army has two types of helicopter pilots: commissioned officers and warrant officers. You must have a college degree to become a commissioned officer. Many people who choose to take this route study physics and aerospace, electrical, or mechanical engineering in college.

However, many people join the Army right after high school and become warrant officers. To become a warrant officer, candidates must complete nine weeks of Basic Combat Training. Then, they attend Warrant Officer Candidate School in Alabama for nearly seven weeks. At this school, they are tested on self-discipline, attention to detail, and time management. Additionally, the program tests decision-making skills in very stressful environments. Once these qualities have been proven, soldiers move on to specific training for helicopter pilots.

Specific flight training takes place at the Army Aviation School. Here students learn basic flying skills. They spend a lot of time in classrooms learning everything about helicopters. There are also in-depth lessons in flight physics, on-board systems,

monitor the cockpit control panels, engines, and other systems on board the helicopter. Additionally, they need to be prepared to perform military operations, transport troops and materials, and evacuate wounded soldiers.

Most experts agree that learning to fly with the military is the absolute best flight training a pilot can get. Upon entering the Army, training is a soldier's job. Soldiers get paid while learning, instead of paying for classes. Generally, a beginning Army salary is about $30,000 a year for an officer. With time and experience, officers have the potential to earn close to $100,000 a year. Army service also makes soldiers eligible for other benefits, such as health care, retirement pay, and free or subsidized food, housing, and education. However, if they pursue this path, pilots must remember that their primary responsibility is to be a soldier first and a helicopter pilot second. The needs of the Army always come first.

Once pilots finish their service with the military, many choose to take their flight skills to a civilian job. Some work as pilots for law enforcement and earn around $90,000 a year. Others become Emergency Medical Services (EMS) pilots. Salaries for this job are about $60,000 annually. Other civilian job opportunities include flight instructors or sightseeing pilots who fly tourists over city attractions. Salaries for these jobs are about $60,000 a year.

David was impressed with all the opportunities available to him. The training will be difficult, but he thinks it will be worth it. Before long, he might be flying in a foreign country, helping serve his country and earning a living doing something he loves.

map reading, map drawing, and emergency procedures.

After the classroom portion of the training, soldiers start their in-flight education. To begin, they spend several hours in a flight simulator. Once this requirement is met, they then complete between 70 and 150 hours of in-flight training. In this phase, students further develop their technique and learn basic combat flight skills.

The last phase of this intense training program requires students to specialize in one of four types of the Army's helicopters. Students do not get to choose their specialty. It is assigned to them by the Army. During this phase, they learn all of the details and characteristics of a Kiowa, Black Hawk, Apache, or Chinook helicopter. The whole program takes about one year to complete.

In addition to having a strong desire to fly a helicopter, pilots must have the ability to multitask and remain calm in stressful situations. During training, they are frequently forced to make on-the-spot choices. Then, they must explain their decisions. Also, there is much more to becoming a pilot than just flying the helicopters. Before taking off, they need to prepare flight plans and check weather reports. While in the air, pilots must

Military Medical Innovations

After the massive freeway accident, emergency workers immediately sprang into action. They quickly arrived at the accident scene. Then, they began to **assess** the damage. The workers evaluated the injured with the triage system. They rapidly identified who needed the most immediate treatment. A few of the injured were placed in ambulances and medical helicopters to be taken to local hospitals. Others with less **severe** injuries would be treated on-site. Some would need blood transfusions, but they would survive this horrible crash. The people on the scene may not have realized it, but all of these modern medical techniques originated from military medical practices.

Triage

Triage is a process for classifying injured people into groups. The word *triage* comes from the French verb *trier*, which means "to sort." The injured are quickly assessed, sorted, and **categorized** based on the severity of their injuries. Today, this system is used **frequently** in emergency rooms and at disaster sites. Triage helps

---

An Army of Progress

1 Make Connections
Think about a time when you felt like someone was treated better than you because of who they were. How did that make you feel?

2 Inference
Why did the soldiers become addicted to the drugs? How do you know?

categorize the wounded; allocate, or distribute, scarce resources; and maximize the number of survivors.

This standard practice did not originate in hospitals. It was **developed** on battlefields in France during the 1800s. A French doctor in Napoleon's army came up with this method to sort and categorize wounded soldiers. This was a huge change in protocol, or procedure. Prior to this, soldiers were treated in order of rank. The highest ranking officers were always treated first, a **concept** that led to many unnecessary deaths. **1** With the triage system, soldiers who could be quickly treated and returned to combat were now the highest priority. Doctors then turned their attention to wounded soldiers who would probably recover in a few days. Those who were severely injured and probably wouldn't live were left to die on the battlefield.

Painkillers

Issuing painkillers to the wounded is another medical technique that was frequently used by military doctors and is standard practice today. Painkillers were often used during the Civil

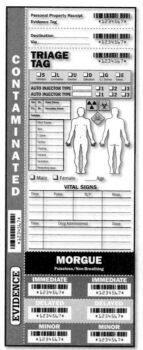

War to keep soldiers comfortable. Many battlefield doctors used morphine to alleviate, or relieve, pain. The morphine was often given in opium pills. Opium is an addictive narcotic that comes from opium poppy seeds. Almost 10 million opium pills, along with 2.8 million ounces of other forms of opium, were given to Union soldiers during the war.

Opium was used to numb the wounded and reduce their pain. The physicians also used it to treat diarrhea, dysentery, and malaria. It provided soldiers with relief from the pain. However, it caused other problems. By 1880, a large number of Union soldiers were addicted to morphine. The newspapers of the day referred to this addiction as "Soldier's Disease." **2**

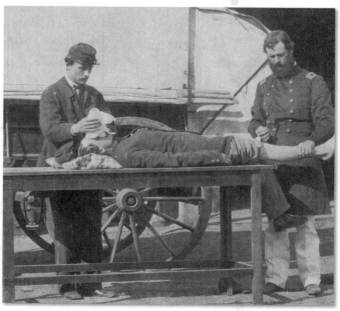

Civil War surgeon at work

A wounded soldier is brought to a mobile hospital by ambulance during battle.

Transporting Blood, Supplies, and Patients

The first known ambulance service was created by the Knights of St. John during the Crusades (decades of wars fought over religion) in the 11th century. They would transport the wounded to medical tents for assessment and treatment. Over time, this concept continued to develop. During French wars in the early 1800s, Napoleon's chief physician improved upon the existing ambulance system. His idea was to remove injured soldiers from the battlefield while fighting was still taking place, instead of waiting for the battle to end. He used horse-drawn wagons to quickly transport the injured. Additionally, he had trained attendants moving the wounded. By doing this, treatment could begin before they arrived at the hospital or medical tent. Previously, the injured soldiers had to wait until the battle ended to receive any medical care. As technology improved, motorized vehicles began to replace horse-drawn ambulances. Soon, this military invention was being used by civilian hospitals. Today, ambulances are used frequently by emergency personnel around the world. Emergency workers arrive on the scene and quickly transport the wounded and ill to the hospital. **3**

During the Spanish Civil War in the 1930s, Dr. Norman Bethune created the first mobile medical unit. Severe blood loss was a frequent cause of death on the battlefield. Bethune realized that he could provide blood transfusions on the battlefront. This could save many soldiers' lives. The very first mobile unit he developed had medical supplies for 100 operations and dressings for 500 wounds. This could all be carried on a mule. Blood and medical supplies could now be transported very close to the front lines. Others quickly saw the benefits of this concept. Bethune's units became the models for American Mobile Army Surgical

3 Context Clues
What clues from this paragraph help you understand the meaning of the word *personnel*?

A patient is wheeled out from the intensive care unit at the U.S. Mobile Army Surgical Hospital (MASH) in November 2005 in Muzaffarabad, Pakistan, after an earthquake.

4 Main Idea

What is the stated main idea of this paragraph?

Hospital (MASH) units, which were used frequently in later wars. In 2006, the last MASH unit was closed and converted, or transformed, to a Combat Support Hospital (CSH). The CSH has improved upon Bethune's concept and provides state-of-the-art medical care near the front lines.

The use of helicopters to transport the injured is another practice used at the accident site that developed during a war. Medical helicopters were first used in the 1950s during the Korean War. When helicopters were used to transport the wounded soldiers, the injured could be even more quickly evacuated to hospitals. Trips that

would have taken hours on the road were reduced to minutes in the air. **4**

A Baltimore doctor wanted to make this military transportation method available to civilian patients. In 1968, he worked to have patients brought into his shock trauma unit by military helicopters. This work opened the doors for faster transportation to hospitals for civilians. A few years later, the first hospital-based helicopter program was started in Denver, Colorado. Today, medical transport in the air is commonplace. Most trauma units have their own helicopters and landing pads. This allows patients to quickly arrive at hospitals for treatment.

As wars wage around the globe, the battlefields will continue to be laboratories for the medical field. As military surgeons conceptualize and perfect new techniques, civilians will benefit from their hard work. **End**

Buffalo Soldiers

Many people are familiar with Bob Marley's hit "Buffalo Soldier." Few know that it is more than just a popular song with a reggae beat. This song, which provides a brief glimpse at a part of U.S. history, speaks of the role of African Americans in the U.S. Army. Marley sings, "I'm just a Buffalo Soldier in the heart of America. Stolen from Africa. Brought to America. Fighting on arrival, fighting for survival; Said he was a Buffalo Soldier win the war for America."

Historians say Marley's song highlights the work of African American soldiers in an Army **dominated** by whites. Despite racism and discrimination, this group of soldiers did its job bravely and with honor.

African Americans Officially Join the Army

After the Civil War, the Army was reorganized and former "all-white" policies were **amended**. Two cavalry and four infantry units of African American soldiers were **established** by the **government**. [1] For the first time, the government made African Americans a part of

the regular Army. Additionally, these men were the first African American soldiers in any peacetime army.

Initially, there were **approximately** 5,000 men in these units. The Civil War brought an end to slavery, and the **primary** reason many freed slaves enlisted was because they feared they wouldn't find other employment. Most of these volunteers were illiterate, and they hoped the Army would teach them to read and write. Others chose to enlist because they felt patriotic. Shortly after the war, the government passed a constitutional amendment to officially abolish, or end, slavery. The government also passed additional amendments that gave African Americans citizenship

Vocabulary

dominated (v) *controlled*

amended (v) *changed*

established (v) *brought about; made firm or stable*

government (n) *those people in control of a nation, state, or city*

approximately (adv) *almost exactly*

primary (adj) *most important*

1 Word Reading

You will come across words you might not know, like *cavalry* and *infantry*. Keep reading. When you finish reading, if you still do not know what the word means, use a dictionary to define the word.

These men pose during a lunch break while on patrol in Montana. The 10th Cavalry was stationed at Fort Custer, Montana, (near present day Billings) from 1892 to 1896.

2 **Make Connections**

Would you have fought to protect the United States after decades of being a slave with a government that protected the slave owner?

and African American men the right to vote. These changes encouraged some to serve their country. **2**

The Nickname "Buffalo Soldier"

The men in these new units soon became known as the buffalo soldiers. The Cheyenne are credited with giving this nickname to the troops. They had never seen African American soldiers before, and the Native Americans were very impressed with their opponents' ability to fight. Some say the Cheyenne gave the nickname to the African American troops out of respect. The buffalo was a sacred, or holy, animal to the Native Americans. They say the Native Americans saw the same fighting spirit in the soldiers as they saw in the buffalo. Others believe the nickname was created because the soldiers' curly hair looked like the buffalo's mane. Even though the

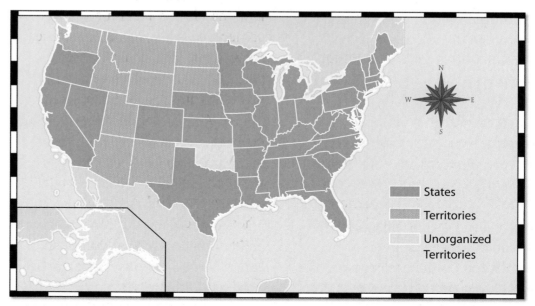

United States Territorial Map, 1880

States

Territories

Unorganized Territories

Expedition 5

Major Charles Young (left), son of slaves, was the third African American to graduate from West Point Military Academy in 1889. He distinguished himself throughout his military career with the Buffalo Soldiers of the 9th and 10th Cavalries.

soldiers rarely used the name to describe themselves, they did take the nickname as a compliment. **3**

The Work and Life of Buffalo Soldiers

The buffalo soldiers quickly established that they were dominant warriors. As the United States was rebuilding after the Civil War, many Americans were moving west. As they moved, the government forced Native Americans from their homes to reservations. The Native Americans were not pleased with this and fought back. Initially, the buffalo soldiers' primary task was to fight the Native Americans in the Indian Wars of the late 1800s. During the Indian Wars, approximately 20 percent of the U.S. troops were African Americans. They fought in more than 177 battles.

After the Indian Wars, the buffalo soldiers fought in the Spanish-American War. They made up approximately 40 percent of the cavalrymen in this war. Many of these soldiers charged up San Juan Hill during the now-famous battle. They also served in the Philippines, Hawaii, and Mexico.

The buffalo soldiers were primarily stationed, or positioned, throughout the Midwest and Southwestern United States. In addition to fighting battles with Native Americans, they were responsible for accompanying settlers, cattle herds, and railroad crews on their journeys west. They were there to protect the settlers from possible attacks from Native Americans and dominating outlaws. **4**

When they were not fighting, the regiments built forts and roads, dug wells, and installed telegraph lines. They also drew maps indicating water sources in the West. They helped establish the groundwork for westward expansion, a concept that the American people believed was

3 **Summarize**
What are the two theories behind the name given to the soldiers?

4 **Visualize**
Think about what you have read. How do you picture the buffalo soldiers looking? Picture their surroundings.

Cpl. Isaiah Mays, a buffalo soldier, is shown wearing the Medal of Honor he received in 1890. Mays, who was born a slave, joined the 10th Cavalry and was stationed in Arizona, where in 1889 bandits attacked a payroll wagon he was guarding. Shot in both legs, Mays crawled two miles to sound an alarm and was awarded the Medal of Honor for his bravery.

the destiny for the country.

Others were assigned to protect what would become Yosemite, Sequoia, and Kings Canyon National Parks. Although national parks did not yet formally exist, these soldiers worked as our nation's first park rangers. **5** Each day, they patrolled the grounds, made maps, and helped build trails. They also enforced, or carried out, laws. The buffalo soldiers made sure that all the natural resources, such as trees, were not destroyed as settlers made their new homes in the West.

Life as a buffalo soldier was difficult. For the most part, their uniforms and equipment consisted of what was left over from the Civil War armies. They generally had to do their jobs with limited resources. They were often given older horses, little ammunition, and malfunctioning equipment. Most of their meals consisted primarily of boiled beef, hash, beans, and cornbread. Occasionally, they had sweet potatoes or a piece of fruit. Finally, they frequently faced discrimination from their commanding officers and the civilians they encountered. Despite these poor conditions, very few buffalo soldiers deserted, or left, the Army. Most enlisted for five years and served their entire term. For their efforts, they were paid approximately $13 a month, plus room and board—much less than their white counterparts.

Honoring Those Who Served

Twenty-six buffalo soldiers have been awarded Congressional Medals of Honor. This prestigious, or respected, award celebrates the bravery and courage of military heroes. Today, many states honor the buffalo soldiers. They hold special ceremonies and reenactments. Artwork of the buffalo soldiers is displayed each February at Guadalupe Mountains National Park. The state of Texas established July as "Texas Buffalo Soldiers Heritage Month." Throughout the month, the memory of these soldiers is honored at exhibitions, living history demonstrations, and festivals. In Houston, visitors can tour the Buffalo Soldiers National Museum. **End**

5 Context Clues

Using context clues, what is a *park ranger*?

Careers in the United States Navy

When people think of joining the U.S. Navy, they often think of life aboard a large ship or submarine. But, the Navy offers much more than life at sea. For those who choose to join this branch of the military, there are many career options available.

Many people enlist in the Navy right after high school. Most initial terms of enlistment are between two and five years. After enlisting, all sailors must complete eight weeks of Navy Boot Camp. This is an intense introduction to life in the Navy. After this, sailors move on to specific skill training for their chosen career path. Navy personnel can pursue a variety of career paths, ranging from cook to civil engineer to foreign language translator.

Air Traffic Controller

Navy air traffic controllers are responsible for directing aircraft from airports or decks of aircraft carriers. They use radios and radar to communicate with other controllers and pilots. They also update aeronautical charts and maps. After their technical training, air traffic controllers spend up to two years in on-the-job training to further develop their skills. They take additional courses and receive individual hands-on instruction. Many sailors earn college credits during this training. New recruits must enlist for five years to pursue careers as air traffic controllers. After their work in the Navy, many move on to become civilian air traffic controllers.

Culinary Specialists

Those with a passion for cooking will be right at home in the Navy. After a four-week training program, sailors can become culinary specialists. They work on every ship and base in the Navy. After starting out in a mess hall, many work their way up to become head chefs. Some even have the opportunity to cook five-star meals for guests at the White House. After their Navy career, many culinary specialists pursue jobs in the hospitality field. They manage restaurants or become chefs. Others become nutritionists or personal chefs.

Diver

The competition to become a diver for the Navy is intense. Candidates must complete an in-depth mental and physical training program. When they are done, a select few men and women will become Navy divers. Divers may

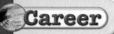

work to deconstruct ocean mines. Some salvage aircraft that were shot down during combat. Others specialize in search-and-rescue missions. Prospective candidates must be in top physical shape and be able to work well under pressure. Divers are given special pay for their hard work. There is an enlistment bonus of up to $30,000. Additionally, these men and women receive dive pay on top of their regular salary each month.

Musician

A musician is another career option available to enlisted sailors. To join this program, enlisted men and women must audition. Then, some sailors have the opportunity to be a part of one of the best music programs in the country. Naval musicians must attend a five-month training program. Upon completion of this course, musicians are then assigned to a Navy Band in the United States, Japan, or Italy. They perform all types of music, from classical to contemporary rock. During this time, training continues. Naval musicians get paid for training while earning college credits and performing around the world. After their service in the Navy, many move on to join professional bands and orchestras as vocalists, musicians, conductors, and composers.

Photographer

Naval photographers use state-of-the-art still and video cameras. They cover news events, ceremonies, and troops in combat.

They also take photos for historical purposes. Some of their work includes aerial photography for mapmaking. Other assignments include editing and producing public relations videos. Photographers may also cover press conferences. Some may work as underwater photographers. Navy-provided training for this job often counts as college credit. As civilians, many Navy photographers pursue careers as journalists, portrait photographers, or film editors.

Salaries

Enlisted salaries start at about $16,000 a year. The earning potential quickly increases with training and years of service. Officers can earn close to $80,000 a year. There are many other benefits involved in joining the Navy. Some of these include bonuses and paid vacations. Sailors also receive health and dental insurance. Retirement savings plans and discounted travel are two other military benefits. Military veterans are also eligible for continuing education benefits, such as the GI Bill. After 90 days of active duty, sailors are eligible to receive full college tuition. Additionally, they get $1,000 a year for books, and a monthly housing allowance.

The Navy offers a wide variety of careers that reach far beyond sailing a ship. The specialized classes and on-the-job training can prepare enlisted sailors for a lifelong Navy career. They also can help people make a smooth transition to the civilian workforce. While developing personally and professionally, many complete college degrees, build retirement savings, and achieve their lifelong career goals.

Now You See It

- How has technology changed visual expression?

- How are graphic arts the same as or different from fine art?

- What graffiti, if any, should be outlawed?

FLY GUY

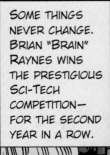

Some things never change. Brian "Brain" Raynes wins the prestigious Sci-Tech competition—for the second year in a row.

Here is your $5,000 check, young man. Congratulations.

Um... thanks... again.

Yeah, Brain. Go! Go away.

Don't even, Chad. You could at least *acknowledge* that he won.

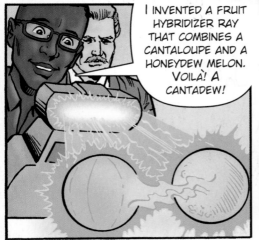

I invented a fruit hybridizer ray that combines a cantaloupe and a honeydew melon. Voilà! A cantadew!

Last year, Brian invented a microfying glass.

I direct a laser beam through the glass onto these spots on the carpet. Voilà! They... shrink!

Too bad he can't get his machine to work on his zits.

Whatever!

You must be very proud, son.

Sure.

Don't spend it all in one place. Ha!

I won't...

My house at eight. Don't be late.

I've won, but I'm still a glork.*

The other kids are going to a party. I'm going... nowhere. Why?

*Glork = geek + loser + dork.

Maybe I should go to the party, anyway, and find out why I wasn't invited.

Nah. They'll just *reject* me.

THE TEEN SCIENCE WHIZ **CONCLUDES** THAT HE NEEDS TO STUDY THE "COOL" KIDS IN THEIR NATIVE HABITAT.

IF I KNOW WHAT THEY LIKE, I CAN BE THE KIND OF PERSON THEY WILL LIKE.

BUT, HOW CAN I GET INTO THE PARTY WITHOUT AN INVITATION?

OF COURSE!

I'LL USE THE MICROFYING GLASS ON MYSELF!

I'LL SHRINK MYSELF DOWN TO THE SIZE OF A BUG.

GO TO THE PARTY... AND BE LIKE THE **PROVERBIAL** FLY ON THE WALL... IF I SURVIVE.

click!

MEANWHILE... A FAMILY OF FAMISHED FRUIT FLIES FEAST ON THE SPOILS OF BRIAN'S HYBRIDIZER EXPERIMENTS.

GO AWAY. SHOO, FLIES.

WHAT IS HAPPENING TO ME? THIS IS **MORPHING** ME INTO A FLY. OH, NO!

COOL! I CAN SEE IN MULTIPLE DIRECTIONS. I CAN LOOK UP, DOWN, ALL AROUND.

THIS ISN'T WHAT I PLANNED, BUT SCIENCE... MARCHES ON! MAKE THAT FLIES ON... OFF TO THE PARTY. FIRST, ONE MORE GRAPE.

ZZZZZZ

CHAD'S HOUSE LATER THAT NIGHT...

I'M BORED.

PLAYING VIDEO GAMES. TALKING ON THE PHONE. NAPPING?

GRAFFITI: VANDALISM OR ART?

Narrator: Welcome to *Sign of the Times*, the talk show devoted to what's going on in our **community** of Westridge. Today, we're focusing on the subject of graffiti. These pictures and words drawn or painted on streets, walls, and buildings are **visible** to us all when we walk or drive through town.

Our two local guests in the studio today feel really strongly about this topic. Muriel Johnson is a longtime resident of our community. She has always been active in community service. Our second guest is a young man, Josh Harding. Josh calls himself an artist. First, let's hear from Muriel, whose apartment building was recently vandalized.

Muriel: Thank you, Ms. Gonzales, for having me on your show. I have lived in Westridge for more than 70 years. What is happening now to the homes and businesses so many of us have owned for years is a disgrace to our community. What I'm talking about is the surge of graffiti splattered on homes and other **residential** properties. Who wants rough drawings and paintings, and sketched words, to cover clean stone, fine red brick, and well-painted buildings?

1 Visualize

Picture how Muriel's apartment building looks with the graffiti.

Narrator: Muriel, tell us about your **experience** with this recent outburst of graffiti.

Muriel: Well, one of my residential buildings, an apartment complex I bought nearly 40 years ago, was recently defaced. One morning last week, I received call after call from the **tenants** who rent my apartments. Each one complained about the disturbing pictures and messages that appeared overnight on the walls of the apartment building. Moreover, the wall across the street also was covered with graffiti. They all have to look at the graffiti because it can be seen from their front windows. The calmness of their homes has been replaced with an uproar over the vandalism. Besides that, my tenants feel personally attacked in what was a safe residential area.

I have a **financial** responsibility to clean up the apartment building. It will take a lot of money. To make my tenants happy, I may even have to pay to have the wall cleaned. I don't make a large profit renting my apartments, and I'm retired. The apartment building is my sole source of income, so this will be a financial burden. These young people who vandalize homes should consider how they affect other community members. They should stop defacing property. The police should find them and make them clean up their damage. They should pay for restoration. **1**

Narrator: Muriel, thank you for sharing your experience. It's easy to see why you find graffiti so

upsetting. I'm sure you aren't alone in your concerns about graffiti. But, our next guest, Josh Harding, has a different perspective on the issue. Josh, I understand you call yourself a "graffiti artist." Do those words really go together?

Josh: You bet. I am working with a group of guys to add art to otherwise drab gray streets in business and residential areas of our community. If Muriel's building and street had been tagged with *our* graffiti, Muriel and her tenants would have been proud of the work of art visible on her building. The art would have enhanced the property. **2**

You see, just because people call my art graffiti doesn't mean it defaces buildings and walls—it improves them, adds living colors and pleasing designs. Even more important, what my group incorporates in our graffiti is a social message. We want to wake people up to the need for tolerance. We want to show people we care about the beauty of the environment. We want to shake people out of

2 **Ask Questions**
A question to ask yourself is: How does Josh's viewpoint compare to Muriel's view?

3 **Visualize**

Picture the graffiti described by Josh.

their gray worlds and bring them light and color. If you've never looked at places we've tagged, you wouldn't know how sad they seemed before. We bring life to them, art to them, and meaning. **3**

Narrator: That is a different way of looking at graffiti—as an art form and social commentary. What do you think, Muriel? Does this change your feelings about your experience?

Muriel: It still won't pay for the cleanup of my apartment building on Summit Avenue. But, I can begin to understand there is more to graffiti than just vandalizing property. I didn't realize these young people feel they are adding art and expressing important messages. I thought they just wanted to destroy other people's property.

Josh: Ah, is your apartment building at 228 Summit Avenue? Is it that gray building across from a concrete wall?

Muriel: Yes, do you know who painted my building?

Josh: Sorry, Muriel, but that's one of the pieces of art and social commentary I was just describing. My group tagged your building and the wall across the street. I'm sorry we've caused trouble and cost you money. We really don't mean to hurt individuals. We just want to express what we feel so others can feel it. Our medium is the gray walls of the community.

Muriel: Josh, thank you for being honest and admitting what you did to my building. What you've said gives me something to think about. Perhaps what you did is art, but you should ask permission from the owner first. Maybe you boys could meet me tomorrow to discuss a cleanup project—at your cost. **4**

Josh: Yes, ma'am.

Narrator: A surprising turn of events here, but our time is up. See you next week on *Sign of the Times.* **End**

4 **Summarize**

How have the opinions of Muriel and Josh changed?

Comic Book Writer

WHAM! BAM! SLAM! KABOOM!

Words with Punch, Images with Pizzazz

If you are a reader of comic books or graphic novels, and you like to write, you might be interested in a career as a comic book writer. Don't let the limited number of words you see in those conversation balloons fool you. Writing comic books involves a clear understanding of language. It requires an ability to use language well to tell a story. Writing also requires knowledge of graphic

arts. You will need to imagine, and explain, how the story will be told visually.

Think about what you see in each frame of a comic. The images that are visible on the page are supported by the words, and the words are supported by the images. An accomplished writer knows how to show just enough and say just enough to tell the story powerfully. Each frame of the comic needs to move logically to the next frame. In this way, a comic book or a graphic novel is more like an animated cartoon you'd see on television than a cartoon in the newspaper, called a still cartoon.

Of course the story itself must be something you, as a comic book writer, want to develop in your own special way. The characters and events will need to seem fresh and exciting, even though most plots—or at least parts of plots—and all the basic themes have been used countless times before:

Batman saves the city, Superman saves the world, Wonder Woman saves the universe. So don't be satisfied with retelling an old story with characters in new costumes. Develop your hero or heroine. Refine the events, focus on unfolding and telling an original story. That's what will bring you readers, and that's where the writing fun lies: creating your own stories.

What kind of training would help you become a comic book writer? Successful writers today advise training in all kinds of writing. Study how to write stories, animations, movies, plays, and speeches. Take courses in creative writing to help develop your own creative skills. Learning the history and technology of movies and animations is also valuable. These help you think about how your still images will merge into a sequence that seems to flow. Classes in which you critique the success of visual media will help you learn what works well and what doesn't. Also, you should practice, practice, practice. The more writing you do, the better you will become at taking your ideas and sharing them

in the format you love. Think of this proverb: Practice makes perfect.

Writing a story is only part of the work needed to create a comic book. You will need to explain clearly to an artist your idea of what belongs in each frame. Some writers provide lengthy descriptions. These leave less chance the artist will misinterpret the details and purpose of the images. Some writers offer less guidance. This allows the artist to contribute more to the creative aspects of the product. Most artists will draw pencil sketches for your comment and approval. A good artist selects the best shading, colors, and angles to capture the emotions, characters, and events of your story. A good artist also adds clues that suggest action—splashed-up puddles, footprints in mud, and so on. You and the artist will work as partners to create the final work.

Last, but very important to your career, is that you will need to publish your work. That way, your effort can turn into a financial success, which can vary widely among writers. Entry-level positions might start at $20,000 a year, while experienced freelance writers could make as much as $95,000 a year. Like other writers, have faith in yourself. Don't be discouraged by rejection. If your stories are creative, exciting, and fun, you will find a way to publish them and entertain readers around the world.

WHEN VIDEOS TURN BAD

How would you define a "film"?

Is it something you have to see in a theater or own on a DVD?

Or, could any video clip, no matter how trivial, be considered a "film"?

What Is a Film?

These questions all **involve** some truth. The word *film* describes the material traditionally, or usually, used to capture images. In that way, anything using the material of film to record the world could be considered a film. But, there are also cultural and historical ideas involved. Film is often seen as necessarily artistic. A great movie may be called a film, but a commercial for a product would not be, even though they are both created with the same media. Whether a film is considered one we can sell depends on what content it will **contain**, not what it's made of.

How Films Began

The motion picture has been around since the 1860s. The earliest films were a series of still frames, or pictures, attached to a spinning drum and viewed through a small window. This is like making a flip book of still images. When you fan the pages quickly, the drawings appear to move. By the 1880s, the earliest motion-picture

Vocabulary

involve (v) *include*

contain (v) *hold within itself; include*

Vocabulary

impact (n) *the power of something such as an event or idea to cause changes or strong feelings*

cameras had been made. These cameras allowed for the creation of movies much like those of today, but they could not record sound. The first films were silent, consisting purely of a sequence of images, nothing else. Dialogue was written on cards and filmed for the audience to read. These popular films had a great **impact** on society because they changed the way people viewed their lives.

Oh, no!
Now what?

Later, inventors figured out how to play sound with the movie. Then the moviegoer could actually hear the dialogue and the sounds of things happening. Eventually, people devised a way to edit film to create special effects, which are illusions that could not be filmed with the rest of the movie. The growth of the film industry has impacted many areas of life, driving the expansion of television and online video services. **1**

Everyone's a Filmmaker

Modern digital technology takes filmmaking from the studio and allows it to be done by individuals. Cell phones, digital cameras, and camcorders all can record video with both images and sound. Affordable computer editing

programs enable these movies to be fixed and changed and published online.

Several Web sites allow members to upload their own content. The video then is able to be viewed by people all over the world. YouTube is one of the best known, with a huge database of user-created content. Some of these videos share interesting news, expose different viewpoints, and create humor. These videos often contain important political or social comments.

However, with these beneficial uses come other uses that are perhaps inappropriate. Some videos criticize

1 Make Connections

Think about what you know about movies. How were early movies different from what you see now?

and attack, just to destroy someone's image or reputation. Individuals or groups may be attacked in ways most people, and sometimes the law, consider unacceptable. Such videos often contain racist, sexist, or otherwise bigoted material. Different people have different **prejudices**. YouTube and similar Web sites are places that can be used to share interesting or helpful information. Unfortunately, people also can post biased and sometimes offensive films.

Where Does It End?

Many of these films can be—and are intended to be—personally damaging. Others may impact people's lives in ways the film creator did not intend. Some filmmakers just wanted to laugh at someone else's mistakes. Some hoped to make a film that gained fame. However, because these films are visible to millions, the films can be incredibly embarrassing for the subjects of the videos. Moreover, the person being portrayed often cannot block or limit the spread of the video.

Even if the "attacked" person can get the site to take down the video, the film could still be circulated. Popular videos are often passed along by individual users. Then the

START/STOP

videos can be published on other sites. This practice can make the spread of the material nearly impossible to stop. The prejudiced, incorrect, and harmful messages these videos contain can be hurtful. How would you like it if your whole school started talking about a video someone had made about you that contained false information? **2**

Free Speech or Slander?

The issue of personal videos becomes a problem of individual rights. The Constitution guarantees citizens freedom of speech, but this freedom does not extend to spreading lies. The force of YouTube and other sites can be positive and powerful. It can spread constructive information about politics or events that make the

public wiser, and help people make good decisions. But, some **reform** is needed, because untrue and damaging content is inappropriate.

The sites hosting the content should be held accountable to remove prejudiced films that spread lies or personally damage people. However, a citizen's right to criticize

3 Summarize
Explain what is the question of great importance mentioned in this paragraph.

must be maintained. This makes reform of the system a difficult and touchy area. Just as we asked, "What is a film?" we also have to ask, "What is appropriate?" Uploading a video of someone slipping and falling on ice, for the purpose of making fun of them personally, is not appropriate. However, a video of several people slipping and falling in front of a business that refuses to clean its walkway might be worthwhile commentary. The second video may actually affect people's lives positively by forcing the business to act.

So if you were to reform the system and remove content, would you remove one, both, or neither? Why? The decision is difficult because it involves both people's right to privacy and their right to freedom. Now that individuals can create films on their cell phones, digital cameras, or other video equipment, this has become a question of great importance. **3 End**

Animation and Gaming Graphics

On the Scene

Suddenly, you feel transported to a mountain. Huge bats—shiny with glaring eyes and sharply pointed teeth—swoop down at you as you cringe in your seat. For a second, the movie made you feel as if you were there. **1**

If you've read graphic novels or comic books, you may have discovered they can be difficult to follow. Sometimes one frame doesn't seem to continue in the next one. People and objects unexpectedly change position from one **image** to the next. The still pictures allow little sense of movement.

Animation is an important **visual** tool for telling a story. It allows viewers to see a story unfold in front of them. It also makes everything realistic and natural.

Early Animation

People began to **produce** animation a long time ago. Beginning in the 16th century, people created objects called "magic lanterns" that would **project** a series of still images onto a screen, much like a modern projector. Images had to be switched by hand. These were very

Vocabulary

image (n) *a picture or other likeness of a person or thing*

visual (adj) *having to do with sight or used in seeing*

produce (v) *make or manufacture*

project (v) *cause to be seen on a surface*

1 Visualize
Picture this scene in your mind.

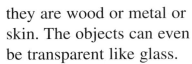

Vocabulary

represent (v) *show or picture something*

primitive animating devices. Flip books, created in the 1800s, showed "moving" drawings—simple animated cartoons. The artist would draw a scene on a page, then redraw the scene with subtle changes to an object on subsequent, or following, pages. When the pages were bound in a book and quickly flipped through, the object in the scene appeared to move.

In the 1860s, people developed mechanical devices to project a series of images in quick succession. This also produced the effect of movement. With the invention of the film camera, animators developed stop-motion animation in which a picture is taken of each image that is redrawn with slight changes. When the images are played back quickly, the objects appear to move seamlessly. This new and different way to **represent** objects showed the world in motion, not at rest. **2**

2 **Summarize**

What is the sequence of how animation developed?

Animation Leaps Ahead

The computer has helped people create new types of visual art. Yet, modern computer animation is done in the same way as stop-motion animation. Design programs allow three-dimensional shapes to be created with the computer by adding shadows and highlights. These can be rotated, stretched, and moved across the screen. The designer can put these shapes together and turn them into representations of objects, such as cars, trees, and people. Images can be applied to the surface of objects to make them look as if

they are wood or metal or skin. The objects can even be transparent like glass.

Complex mathematical equations are used to determine how light reflects from these surfaces. These math equations compute how much shading or highlighting is needed on an object. This allows the production of realistic visual effects. As the objects change and move, a still image is recorded every fraction of a second. When these images are strung together into video, the objects appear to move. These techniques are used in movies to create amazing things, such as alien worlds, spaceships, futuristic cities, and gigantic bats. Also, computer animation is used to film scenes that would be too difficult or dangerous to do in reality, such as jumping off a building or going over a waterfall.

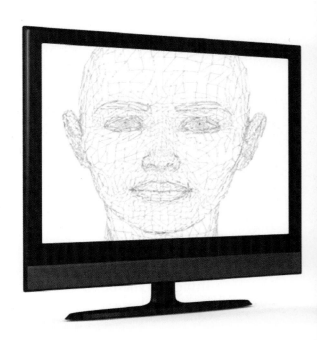

Graphics Take to Gaming

As computers became more powerful, these techniques of movement, shading, and highlighting were adapted to computer gaming. Colorful lines and circles made up early computer games such as Pac-Man. The user, as if looking down on the action from above, manipulated a yellow dot to chomp up blue dots through a labyrinth of paths. Computer game users now get to **participate** in the action as if they were immersed, or put into, the game. They are no longer remote from the world represented on screen, but feel as if they are walking through it. Users interact with this animated world and affect it.

Computer games work similarly to the earlier computer animation software. As the player's character moves, objects appear to move past, getting bigger as they come close, just as objects do in real life. Making the object grow bigger creates the illusion that the object is coming closer. Each fraction of a second, a still image is displayed on the screen. These images show the objects around the player with their correct locations and sizes, making the world appear realistic. These frames are shown one after the other. The eye cannot tell they are still.

Years ago, the most advanced games had only simple geometric shapes like cubes and triangles. Many old games used wire-frame graphics, showing the edges of objects but not filling in their faces. However, modern games have become incredibly realistic. Using lines, shadows, and highlights to create visual illusions, graphic artists trick the eye into seeing movement. Reflections on water look real, characters have flowing hair and rippling clothes, and the textures of brick walls and tree bark are lifelike because of creative uses of lines, shadows, and highlights. **3**

Vocabulary

participate (v) *take part in something with other people*

3 Summarize
Explain the techniques used by graphic artists to make animation look 3-D and move.

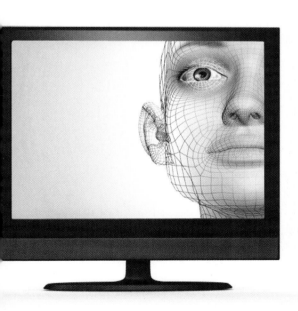

Today, game development doesn't stop when the game leaves the game studio. Participants in the game can add their own content. This addition of user-generated content is called *modding*, from the word *modify*, meaning "change." Players, using the same design software as the developers, can create new objects, new characters, or even new worlds. For example, a player can create a building that looks like his or her school and insert it into the game. This used to be impossible. But, computers have advanced so much that even complicated visual design software runs on many home computers. This trend, in which a game's participants create added objects, has become part of video game culture. A person can use the software to design a map for a popular Internet game and put it on his or her personal Web site for others to download and use. Some people have become so good at this kind of designing that

game companies have hired these "modders" based on their work on the Internet, not on any technical education.

Engaging Other Senses

The visual aspect of games, creating three-dimensional objects, is a vital part of the development process. However, anyone who has played a game with the sound turned off knows that makes the experience less exciting. The creation of music to heighten the sense of game excitement is an important step. Also, each action in the game must have an associated sound. No matter how realistic the game looks, walking and jumping will never seem real if there is no sound. Recently, game developers have designed controllers that vibrate. These give tactile feedback the player can feel, enhancing the realism. **4**

Animation is the most fundamental aspect of computer gaming. However, only by combining visual input with audible and tactile input does a game seem real. What started as a simple attempt to show movement on a page has evolved into a complex virtual world. We can see, hear, and seemingly feel as if we are walking through this world by the creative use of lines and shadows. **End**

4 Context Clues

Reread the last two sentences. What clues help you understand the meaning of *tactile*?

Design Your Own Career

When your brother asks you for directions to the mall, you draw a map. Your random sketches and doodles really impress your friends. As you whiz around buildings in a video game, trying to find and destroy the enemy, you wish the graphics were more varied and realistic. These are examples of skills and interests in art and design that could be applied to the job of a graphic artist. You would find the career competitive, challenging, and personally rewarding.

Graphic artists, or graphic designers, work for many groups, either alone or with a team. They may design for businesses, Internet companies, nonprofit organizations, or the government. They may work for printers as well as publishers of newspapers, magazines, and books. Some artists are hired to work full-time in-house, or at an office. They may participate in a team that creates designs. Others are freelance designers, meaning they are self-employed and often work from home. Representing themselves, they seek out contracts for work. This freedom enables them to select the types of projects they are skilled at and find enjoyable. A few graphic artists work entirely for themselves. They may, for example, create graphic novels, animate cartoons, or design multimedia shows.

Graphic artists at work "in-house." They work for a company at its office.

Graphic artists are the people who create visual images to communicate ideas. As a designer, you would use varying forms of media for your work. You might produce print materials such as posters, logos, and pamphlets for an advertising campaign, or sketch the illustrations for a children's book. For a textbook publisher, you might draw tables, maps, and graphs. You might lay out the photos and information for magazine pages, or create computer-generated art or edit photos for a calendar. Think of the art you see on Web sites, on a video or DVD, on television, and so on. A graphic artist designed that art.

If you were a graphic artist, you would create images that inspire the trust of your client and spark the interest of the target

audience. Your ideas would have to be presented with a keen sense of design. Your knowledge of color theory and typography—the type of lettering—would help. Moreover, you would need to communicate verbally to understand what clients want and to explain what you can do. Your willingness to incorporate others'

ideas would show in your sketches and finished art. You would use problem solving to get your ideas to mesh with the job's requirements. And, you would apply technical skills related to the media you work in.

A graphic artist also needs to be open to change. The artist reforms concepts and styles as jobs or consumers change. You may have been creating advertising for a huge automobile manufacturer. Suddenly, you are called on to design a Web site for a company that sells an automobile with a low impact on the environment. You might have been designing brochures for a fishing company. Next, you are planning a multimedia show for a nonprofit group. If you work in technological design, you could be asked to create an entirely modern cellular phone. If you work in industrial design, you may be hired to draw a plan for a better chair.

Education and Salary

A graphic designer is educated in the terms and technology necessary for the job. The designer studies common design practices and many graphic styles and forms. Most companies require a degree from a four-year college or a two- to three-year design school. Computer graphics and design software knowledge are essential. And, the designer must stay on top of technological advances. Most beginning designers receive on-the-job training. Some achieve higher levels in companies, becoming team leaders or managers. Some teach design at schools and colleges. Average annual salaries for graphic artists in 2008 ranged from $35,000 to $45,000.

Or, maybe this really is your dream job: You are sitting at a computer, and instead of hunting for the enemy, you are creating the background in which an exciting new video game takes place. If you train to be a graphic artist, this dream could become reality.

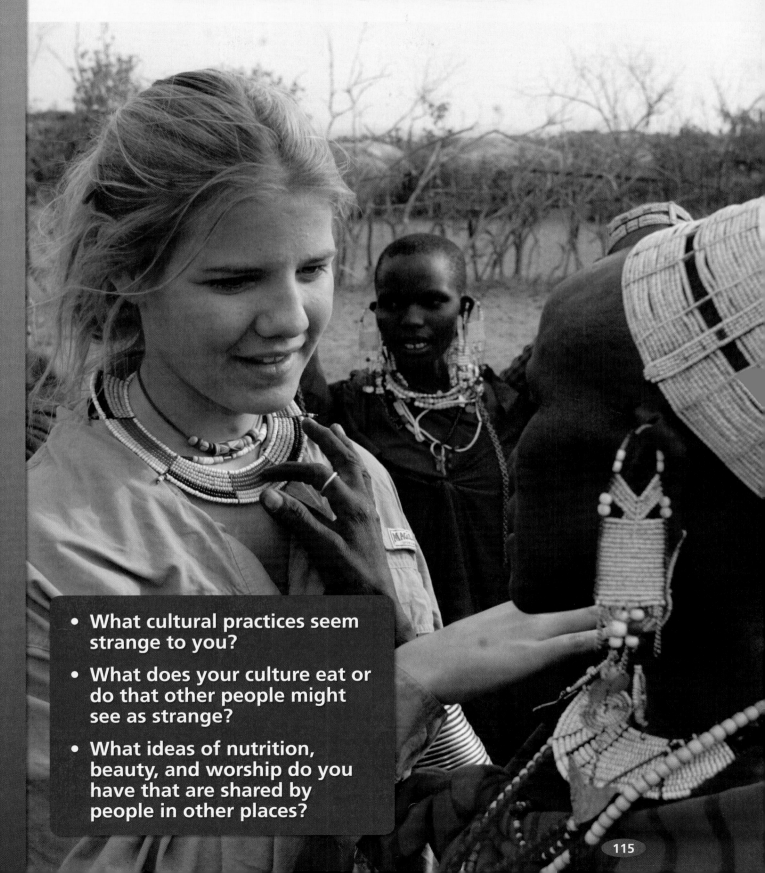

Across Cultures

- **What cultural practices seem strange to you?**

- **What does your culture eat or do that other people might see as strange?**

- **What ideas of nutrition, beauty, and worship do you have that are shared by people in other places?**

Rats Rule!

Vocabulary

culture (n) *a way of life, ideas, customs, and traditions specific to a group of people*

---

1 **Make Connections**

Have you ever seen a menu in a Chinese restaurant with the signs of the zodiac? What other animals are represented?

Rats! In the sewers, in the Dumpsters, and in the streets, rats feed on the leftover food and scraps of humans. They dwell in the filthiest places imaginable. Few creatures in the animal kingdom have a more negative image than the rat. Around the world, rats are seen as revolting, vicious, unclean animals that damage food supplies and spread deadly diseases. However, some people actually keep rats as pets. What's more, the view of rats varies from **culture** to culture more than you might think.

Span the globe and you'll find cultures in Southeast Asia, Australia, and Africa that eat rats as part of their daily diet. In China, the rat is the first of 12 animals in the zodiac. People born in the Year of the Rat are thought to possess such admirable qualities as creativity, honesty, and generosity. **1**

Of all the different ideas about rats, however, one of the most

Rats scrounging the sewers for food

unusual is found in northwest India at the Karni Mata temple. Throughout the year, worshippers **trek** to this 600-year-old temple to show their devotion and pay their respects to its holy residents—20,000 brown rats!

Durga, the Hindu goddess of power and victory

The Legend of Karni Mata

Why on earth would anyone want to worship rats? To **fathom** the answer, you must first know the story of Karni Mata, the Hindu mystic. Born in the 14th century, Karni was believed to be the reincarnation of Durga, the goddess of power and victory. From a young age, this reborn goddess performed many miraculous, or unexplainable, healings, which earned her a **devoted** flock of followers.

As the legend goes, one day a child of one of her tribesmen drowned. When Karni attempted to revive the child, Yama, the god of death, informed her that the child had already been reincarnated. She

was too late, so she made a deal with Yama and rats began emerging, or coming forth, from her small sanctuary. Word of the event spread near and far—Karni had made a deal with Yama. From that day forward, Karni's tribespeople would be reborn as rats until they could be born back into the tribe as humans. "Karni's rats" have been treated like royalty ever since.

A Temple for Rats

In the early 1900s, a local ruler named Maharaja Ganga Singh constructed the temple as a tribute to Karni Mata. He generously donated huge silver gates and **intricate** marble panels. Silver and gold ornaments **adorn** the interior walls of the structure. In the inner temple is a small shrine that many believe Karni Mata made herself, some 600 years ago. Today, the temple is one of India's most famous religious sites. **2**

Rats are treated like royalty at the Karni Mata temple in India.

Royal Rodents

The temple's rats are known as *kabas*, and they rule like kings and queens! Priests set bowls of milk and water around the temple, and

Vocabulary

trek (v) *make a slow, difficult journey*

fathom (v) *understand*

devoted (adj) *loyal and loving*

intricate (adj) *detailed and complicated*

adorn (v) *decorate*

2 Main Idea
What is the main idea of this paragraph?

A baby splashes in the milk set out to feed Karni's rats.

3 | Ask Questions

Think about what you have read. Could you tell a friend about the rat temple?

pilgrims who have made the trek to the temple feed the rats sweet treats called *prasad*. Worshippers drink milk and eat food that's been sampled by a rat; it's considered a great blessing.

However, there is one blessing that's very rare: the sighting of a white rat. **3** Of the thousands of rats that inhabit, or live in, the temple there are said to be only about five white ones. They are thought to be especially holy. Seeing one of these rats is considered very lucky because they are believed to be the manifestation of Karni Mata and her family.

The creation of a rat temple may be hard to fathom, especially given the animal's link with disease. But, during the last century, there has never been an outbreak of illness among the devoted pilgrims who have visited, which may be a miracle in itself! The Karni Mata temple is not for the squeamish. But, if you could transform into any animal, you might consider becoming one of the temple's royal residents. After all, few animals live such charmed lives as the followers of the rat goddess. **End**

Some people believe a sacred white rat could be Karni Mata herself.

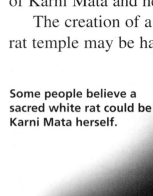

Adventures in Eating

A street vendor offers Cambodia's latest food fad, fried tarantulas basted in oil and garlic.

Everyone has a favorite food. Whatever yours is, chances are that food would seem pretty strange to some people. Every culture around the world has delicious food, but most cultures also have a few recipes that sound odd or even **revolting** to other people. Fried spiders are favorite snacks in the Cambodian town of Skuon. These spiders are specially bred, or raised, in holes in the ground, and each is about as large as a human hand. Eating iguanas is an ancient tradition for the people of Costa Rica. Fried grasshoppers are popular in Africa, and many cultures enjoy chocolate-covered ants.

You're Eating What?

These foods might sound a little **peculiar** to you. But, some of the strangest foods Americans eat have been around for so long that nobody gives them a second thought. Take cheese, for instance. Many Chinese people do not include milk in their diets. They might find the idea of milk ripened by bacteria, an organism that can sometimes cause disease, rather gross. It may not seem peculiar for you to imagine eating crab legs or lobster tails, but in other parts of the world these foods are disturbing.

Across Cultures

Vocabulary

recipes (n)
*instructions
for preparing
something*

ingredient (n) *one
of the items
that something
is made from*

1 Context Clues

Using context clues,
define *blubber*.

2 Ask Questions

Think about what
you read. How are
the foods described
different from what
you eat?

In fact, plenty of dishes in the United States, such as scrapple or head cheese, created out of a pig's head and organs, are positively revolting to people of other cultures.

Fans of Fat

It's not surprising that the food of a culture reflects what is close at hand and what makes the most nutritional sense. For the Inuit, who live in parts of Alaska, Greenland, and Canada, seal and whale blubber have long been an important part of their diet. Plain fat from other animals is also popular in other cultures with cold climates. **1** In the Ukraine, *salo*, or salted pig fat, is eaten raw, smoked, fried, or boiled. **2**

It's in the Blood

Then there's blood. Many cultures around the world include blood in some of their favorite **recipes**. Blood sausage is exactly what it sounds like and is eaten for breakfast in various European countries. It's a sausage made of pigs' blood, fat, and organs and is usually fried. Some places call it blood pudding or black pudding, but it's pretty much the same dish. In Sweden, cooks make blood dumplings out of flour, blood, and salt and serve them with butter and jam. Many Chinese cook with jelled, or firmed, duck or pigs' blood. In the Philippines, a favorite dish is blood stew, which is made with pork and blood. **3**

The Maasai of Tanzania drink a mixture of cow's blood and

Making blood sausages after slaughtering a pig at the Wushi Village, China

milk. Different cultures in Asia and Eastern Europe also include blood soup among their favorite dishes. In Mexico, a special type of soup uses goat's blood as the main **ingredient**. Why blood? It has plenty of iron, and it helps thicken sauces and soups. It is truly a multipurpose food. But, some cultures do not allow blood in their meals. In Jewish and Muslim cultures, religious law forbids people to eat blood. Instead, the preparation of meat must be supervised to make sure that as much blood as possible is removed before cooking.

Heads to Toes

Eating the ribs of a cow or pig is normal in the United States. What other animal body parts are enjoyed around the world? Jellied cow's foot is a Polish dish that is just what it sounds like: a cow's foot cooked for many hours in water with garlic and spices until it takes on a jellied **texture**. Norwegians have a traditional dish of sheep's head that is often served around Christmas. [4] The head is boiled and all of it is eaten, including the eyes, tongue, and ears. The French counterpart to this dish is called *tête de veau* or "calf's head." The brain is served on a plate with the head. Mexicans also serve brains in a similar dish called *tacos sesos*, or tacos made with cow's brains. A traditional Scottish dish called *haggis* is basically a sausage, except the sausage casing is made from a

Raw haggis

sheep's stomach. Seal flipper pie is traditionally eaten at Easter in Newfoundland, Canada. What is the secret ingredient? You guessed it: seal flippers!

An Unusual Nest

Some delicacies around the world are not only unusual, they're extraordinarily expensive. For hundreds of years, Chinese cooks have made a dish called "bird's nest soup." The main ingredient in this recipe is the nest of tiny birds called cave swifts. If you're thinking of a textured structure made of twigs and straw, think again. Cave swifts make nests entirely out of their own spit, which hardens in the air. When combined with water, the hard nests

Vocabulary

texture (n) *the look and feel of something*

4 Make Connections
What traditional dish does your family serve for special holidays?

A man collects nests for bird's nest soup.

Vocabulary

excretes (v) passes
   waste matter out
   of the body

The Asian Palm Civet plays an important role in making the world's most expensive coffee.

become squishy in texture and a lot like gelatin. Millions of cave swifts' nests are pulled off cave walls each year. Then they are cleaned and sold to restaurants, where they are served as bird's nest soup. The work of pulling the nests off cave walls is extremely dangerous. Because of this, cave swifts' nests are one of the most expensive animal products people can buy. Eating bird spit may seem revolting to you, but people in Hong Kong will pay between 30 and 100 U.S. dollars for a bowl.

Beastly Beverage

People all over the world drink coffee, but Kopi Luwak is the most expensive coffee in the world. Most coffee comes from berries picked from coffee trees. The seeds inside the berries are roasted to make coffee beans.

But, Kopi Luwak goes a step further. In Indonesia, the Asian Palm Civet, an animal that looks like a cat, eats coffee berries as part of its diet. Then, it **excretes** the partially digested beans. The excreted beans are washed and lightly roasted. These beans are used to make this incredibly expensive coffee. It is said that the process of going through the Asian Palm Civet's digestive system gives the coffee beans a very peculiar flavor. It's got to be special because people are willing to pay astonishing prices for it. **5**

The next time you eat a cheese sandwich or a burger and fries, just think—someone across the world who is snacking on fried spiders might think your dinner is really disgusting. **End**

5 Ask Questions

Think about what you read. Ask yourself questions about things you don't understand or things that leave you wondering. For example, how did people discover these foods to be tasty?

Chef

If you enjoy preparing food and presenting it in an attractive way, then you might consider a career in the culinary arts. Chefs and cooks can be artists with food, using their skills to prepare and serve meals in a variety of situations. When people think of chefs, they often picture someone in a tall white hat cooking delicious food in an upscale restaurant. This can be an accurate portrayal because many chefs work in fine dining establishments. However, the world of culinary careers is much broader than that.

There are as many different types of restaurants as there are people who like to eat. From elegant and expensive steakhouses to friendly cafes and local diners, beginning chefs have a wide variety of restaurants from which to choose. Chefs also can find employment in hotels, catering facilities, and conference centers. Many corporations have cafeterias where their employees often eat lunch and breakfast. Hospitals, nursing homes, and assisted living facilities need talented chefs to prepare food for residents and their guests. Personal chefs prepare food for one family on a full-time basis.

Each situation can offer a different set of benefits and advantages. When you're thinking of a career as a chef, it is smart to look beyond the restaurant.

The educational requirements to become a chef are as diverse as the jobs themselves. Many chefs get their start in vocational schools where they learn basic cooking skills, nutrition information, and food handling and sanitation procedures. These courses can range from a few months to two years and are open to high school students and beyond. Many community colleges offer a two-year food

chef's responsibilities may include preparing menus and ordering food. Many chefs visit local farmers' markets or other suppliers to get the best selection of ingredients for that day's menu.

Most chefs work long hours, especially those who work in restaurants, where the last customer might not leave until midnight. Cooking is also a physically demanding job. Chefs must spend a lot of time on their feet in very hot kitchens. The job also involves a lot of heavy lifting—think of all those huge sacks of flour or sugar. It can be dangerous, too, because chefs handle extremely hot food and sharp knives.

Sometimes the monetary rewards for the hard work are not great. An entry-level chef might make only a few dollars more than minimum wage. However, a top chef or restaurant owner can earn a much larger income. Some chefs can earn more than $100,000 a year. Your skills, where you work, and the type of chef you are will determine where your pay will fall in the salary range from just above minimum wage to more than $100,000.

If you can stand the heat and love to cook, a career in the culinary arts can be a fulfilling path in life.

services or culinary arts program resulting in an associate's degree.

Some colleges and universities also offer a culinary arts curriculum. These schools usually pair cooking classes with a course in business and hospitality. They may have a four-year program for those who plan to own or manage a restaurant or other food-service business.

Culinary arts schools offer a highly specialized education in various cuisines and cooking styles. If you aspire to be a top chef in a fine restaurant, a culinary arts school might be your best choice. Students usually need from nine to 24 months to complete a culinary arts program at one of these schools.

Chefs do a lot more than just cook. A

The Multicultural Search for *Beauty*

The 15-year-old was getting ready for a party. First, she painted her nails with a dark red polish and let it dry. Then, looking in a mirror, she applied light powder to her face, ruby red lipstick to her lips, and brown pencil to her shaved eyebrows. Next, she combed her hair, using gloss to make it shine. That done, the girl dressed, and as a finishing touch, fastened a heavy gold necklace around her neck. She checked her reflection once again in the mirror. It was perfect!

This scenario could happen here today. But, you may be surprised to learn that the 15-year-old who used cosmetics, hair product, and jewelry to **alter** her appearance lived in China about 2,000 years ago.

For thousands of years and in different parts of the world, men and women have found ways to enhance their looks for different reasons. Sometimes they altered their body to appear more attractive to the opposite sex. For example, women all over the world wore corsets around their waists for many centuries. The corset was designed to give women a small waist that was considered beautiful. Women wore this unbelievably tight garment under their clothes. Many stories have been told of organ damage and broken ribs in the name of beauty. Other times, people modified their bodies to **assert** their **status** in

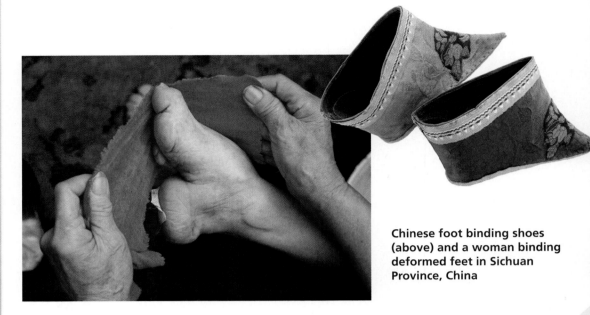

Chinese foot binding shoes (above) and a woman binding deformed feet in Sichuan Province, China

society. Decades ago, wealthy women in China practiced foot binding. Small feet were not only a sign of wealth, they were a sign of beauty. Between the ages of 3 and 11, girls would have someone tightly wrap, or bind, their four small toes on each foot. Done correctly, this would keep the foot from growing, and the toes would actually be wrapped under the foot. Women would end up with tiny feet, one-third the size of normal feet. Many times women would be crippled and left to depend on others for many things. In both cases, extreme measures were taken to be beautiful in the eyes of society. **1**

Different cultures emphasize different parts of the body. One culture appreciates full lips. Another culture values long, slender necks. And, what is attractive to one culture may seem odd to another. What stays the same is that some people in all cultures go to great lengths to have others in their society say, "Wow!"

A Necklace of Another Kind

Welcome to Myanmar, a large country in Southeast Asia. This country is known for its majestic mountain ranges, historic temples, and secluded beaches. But, it is also known for a **distinct** tribe of people, the Kayan. The women in this tribe in the northeast of Myanmar have necks that resemble that of a giraffe.

Achieving that look isn't easy, for the women are born with necks that are normal sizes. To attain it, a Kayan woman wraps her neck in a series of high brass coils. The result is that the woman's head stretches very high up and her chin juts out in front, giving the impression that she has an elongated neck. With the coils in place, the distance between her chin and her shoulders can be as great as 12 inches. Made of brass, the coils are smooth and can weigh as much as 12 pounds.

There are theories as to how and why the neck coils originated.

1 Main Idea

Find the main idea sentence in this paragraph. What details support it?

Kayan women show the various stages of neck rings.

Some say it was to protect women from being bitten on the neck by tigers or from attacks by rival tribes competing for land and status. Others say it had religious significance, a **tribute** to an ancient deity, or god. No one knows for sure.

The neck coils require maintenance. The women scrub them clean with a solution of lime, straw, and tree bark. Then, the women go about their work, never letting the coils interfere with their chores and everyday living.

You may wonder when Kayan females start wearing neck rings. At age 6, an older woman places a short coil around the girl's neck. Then, at about age 10, the coil is replaced with a longer and heavier spiral. By the time the girl has grown into adulthood, she is wearing a full set.

Admittedly, the rings are uncomfortable, yet women wear them anyway. "It's **tradition**," explained one. Neck rings can be hot, especially in very warm weather.

"We get used to them," said another. Clearly, the practices of one's ancestors have a powerful hold on a culture and its people today. **2**

Piercings Abound

While some people adorn their bodies, other people pierce them. People all over the world pierce ears, noses, lips, tongues, and various other body parts. Where did these practices come from? Nose piercing has been traced back 4,000 years. But, its popularity arose in the 16th century when women in India often wore nose rings. Back then, rich women used nose rings to assert their wealth and status. As the family became richer,

2 Visualize
As you read the descriptions, picture in your mind what you or someone you know would look like with neck rings.

the woman wore an increasingly larger ring.

Traditionally, the nose ring was placed in the left nostril, rather than the right. According to Indian medicine, the left side is associated with the female reproduction process and a nose ring is said to lessen the pain of childbirth. Today, however, the nose ring—whether worn in India or in the United States—is often used as decoration. Earlobe piercings are one of the world's most popular piercings and have been around for centuries. The tradition probably started as a way to keep demons and evil spirits out of the body because metal repelled demons, which entered the body through the ears—or so people believed. The oldest mummified body in the world was found frozen in an Austrian Glacier in 1991. Tests showed the body to be more than 5,000 years old. The body

had pierced ears, and the holes had been enlarged to roughly the size of a pea.

Though it, too, began with ancient civilizations, the piercing of the lips is common throughout the world. Many people insert objects into the piercings, such as rings, pins, or disks. The Dogon tribe of Mali and the Nuba of Ethiopia wear rings in their lips for religious purposes. Among tribes of Central Africa and South America, piercings are stretched to extremely large proportions, and large wooden or clay plates are inserted. Women in the Makololo tribe of Malawi wear lip plates in the upper lips to make them beautiful.

Tongue piercing also began with ancient civilizations like the Mayas and Aztecs. The tongue was pierced to draw blood to appease angry gods and to create an altered state of consciousness, allowing communication with the gods. **3**

3 **Ask Questions**

After reading the last three paragraphs ask yourself, "How are these cultures' views of beauty similar and how are they different?"

This African tribal woman is a model of beauty in her culture with her enlarged ear piercing and lip disk.

The Greatest of Tattoos

You have probably seen people who sport a tattoo, perhaps a bird in flight or a small heart. The tattoos are a way to distinguish themselves. But, some men in Japan take tattooing to an extreme, covering nearly the whole body—chest, shoulders, upper arms, back, buttocks, and legs—with a full body tattoo. While tattoos in the United States often have personal significance, or importance, such as a tribute to a friend or family member, full body armor, as it is known in Japan, is based on traditional folktales from Japanese theater. As a result, a typical full body tattoo shows one large image from a story of long ago—perhaps a fire-breathing dragon, a savage tiger, or a supernatural being, with abilities beyond that of natural man. The effect can be scary and threatening.

Getting a tattoo is painful, yet men put up with the discomfort. Some do it to test themselves, trying to prove they are "real men," able to endure months of weekly visits to the tattoo artist. Others simply appreciate the beauty of an image from literature.

Whatever their motivation, today, full body tattoos are discouraged in Japan. As a result, few men show their tattoos in public. In fact, to conceal a large tattoo for their customers, tattoo artists cover most of the body with the body art, but leave a blank space down the middle

of the customer's chest for occasions when the man wears an open-collar shirt.

American Beauty

Many Americans also go to extremes to become "beautiful." They starve themselves to become thin, lose sleep to keep from messing up their hairdos, undergo risky cosmetic surgery, risk skin cancer to become tan, suffer through piercings and tattoos—all in the name of beauty.

The next time you see a TV ad in America for some sort of body enhancement—like chandelier earrings or musk-scented cologne—think back to body alterations done around the world to achieve a desired effect. Keep in mind that through the years and across many cultures, people have found different ways to assert their status and say, "Check me out!" **4** Practices differ because of each culture's distinctive values, lifestyle, and history. **End**

4 **Make Connections**
What do you do to enhance your beauty? Why do you think it makes you more beautiful?

A Big Mac for Everyone?

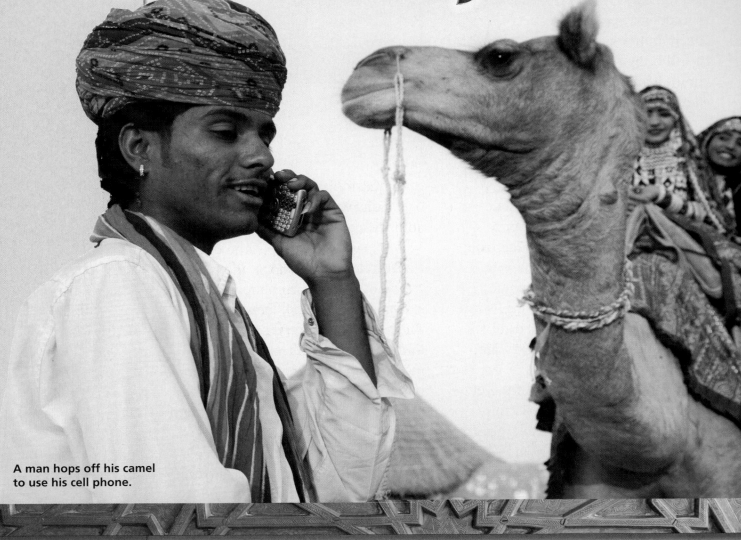

A man hops off his camel to use his cell phone.

Vocabulary

originated (v) *began from somewhere or something*

Westernization and Americanization

A tribesman in a remote village in Papua New Guinea wears a Led Zeppelin T-shirt. A goat herder in Ethiopia makes a call on a cellular telephone. A child in Peru opens a bag of Cheetos. What do these events have in common? They are all examples of Westernization.

Westernization occurs when cultures adopt customs or technologies that **originated** in North America and Western Europe. Denim jeans, rock music, and junk food have been some of the most

American-made washing machines are imported around the world. Why do you think this modern convenience is so popular?

popular fashions and trends that Western culture has brought to the rest of the world. Technologies, like washing machines, refrigerators, cell phones, and computers, have also made their way into other cultures.

Often a culture will adopt some elements of another culture and **incorporate** those elements into their own traditions. Heavy metal music, for example, originated in the United States, but there are countless bands in the Middle East that have made that form of music their own. Many countries have incorporated some elements of Western dress along with their classic clothing. As a result, you might see a Fijian woman wearing Nikes with her traditional grass skirt.

Americanization is Westernization that comes specifically from the culture of the United States. All over the world, American movies, music, clothing, and even foods are **prevalent**. If you visit places as far away as Jerusalem, Cape Town, and Beijing, you will recognize the same chains of restaurants and shops, the same styles of clothing, and the same kinds of technology. However, Americanization is not limited to big cities. In fact, aspects of American culture have made their way to some of the most **remote** places on the planet. **Imported** VCRs or DVD players bring American movies to any town or village with electricity. The products and technology that viewers observe in those movies are often considered modern and desirable, particularly by young people.

However, American culture is often at odds with traditional cultures. Short skirts and tight shirts, for example, are prohibited in many cultures. Graphic song lyrics are offensive; food items may be forbidden. On the other hand, cell phones make communication easier,

A Chinese man delivers Coca-Cola. How is soda transported in the United States?

1 Context Clues

Using context clues, what do you think *conveniences* means?

and conveniences like washing machines and refrigerators make daily tasks less time-consuming. **1**

Some people say that the importation of Western or American technology, foods, medicines, and clothing make people's lives in non-Western countries easier and better. Other people say that Westernization is bad—stripping cultures of what makes them unique and self-sufficient. Many elders believe that the incorporation of any Western way of life is destructive and forces them to rely on other countries, which is perceived as bad. Most likely, the truth is somewhere between those two extremes. Let's take a look at an example

of Americanization that may be familiar to you.

Case Study in Americanization: McDonald's

With more than 13,000 restaurants in the United States, it is likely that there is a McDonald's in your neighborhood. But, did you know that there are McDonald's restaurants in 119 countries and territories across the globe? What started in 1940 as a hamburger stand in San Bernardino, California, became a symbol of American culture throughout the world. When McDonald's opens its first restaurant in a new country or

A McDonald's in Jordan. Do you think they serve any specialty items here?

community, it is generally welcomed as a sign of modernization. People line up to be among the first to eat at the new restaurant. At the grand opening of McDonald's in Kuwait City, the drive-thru line was 7 miles long. **2**

There may be benefits to a community when McDonald's opens a restaurant. Among these benefits is that McDonald's brings money into a community by providing jobs for local employees. In addition, the McDonald's Corporation donates money to local charitable **organizations**. Finally, McDonald's holds to high standards of cleanliness and food quality. A study in Hong Kong showed that the clean public bathrooms available in McDonald's restaurants put pressure on other restaurants to

provide the same level of service and hygiene.

There also may be drawbacks, or disadvantages, for a community when McDonald's arrives. Often, elders in a community mourn the loss of traditional foods and ways of life. Rather than eating a home-cooked meal made with local ingredients and taken with extended family, young people can grab a hamburger imported from far away. Although McDonald's makes an effort to include local dishes on its menus, such as rice and beans in Costa Rica and a vegetarian burger in India, those choices are not as prevalent as burgers, fries, and shakes. In addition, the food that McDonald's sells is often higher in fat, salt, and sugar than traditional foods. This unhealthy food can

Vocabulary

organizations (n) *groups of people joined for particular purposes*

2 Make Connections
What would you be willing to wait in a 7-mile long line for?

3 Summarize

Summarize the drawbacks of an American restaurant moving into a new country.

lead to increases in fatal health conditions, such as heart disease, obesity, and diabetes. **3**

Clearly, Westernization is a complicated issue. While there are benefits, like simplifying household tasks with imported technology, there are also drawbacks, like changing ways of life that have worked for thousands of years.

Un-Westernized Cultures

Whether by choice or because of forces beyond their control, some cultures have not had much contact with the Western world. A map of McDonald's locations shows a number of countries in Africa and Central Asia without McDonald's restaurants. **4** There are probably multiple reasons for this. Perhaps the local people or governments are resistant to Westernization. Equally likely, those places do not have the infrastructure, or basic facilities, to support a McDonald's. Perhaps there are no paved roads, or the roads are damaged or

4 Text Features

Using the map can help you understand the text. Why do you think these areas have no McDonald's? What do they have in common?

dangerous. Perhaps people do not have enough money to eat at a restaurant because their economy is not money-based. The most remote cultures tend to resist the advances of Westernization most successfully just because they are difficult to access. Imagine trying to set up and stock a McDonald's in a Pakistani village that's an 8-hour hike from the nearest paved road!

As it becomes easier to access technology, even the most remote cultures are likely to be affected by Westernization. This can be good and bad. People would like to have the freedom to choose the things that will make their lives easier and better, regardless of where they originated. At the same time, it would be a very boring world if everyone wore the same clothes, listened to the same music, and ate the same foods. Perhaps a Big Mac should be a choice, but it should not be the only choice. **End**

McDonald's Spans the Globe

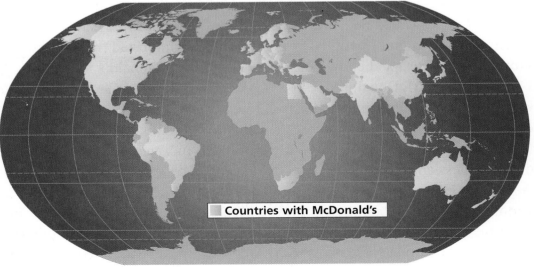

Countries with McDonald's

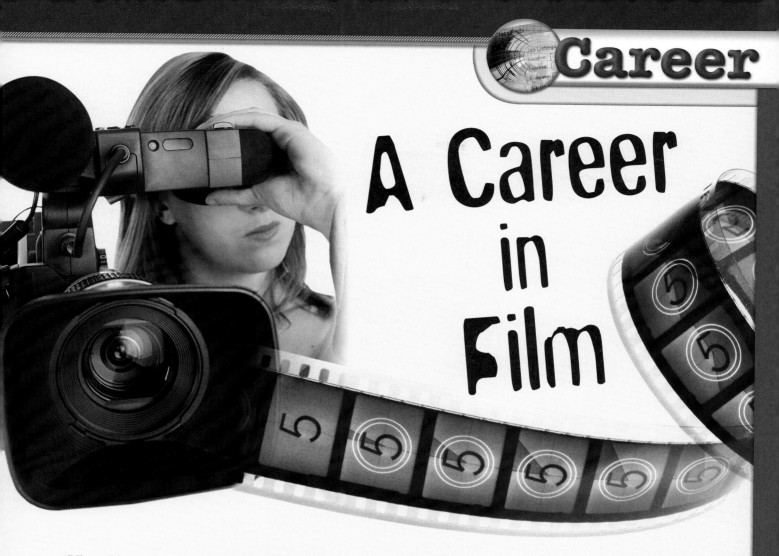

A Career in Film

Visual images are all around us. Many people enjoy capturing moments and events on camera or video. These experiences can range from taking photos at a family gathering to videotaping a sporting event. But, what if you think bigger? What about shooting video or taking pictures in unusual places at unusual events? Millions of people make their living doing just that. They work on camera crews to shoot documentaries, TV shows, commercials, movies, or music videos.

A camera crew has opportunities for many different kinds of work. The camera operator—the person who takes the photos or shoots the video—is just one part of a large team.

A film loader is one of the most important people on a camera crew. You've probably already figured out that this person's job is to load the film into the cameras, but the job

entails much more than that. The film loader needs to make sure the right film is used. He or she has to load the film in a light-free environment, following specific technical instructions so that the film is not damaged. Then, when the film shoot is done, it's up to the film loader to download the film without exposing it to light and dust and send it into production. Film loaders also order all the equipment and film required for a day's photo shoot, coordinate film and equipment deliveries, and inventory all the film at the end of the day before it is handed over to the production crew.

The assistants on a camera crew get the set ready for the cameras to start rolling. Assistants set up the shots, tell actors where to stand, mark the studio floor to indicate actors' positions, and monitor rehearsals to ensure that every actor is in focus while filming a scene.

There are different levels of assistants. The first assistant camera person is the top of the ladder, making sure that everything runs properly and managing the set or photo shoot. He or she reports to the project's director of photography, while other assistants and crew people report to the first assistant.

The camera operators are the people who actually film the scenes. The director of photography and the first assistant tell the camera operator what kind of shot they want. They discuss which angles are best, what features to highlight, and what they want the finished product to look like. Then it's up to the operator to film the scene to those specifications. Most movies, music videos, and TV shows have multiple cameras to film scenes, and each camera has its own operator.

A typical workday for a person on a camera crew might go like this. He or she comes to the set and reviews which scenes are being shot that day. The crew person needs to know what type of film and which cameras are being used that day. He or she is responsible for being sure that all the equipment is set up, loaded, and ready. Some test shots are taken to ensure everything is working properly. Then, when the actors arrive and are in place, filming starts. A scene may be filmed more than once to ensure no one makes a mistake, the lighting is just right, and everything looks as the director wants it.

The best way to learn how to be a camera crew person is to train your eye. Begin capturing still images with a camera, then improve your skills from there. Many high

schools have video production on campus, and students are involved in all facets of the production. After high school, some vocational schools and community colleges offer courses in this field, as do four-year universities. Get as much experience as you can by working on school productions or making your own films or music videos.

You can volunteer or take a job at a film or video production house and attend workshops, seminars, and classes. Introduce yourself to people you meet who are already in the industry and ask for their advice and assistance—networking is key in any industry, but especially in film.

Working on a camera crew is not the steadiest job because crew people usually work on a project-to-project basis. Every time a project ends, you can be out of work until you find a new assignment. Having a supplemental part-time job can help financially. Salaries vary widely based on job type, region, and experience.

With hard work and the right connections, you might find yourself behind the camera in the career of your dreams. Take your best shot!

Back in Time

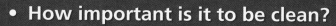

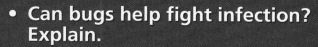

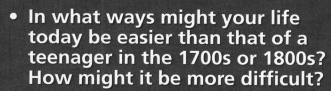

- How important is it to be clean?

- Can bugs help fight infection? Explain.

- In what ways might your life today be easier than that of a teenager in the 1700s or 1800s? How might it be more difficult?

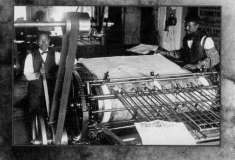

1600s   1700s   1800s   1900s   2000s

137

Clean as Can Be?

1 Main Idea

What is this paragraph mostly about?

Like most Americans, you would probably agree that taking a daily shower or brushing your teeth is a **rational** way to stay clean and healthy. These **customs** would have been a shocking idea just a few hundred years ago. It might be hard to imagine, but our **current** customs about cleanliness are not what they were in the past. Until the 1700s, most people saw no **purpose** in bathing. They believed that simply changing your linen underclothes would keep you clean. **1**

By the following century, more Americans began to see the purpose of bathing, but many Europeans still stuck to their customs regarding clean linens. Without indoor plumbing, hot baths were a rare luxury in America, and most people took cold baths instead. Soap was so hard to make that it was often more rational to save it only for the laundry. People were usually most concerned with having a clean face and hands because those parts were what others could see. No matter how dirty you were everywhere else, a clean face and hands equaled perfect cleanliness.

As for hair care, this too was much different in the 18th and 19th centuries from current practice. People rarely washed their hair, and when they did, they typically used only water. During the 1700s, powdered wigs were all the rage. The first wig was created as a rational solution for French King Louis XIII, who was balding. Suddenly everyone wanted to follow his example. Both men and women wore wigs, especially the upper classes, or rich people. The most expensive wigs were made of human hair, but horse and goat hair also were used. Though there was no real purpose for powdering wigs, people just liked the way they looked. Wig owners also used pomade. This fragrant ointment was a **substance** made of mashed apples, honey, and other sticky ingredients such as bear grease to keep the powder sticking to the wigs. But, this made wigs attractive to moths and other vermin, which often nested right inside the wigs. **2**

King Louis XIII

Vocabulary

substance (n)
something that has weight and takes up space; matter

2 Summarize
What are the old-fashioned practices for staying clean mentioned in the passage?

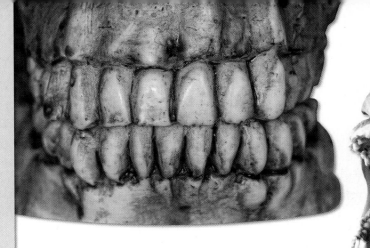

By now you may be wondering what substance—if any—Americans used on their teeth a couple of centuries ago. It was certainly nothing like the current forms of toothpaste we all use. Some early toothpastes were made from urine. The ammonia in urine was found to be very cleansing. By the 1700s, tooth powder was introduced. This was a substance that included harsh abrasives, such as brick dust and crushed pottery, that probably did more harm than good.

By the 1800s, tooth powders evolved and contained chalk, soap, and some kind of sweetener to enhance the taste. Even so, not many Americans understood the importance of regular brushing. It is not surprising then that many people lost their teeth and needed false teeth called dentures. To make the dentures, dentists in the 1700s and 1800s often used the teeth of corpses. Teeth were sometimes stolen from the dead on battlefields during wars. People also could sell their own teeth for money. George Washington himself wore dentures, but they were not wooden as some people believe. They would have been made of metal and ivory or human or animal teeth. **3**

It's likely these old customs of cleanliness would not appeal to many Americans today. Reading about them might send some running to the shower. **End**

George Washington's actual dentures

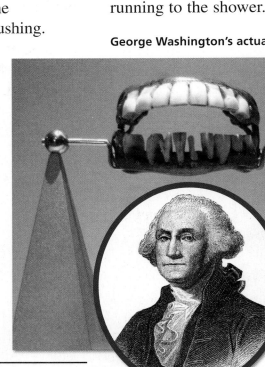

3 Ask Questions

Think about what you read. What questions might you have about early toothpaste and dentures?

Strange Medicine
—Believe It or Not

Many people fantasize about traveling back in time. But, if you could transport yourself back to 18th century America, you had better not get sick. There were few doctors in those days, and most never earned a medical degree. You may wonder how they determined a good health **treatment** from a poor one. The most popular health treatments—bloodletting, blistering, and purging—were often harder for a patient to **tolerate** than the illness.

During this period, doctors had no knowledge about microscopic organisms that cause diseases, such as bacteria, germs, or viruses. Instead, they relied on common medical theories of the day to explain diseases. One theory claimed that diseases could be caused by three conditions. They believed a diseased body was salty, putrid, or oily. Doctors would **prescribe** bleeding and purging, or making a patient vomit, to flush out the impurities that caused these conditions.

Another painful but widespread practice in the 1700s was blistering. Also known as cupping, this remedy was frequently used to treat respiratory illnesses. It involved heating a glass cup to a high temperature and placing it on the

The practice of cupping would cause blisters such as this one.

Vocabulary

treatment (n) *medical method to try to cure or heal*

tolerate (v) *put up with; bear*

prescribe (v) *advise to take a certain medicine or treatment*

Vocabulary

gruesome (adj)
*causing fear and
disgust; horrible*

survive (v) *stay alive
through or after a
dangerous event*

1 Summarize

Explain the treatments
described and why they
were used.

patient's back. When a blister formed, the sores were opened to release the thick, yellowish matter known as pus. Considering the lack of basic knowledge about the human body, it's no wonder the average life expectancy was only 35 years. **1**

The Practice of Bloodletting

Bloodletting was one of the most popular medical treatments in history up to the late 1800s. This **gruesome** practice involved drawing large quantities of "bad blood" so new, healthy blood could refill the body. This procedure was thought to cure everything from high blood pressure to fevers to disease. The more serious the health problem, the more blood they would remove.

Although doctors often prescribed bloodletting, barber-surgeons usually performed the

This bloodletting device with spring-loaded lancets was called a scarificator.

procedure. The red-and-white striped pole of the barbershop, which is still used today, is a symbol of this old-fashioned practice. The red represents the blood that is drawn, the white represents the tourniquet used, and the pole represents the stick the patient squeezes to dilate, or expand, the veins.

Strange devices were used to draw blood. Spring-loaded lancets came into use in the early 1700s. The lancet, a double-edged surgical blade, was cocked and a "trigger" fired the blade into the vein. The blood was caught in shallow bowls. Often, blood was drawn from multiple incisions, or cuts, in the body. When the patient became faint, the "treatment" was stopped. Thankfully, bloodletting was exposed as a risky and undesirable practice by 1900.

George Washington was a great believer in bloodletting, but it led to his death in 1799. After suffering from a severe throat infection, doctors drained nearly 8 pints of the vital fluid from his body within 24 hours. Sadly, the president didn't **survive**. The treatment proved more fatal than the disease.

Taking blood from the human body is a common practice today, but for different reasons. Also, the procedure has been renamed and vastly improved. A skilled technician, known as a phlebotomist, draws a small amount of blood for laboratory tests or blood transfusions. Having your blood drawn today is relatively painless, and they won't take too much. **2**

2 Main Idea

What is main idea of
this section?

Hospital tents in rear of Douglas Hospital in Washington, D.C., during Civil War time

Civil War Medicine: Amputations

By the time of the American Civil War in the 1860s, medical knowledge was still quite primitive. Doctors didn't understand the basic causes of infection and could do little to prevent it. This was a time before antiseptics and sanitary practices were required during surgery. As a result, minor wounds easily became infected and fatal. Twice as many soldiers died of disease during the Civil War than of gunshot wounds.

The most painful scene to observe on the battlefield was the surgeon's camp. The number of wounded was staggering. Amputation became the treatment of choice for injuries to a leg or an arm. Many amputations were performed within 10 minutes.

Chloroform was used as an anesthetic to reduce the trauma of the gruesome procedure. Doctors applied the sweet-smelling liquid to a cloth and held it over the soldier's

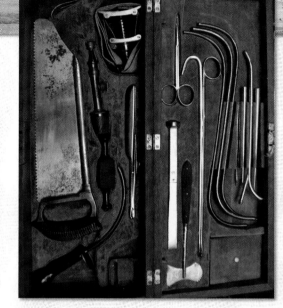

An amputation kit

nose and mouth until he was unconscious. When chloroform was unavailable, wounded soldiers would drink whiskey or simply bite a bullet to help them tolerate the excruciating pain. After the patient was sedated, a tourniquet was placed around the soldier's arm or leg to control bleeding. Surgeons made circular incisions with a scalpel and finished severing the arm or leg with a bone saw. **3**

Surgical camps were busy around the clock. Stacks of amputated limbs sometimes piled up to 5 feet high. Despite these horrible conditions, as many as 75 percent of the Civil War amputees managed to survive.

3 **Context Clues**
What context clues in this section help you figure out the meaning of *amputation*?

What's Old Is New: Leeches and Maggots

When it comes to old remedies, leeches and maggots could qualify as the most revolting. Leeches are bloodsucking worms usually found in lakes, ponds, and streams. They were used in ancient times to treat many ailments including headaches, ear infections, and hemorrhoids. In the 1800s, leeches were back in use for bloodletting. But, they fell out of favor when doctors realized that the patients they bled often did worse than other patients.

4 Summarize

Explain how leeches and maggots help fight infection.

The use of maggots, the wormlike larvae of flies, for wound care also can be traced back hundreds of years into antiquity. In America, the first therapeutic use of maggots was made during the Civil War. A doctor noticed the high survival rate in patients whose wounds had maggots. The flesh-eating bugs helped to cleanse the wound and keep it free from infection—aiding in the healing process. The treatment was replaced by the introduction of antibiotics in the 1900s.

Today, leeches and maggots are making an amazing comeback. These tiny creatures are examples of a practice called biotherapy—the use of living animals to treat illness. Turns out, there could be truth to these old remedies.

Leech saliva is made up of 30 different proteins that help numb pain, reduce swelling, and thin blood. Leeches are effective in helping tissue and limbs survive better after reconstructive surgery. Maggots are useful because they help remove dead tissue and reduce infections. Some doctors are now prescribing maggots to treat burns, skin cancer, and diabetes-related infections, often with miraculous results. **4**

Dawn of a New Medical Era

During the 1800s, microscopes gave doctors a better understanding of how bacteria, germs, and viruses spread disease. As a result, sterilization and hand washing became standard practice in medicine. New vaccinations were administered to protect the general population from deadly diseases. The exploration of antibiotics—a new kind of drug—opened the doors to what appeared to be the miracles of modern medicine.

Today, most of us take these medical breakthroughs for granted. But, if you could take that trip back in time, you'd realize just how far the practice of medicine has come in a little more than a century, and you would breathe a huge sigh of relief. **End**

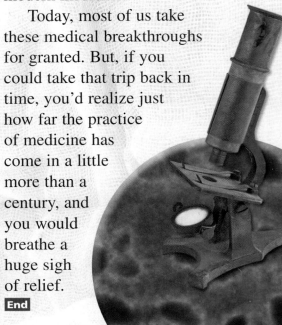

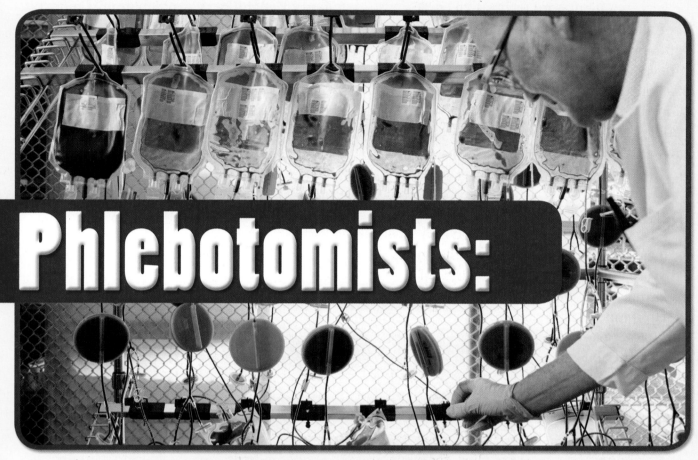

Phlebotomists:

THE MODERN BLOODLETTERS

In ancient times, people believed that drawing blood from a patient would make the sick person get well. People who practiced this art were called *bloodletters*. In current times, we know that taking a lot of blood from a patient is usually not a good idea. However, drawing blood is still a necessary and important skill. Today, we call bloodletters *phlebotomists*.

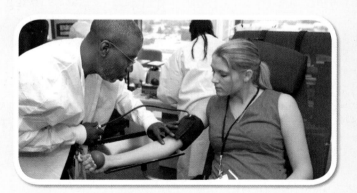

Blood may be drawn by a phlebotomist for a variety of reasons. A patient may be in the hospital or doctor's office and need his or her blood tested. Doctors may want to check for disease or to see if a medical treatment or drug therapy is working. Blood also is drawn for transfusions, the introduction of blood from one person's body to another, usually to replace blood lost because of an accident or serious illness. Blood may be drawn for blood donations or to be studied for research purposes.

Phlebotomists are responsible for handling the blood after it is drawn. They carefully

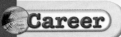
transfer the blood into tubes and prepare it to be sent to a laboratory or hospital.

Phlebotomists may work in a variety of settings. Some work in hospitals, doctors' offices, or laboratories where medical tests are done for the public. Others may staff blood banks where people go to donate blood, or they may be part of a research team at a laboratory or university.

Several practical skills are required for this career. First and most important, the phlebotomist must be comfortable around blood and medical procedures. If he or she is bothered by needles, this is not the best career choice.

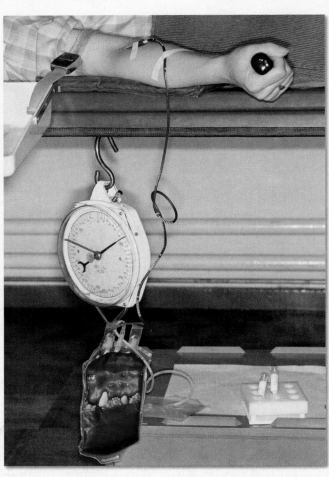

Phlebotomists also must be detail oriented. They must follow strict guidelines at every step of the blood-drawing and collection procedure. Blood samples can contain bacteria, poisons, and other dangerous elements, so great care must be used when handling blood. Safety precautions are important to prevent the spread of disease or infection. Government rules require that all equipment be sterilized and properly handled.

It is important that phlebotomists work well with people, as many of the patients are ill or may be upset. Because many people are scared of needles or uncomfortable at the sight of blood, a phlebotomist never knows when a patient might become upset, cry,

or even faint. It is especially hard to draw blood from children. A phlebotomist must be understanding and able to calm the patient's fears while working quickly and efficiently to complete the procedure with as little stress to the patient as possible. He or she should be able to tolerate pressure and deal well with the unexpected.

Educational requirements vary from state to state. Most states do not require a phlebotomist to be licensed, but many require these professionals to be certified. Various organizations offer certification, which generally requires the student to complete class work and perform a certain number of blood draws under supervision. Some schools offer a one-year program, which includes basic medical courses and hands-on training.

There are many excellent reasons to become a phlebotomist. The average annual salary as of 2008 was $30,000. Many phlebotomists set their own hours, working evenings or weekends or accepting extra work when they like. There is a strong demand for this type of work as more medical tests are performed, and drawing blood is a skill that will always be needed. If you enjoy working with people and being an important part of the medical community, a career as a phlebotomist may be a great choice for you.

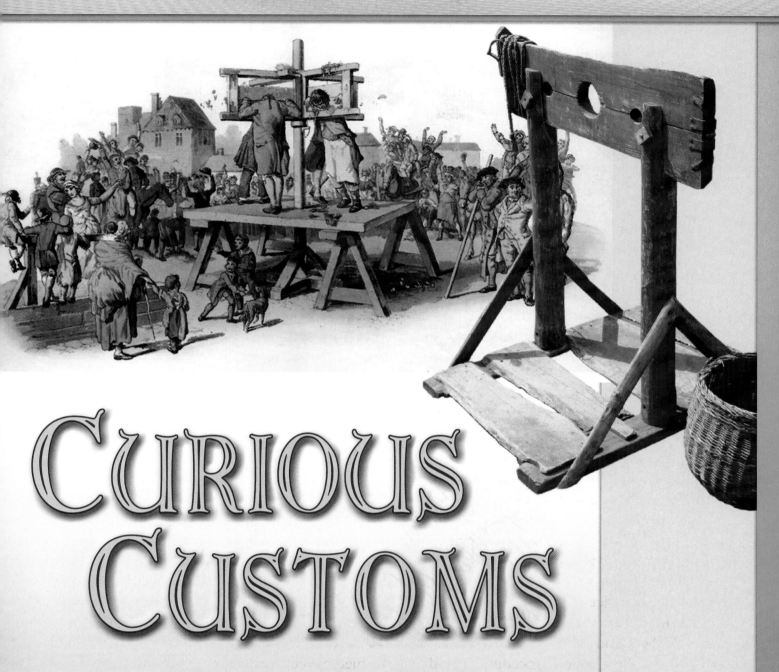

CURIOUS CUSTOMS

The year was 1785. Eighteen-year-old Jonathan from Boston, Massachusetts, was arrested by a sheriff for "public drunkenness." Although being drunk was against the law, Jonathan was not hauled off to jail, fined, or sent home to sleep it off.

Instead, Jonathan received a punishment that today seems cruel. He was brought to the center of town and placed in a wooden contraption called a pillory, in which his arms and legs were locked. All day he was stuck in this strange device while the townspeople came by insulting and taunting him. Certainly, Jonathan was embarrassed by the insults and teasing, but there was more to endure. Throughout the day, townsfolk threw rotten tomatoes at him, making his day even more difficult to handle. At sundown, after a harrowing day in the pillory, Jonathan was released and allowed to return home. **1**

1 Inference
How would the pillory discourage other people from "public drunkenness"? What evidence from the text helped you make your inference?

Many customs from colonial America seem unusual compared with **contemporary** American life. These include customs related to jobs, courtship and marriage, church life buying and selling goods, and manners.

Jobs

In the 18th century, most children did not go to school as they do today. Back then, some boys were fortunate to be apprenticed, or trained, by a professional, such as a shoemaker or a blacksmith. An apprenticeship was an arrangement sealed by contract between a boy, his parents, and the tradesman. The agreement stated that the professional would teach the boy a skill. The plan was that one day, when the boy was older, he would be **qualified** to earn a living in that field.

This is how the apprenticeship worked: At the age of about 10, the boy moved out of his parents' house and in with the tradesman. The boy worked alongside the tradesman for about 10 years. While there, he learned everything about that occupation. So, a boy working with a shoemaker learned practical skills such as how to use a hammer and sew leather. The tradesman also would **instruct** the boy in reading, writing, and arithmetic. When the boy turned 20, the **transaction** was complete. He was free to work for compensation for another shoemaker, or he could open a shoemaking business of his own. Either way, he could finally receive money for his work.

Unlike the training boys received outside the home, girls usually learned skills at home. A girl's mother instructed her in cooking, sewing, gardening, and **various** other domestic skills. Because families in colonial America were quite large, with as many as 10 children, girls had plenty of family members for whom to practice homemaking skills. A few girls were apprenticed in such jobs as milliners, or makers of hats and gloves. In addition to sewing skills, the girls learned basic reading, writing, and math so they could conduct various business transactions with customers.

Young men were apprenticed to a master craftsman to learn a trade such as carpentry.

Courtship and Marriage

As young men and women grew up, they were often interested in marrying and having children of their own. Couples did not date as they do today. Instead, if a couple wanted to marry, the girls' parents showed their approval by posting banns in church. Posting banns meant that the parents put up a written notice in church that the couple planned to get married.

Unlike most contemporary marriages, choosing a partner wasn't a matter of romance; it was a matter of economics. Without modern conveniences, life was hard. It took a family to keep a farm running. Wives kept the household working while husbands worked in the fields. It was beneficial to have large families to help work the farm.

Men were in control of all the family finances and property. Women in the 18th century had a difficult and unappreciated existence. Treatment for women under the law reflected their status. For example, a woman who left her husband was guilty of stealing for taking the clothes she wore. If a husband killed his wife, he was hanged. However, if a woman killed her husband, she was burned alive.

Church Life

Attending church on Sundays was a large part of life in colonial **society**. Rich or poor, people were expected to attend services at the meetinghouse, where worship took place. After a hard week of work, many worshipers walked for miles to reach the meetinghouse. By the time they arrived, they were exhausted. They sometimes fell asleep during the sermon. To prevent this, a man was assigned by the church to keep folks awake. What were his qualifications? He had a stick with a knob on one end and a feather on the other. With it, he poked the drowsy men with the knob and tickled the sleepy women with the feather. **2**

New England winters were cold, and the meetinghouses unheated. To keep themselves warm, families brought hot bricks or little stoves to warm their hands and feet during the service.

Buying and Selling

There were also fascinating customs about buying and selling goods. The Johnsons, a large farming family from Virginia, lived far out of town. As part of their work, they used a pitchfork to stack and feed hay to their horses. One day, Mr. Johnson noticed that his pitchfork handle had turned rusty and was falling apart. The family needed a new pitchfork to continue its labors.

Vocabulary

society (n) *people living together as a group with the same way of life*

2 Context Clues
What context clues can be used to determine the meaning of the word *drowsy*?

If this happened today, a farm family might buy a new tool with cash or credit. Back then, it was the custom for people to barter, or exchange goods, with others. **3** So, the Johnsons offered a storekeeper three loaves of bread for a new pitchfork, and no money was exchanged in the transaction.

3 **Context Clues**
What helps you determine the meaning of *barter* in this sentence?

Manners

Men, women, and children in colonial society had strict rules about how to conduct themselves around others. George Washington once recorded various rules he had learned as a child about how to behave. Although we speak differently today, a good sense of manners in the 18th century is obvious from two of Washington's guidelines:

1. When you sit down, keep your feet firm and even without putting one on the other, or crossing them.

2. In the presence of others, sing not to yourself with a humming noise, nor drum your fingers or feet.

Another custom developed because of the unpaved, sandy streets of colonial times. When it rained, carriages splashed sandy mud on the long skirts of women walking about. To prevent the women's dresses from becoming mud-stained, men walked on the street-side of their wives. Many people still observe this custom today.

Much has changed in American society since the 18th century. The people of colonial America wanted to punish wrongdoing and provide their children with opportunities for good jobs. Church leaders wanted their congregations to stay awake, and men looked out for the women in their family. They wanted to be able to exchange goods or trade services and be polite to one another. On second thought, maybe life hasn't changed that much. **End**

Teen Life—

Blast to the Past

Your life probably includes **activities** such as going to school, spending time with family and friends, playing video games, watching TV, or playing sports. All these aspects of daily life seem normal for American teenagers growing up in the 21st century. Teens growing up 200 years ago also thought about school, work, and having fun. However, their lives were radically, or extremely, different from the lives you and your friends live today.

Going to School 1

Today, laws require students to stay in school until they are 16 years old, and most students stay at least until they are 18. Many continue on to college. In the 1700s and 1800s, going to school until 18 was almost unheard of. Education for most people at that time was much more **fundamental**, and students learned only the basics of reading and math. Education was not as **crucial** to a person's success as it is today.

During the 1700s and 1800s, most children went to one-room

1 Text Features
Pay attention to the headings in this text to help you organize the information.

schoolhouses where students of varying ages and abilities studied together under the watchful eye of one teacher. Older students were expected to help younger ones, and the class spent most of its time memorizing facts and reciting lessons in front of the teacher and the rest of the class. Students did not participate in activities like class discussions or work together on projects the way most students learn today. Unlike contemporary classrooms, there were no computers in the schools of the 18th and 19th centuries. Students would write out exercises in longhand.

Classrooms did not have textbooks for every subject. Instead, students learned to read from the Bible and other religious books. During the mid-1800s, a series of textbooks called the *McGuffey Readers* educated students through classic stories and religious tales. Attendance at school was not as important as helping the family. During the 1700s and much of the 1800s, America was a largely agricultural society rather than an urban society as it is today. Much of the population raised crops or livestock and provided most of their own food and supplies. Planting and harvesting crops were so crucial for the family's survival that most students, especially boys, did not come to school when their

labor was needed on the farm. By the time they were preteens, many children left school to be an apprentice, work at home, or get a job to help support the family. Their families needed the compensation, or money, they earned from these jobs.

A privileged few could continue their education in high school or even college. These students mostly came from wealthy families who could afford expensive school fees. Most high schools and colleges were located in urban areas with larger populations, and students often had to move away from home to attend. For most teens, however, leaving school meant it was time to work. **2**

Teens at Work

Because America was a mostly agricultural society, many teens found work on farms. Other teens took jobs in the community. Often, boys were apprenticed to someone who held a job. An apprentice did

2 Summarize

In your own words, describe education in the 1800s.

Expedition 8

not receive any compensation for his work, but he learned the trade and, after a set period of time, was qualified to work for pay or open his own business. Some common jobs were blacksmith, miller, silversmith, tailor, and merchant. Girls were limited to domestic jobs, such as dressmaking, house cleaning, or cooking.

Society began to change in the late 1800s as America became more industrialized. There was a great demand for workers in factories that produced textiles, shoes, and other articles. At the same time, machines took over more of the work on farms, freeing teens to leave home and look for new opportunities in faraway towns or cities.

For the first time, women had **employment** opportunities outside the home. Thousands flocked to mill towns, especially in New England, to work in textile mills. These girls ran huge looms that spun and wove cloth. The work was hard and repetitive, and most workers toiled 12 hours a day, six days a week, doing the same thing over and over. Working conditions could be dangerous. The air was filled with cotton fibers that made it hard to breathe, and the machinery could seriously injure a careless worker. **3**

Men also worked in mills and factories or found work in coal mines. Coal mines and factories provided employment for the waves of immigrants coming to the United States during the late 1800s. Although working conditions were harsh and the pay low, these jobs provided more money, freedom, and opportunity than working on a farm ever could.

Vocabulary

employment (n) *a person's work; job*

3 Context Clues
What does the word *textile* mean? What context clues helped you determine the meaning?

A blacksmith pounds metal on an anvil.

Women working at a textile factory

Recreation

Every teenager wants to have fun, and this was as true 300 years ago as it is today. Although today's teens often look for fun on computers and game consoles, teens who lived a few centuries ago had to find more fundamental ways to entertain themselves.

The most common way for teens to have fun during the 1700s and 1800s was to participate in **social** gatherings. People often met to socialize at community suppers or dances. The school was often a center for other social events with entire families coming to see students participate in a spelling bee, perform music, or read essays and poetry to the crowd.

Social gatherings also took place in people's homes. Young women might get together to enjoy a quilting bee or a sewing circle. These events allowed young people to talk while they did vital household work. Young men might work together to build a barn.

Social gatherings involved the whole family.

Sports, such as ball games and races, also were popular.

Different or the Same?

Life was very different 300 years ago from what it is today. However, in some ways, things are the same. Teens always have had fun with their friends, attended school, and worked at whatever jobs were available. Although you've probably never worked 12 hours in a mill or joined your neighborhood for a barn raising, you've probably shared good times with family and friends, and performed hard work in school or on the job. Some things never change. **End**

	18th and 19th Centuries	21st Century
Types of schools	One-room schools	Large schools with many classrooms
Completion of education	Most left school as preteens	By law, must attend school until age 16
Learning a trade or job skills	Apprenticed to a master to learn job skills	Learn job skills at trade school or college
Types of social activities	Participated in community gatherings	Take part in virtual communities via Internet

MUSEUM CURATOR

Did you know there are more than 17,000 museums in the United States alone? Museums have something for just about everyone, whether you like art, science, history, music, or even sports. Large art, natural history, and science museums are in every major city in this country. There also are museums for specialty interests, including antique cars, glass objects, Native American crafts, and even footwear.

As you browse collections of antique photographs or 100-year-old baseballs, you probably don't think about the person who designed the display. Nor do you think about who feeds the snakes in a live animal exhibit. But, someone knows exactly how the bones in dinosaur skeletons must be arranged. All of

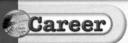

these tasks are performed by museum curators. The word *curate* comes from a Latin word that means "to care," and that's just what curators do. Museum curators are the people who plan, design, set up, and take care of exhibits in museums. If the exhibit is permanent, they also make sure it's well maintained and kept up-to-date. If there is a dinosaur exhibit and someone finds a new Tyrannosaurus rex skull, the museum curator is the one to decide whether to include it and how to display it.

Museum curators usually have one special field of interest. They might like natural science or more specifically, reptiles and amphibians. After college, museum curators go to graduate school to become experts in their field, but many also work in museums to get hands-on experience. There they can learn from more experienced curators exactly what the work entails. The average annual 2008 salary for this work ranged from $40,000 to $50,000.

The work of a museum curator changes continually, but it generally involves collecting items for exhibits and setting up these objects for the public. Sometimes the work can seem like a treasure hunt for ancient objects and art to include in the exhibits. Curators might travel to other museums

and other parts of the world to gather the materials they need. Some museums, like the Museum of Science in Boston, include live animals in their exhibits, so the museum curators are responsible for every one of the animals. Part of the job also is helping the public get the most out of the exhibits, and this takes some thought. What's the best way to mount a 1,000-year-old tapestry on a wall? How should an exhibit of baseball cards be arranged—by year or by player? How can one show off the elaborate stitching in a wedding dress from 1925? How should a diorama of an ancient Navajo village be placed in the Native American wing of a museum? These are the kinds of questions that must be worked out so people who visit museums will enjoy what they see and learn a lot in the process.

If you have a desire to preserve and display some of the world's most outstanding cultural, historical, and scientific treasures, then being a museum curator may be the right job for you.

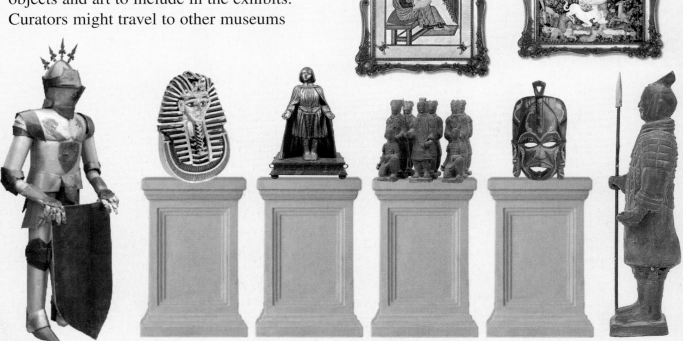

The Future of Our Past

- How does fiction shape the future?
- What does the future hold for us?
- What possibilities of the future are scary?

FROM
1984
BY GEORGE ORWELL

It was a bright cold day in April, and the clocks were striking thirteen. Winston Smith, his chin **nuzzled** into his breast in an effort to escape the **vile** wind, slipped quickly through the glass doors of Victory Mansions, though not quickly enough to prevent a swirl of gritty dust from entering along with him. The hallway smelt of boiled cabbage and old rag mats. At one end of it a colored poster, too large for indoor display, had been tacked to the wall. It **depicted** simply an enormous face, more than a meter wide: the face of a man of about forty-five, with a heavy black mustache and ruggedly handsome features. Winston made for the stairs. It was no use trying the lift. Even at the best of times it was **seldom** working, and at present the electric current was cut off during daylight hours. It was part of the economy drive in preparation for Hate Week. The flat was seven flights up, and Winston, who was thirty-nine, and had a varicose ulcer **1** above his right ankle, went slowly, resting several times on the way. On each landing, opposite the lift shaft, the poster with the enormous face gazed from the wall. It was one of those pictures which are so **contrived** that the eyes follow you about when you move. BIG BROTHER IS WATCHING YOU, the caption beneath it ran. **2**

Inside the flat a fruity voice was reading out a list of figures which had something to do with the production of pig iron. The voice came from an oblong metal plaque like a dulled mirror which formed part of the surface of the right-hand wall. Winston turned a switch and the voice sank somewhat, though the words were still distinguishable, or understandable. The instrument (the telescreen, it was called) could be dimmed, but there was no way of shutting it off completely. He moved over to the window: a smallish, **frail** figure, the meagerness of his body merely emphasized by the blue overalls which were the uniform of the Party. His hair was very fair, his face naturally red, his skin roughened by coarse soap and blunt razor blades and the cold of the winter that had just ended.

Big Brother Is Watching You

Vocabulary

frail (adj) *weak*

Outside, even through the shut window pane, the world looked cold. Down in the street little eddies of wind were whirling dust and torn paper into spirals, and though the sun was shining and the sky a harsh blue, there seemed to be no color in anything except the posters that were plastered everywhere. **3** The black-mustachio'd face gazed down from every commanding corner. There was one on the house front immediately opposite. BIG BROTHER IS WATCHING YOU, the caption said, while the dark eyes looked deep into Winston's own. Down at street level another poster, torn at one corner, flapped fitfully in the wind, alternately covering and uncovering the single word INGSOC. In the far distance a helicopter skimmed down between the roofs, hovered for an instant like a blue-bottle, and darted away again with a curving flight. It was the Police Patrol, snooping into people's windows. The patrols did not matter, however. Only the Thought Police mattered.

3 Visualize
Picture the outside scene that seems colorless. What do you see that is in color?

Behind Winston's back the voice from the telescreen was still babbling away about pig iron and the overfulfillment of the Ninth Three Year Plan. The telescreen received and transmitted simultaneously, or at the same time. Any sound that Winston made, above the level of a very low whisper, would be picked up by it; moreover, so long as he remained within the field of vision which the metal plaque commanded, he could be seen as well as heard. There was of course no way of knowing whether you were being watched at any given moment. How often, or on what system, the Thought Police plugged in on any individual wire was guesswork. It was even conceivable, or possible, that they watched everybody all the time. But at any rate they could plug in your wire whenever they wanted to. You had to live—did live, from habit that became instinct—in the assumption that every

4 **Make Connections**

How would you change if you were constantly being watched or listened to?

READER'S NOTE

This passage was taken from the novel *1984* by George Orwell, first published in 1949. The story takes place in 1984 and presents an imaginary future where government controls every aspect of life, including people's thoughts. The state is called Oceania and is ruled by a group known as the Party; its leader and dictator is Big Brother. The phrase "Big Brother is watching you" came from this novel and means that government is getting too involved in an individual's life.

sound you made was overheard, and, except in darkness, every movement observed. **4**

Winston kept his back turned to the telescreen. It was safer; though, as he well knew, even a back can be revealing. A kilometer away the Ministry of Truth, his place of work, towered vast and white above the grimy landscape. This, he thought with a sort of vague distaste, this was London, chief city of Airstrip One, itself the third most populous of the provinces of Oceania. He tried to squeeze out some childhood memory that should tell him whether London had always been quite like this. Were there always these vistas of rotting nineteenth-century houses, their sides shored up with balks of timber, their windows patched with cardboard and their roofs with corrugated iron, their crazy garden walls sagging in all directions? And the bombed sites where the plaster dust swirled in the air and the willow herb straggled over the heaps of rubble; and the places where the bombs had cleared a larger path and there had sprung up sordid colonies of filthy, wooden dwellings like chicken houses? But it was no use, he could not remember: nothing remained of his childhood except a series of bright-lit images, occurring against no background and mostly unintelligible, or impossible to understand.

The Ministry of Truth—Minitrue, in Newspeak—was startlingly different from any other object in sight. It was an enormous pyramidal structure of glittering white concrete, soaring up, terrace after terrace, three hundred meters into the air. From where Winston stood it was just possible to read, picked out on its white face in elegant lettering, the three slogans of the Party:

WAR IS PEACE

FREEDOM IS SLAVERY

IGNORANCE IS STRENGTH. **End**

Science Fiction... or Fact?

Vocabulary

predict (v) *declare that something is going to happen in the future*

coincidence (n) *when things happen by accident and are not connected to each other*

develop (v) *work out the possibilities of something*

Everyone likes to imagine what our lives might be like in the future. How will we get from one place to another? What will our homes look like? What kind of new technologies will be available? There's no exact way to **predict** what lies in store for us in the future. Yet, did you know that science fiction writers in the past tried to make such predictions?

You may not realize it, but some modern technology was first described in books or movies by science fiction writers many years ago. Could this be an accident or a **coincidence**? Or, did some of these writers really predict the future? It might be a little of both.

From Fiction to Fact

Reading science fiction books or watching science fiction movies allows us to enter an imaginary world of the future. But, what happens when this imaginary world turns out to be true? Sometimes science fiction writers **develop** ideas for future technology from things that already exist. Take credit cards, for instance. They first became popular in the United States in the 1950s. Yet, in

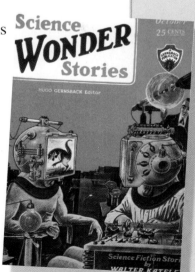

1 Main Idea
The stated main idea isn't always the first or last sentence in the paragraph. Which sentence in this paragraph is the main idea?

2 Context Clues
Using context clues, determine what the word *resemblance* means.

1888, author Edward Bellamy had described credit cards in his book *Looking Backward*. In Bellamy's invented world, people use credit cards to purchase what they need. During Bellamy's time, the concept, or idea, of credit already existed. Sometimes metal coins were used to record store credit. So credit cards might have seemed to him like the next logical step. We can only imagine Bellamy's **reaction** to the commonness of today's plastic credit cards and how widely they are used. **1**

In Ray Bradbury's novel *Fahrenheit 451*, published in 1953, the characters spend a lot of their time watching large flat-screen televisions with **elaborate** and complex sound systems. Their descriptions make them seem very much like today's flat-screen TVs. At a time when television screens were tiny and picture quality was poor, Bradbury's imagined TVs must have sparked, or activated,

some envious reactions in his readers. Speaking of TV, if you ever saw an episode of the 1960s TV show *Star Trek*, you would notice that the crew uses eerily familiar flip-open communicator **devices** to speak to one another. This might just be a coincidence, too, but today our wireless flip phones bear a striking resemblance to these devices. **2**

What about computers? It would be almost impossible to imagine life today without them. Believe it or not, as late as the 1980s, very few

Star Trek communicator devices look similar to today's flip phones.

households had a computer. Computers were found mostly in office buildings. Many actually looked like large typewriters with a small TV screen attached. Yet, in the 1977 science fiction novel *Inherit the Stars*, James Hogan first wrote about a computer that fit in a briefcase. This machine was completely unheard of at the time. Hogan couldn't have known this, but he was describing something very much like the laptop computers prevalent today.

Inventing the Future

Some science fiction authors of the past had unusually good ideas about where technology was headed. Hugo Gernsback is sometimes called the "Father of Modern Science Fiction." In fact, the major award for science fiction literature, the Hugo, is named for him. His early novel *Ralph 124C 41+* was first written as a series of stories for *Modern Electrics* magazine in 1911. The stories were set in the year 2660. Gernsback imagined a futuristic world full of elaborate technologies that were completely unknown then. Today,

they are a part of our culture, or a part of our past. These include television, tape recorders, and space flight. **3** Not everything was entirely accurate, however. For example, in Gernsback's world, people watched "tele-theater," much like television today, except that the audience could interact with the actors. Still, the idea for television had not even been developed at the time of Gernsback's writing.

If some science fiction writers predict future technology, others influence how it will develop. The author Victor Appleton described a "stun gun" in his book *Tom Swift and His Electric Rifle*, written in 1911. By the late 1960s, Jack Cover had invented the first real stun gun, called a "TASER." These are now used in police departments across the country. Cover had loved Victor Appleton's science fiction books as a boy. He

actually based his work on the TASER on the stun gun he had read about years earlier. In fact, it's no coincidence that the acronym TASER stands for Thomas A. Swift Electric Rifle!

3 Predict
If some of Gernsback's predictions for 2660 have come true already, what do you think life will be like in 2660?

Jules Verne's Amazing Predictions

Without question, the science fiction writer who described the greatest range of technologies that we take for granted today was French author Jules Verne. Verne wrote most of his books in the late 1800s. His most famous novels include *20,000 Leagues Under the Sea*, *From the Earth to the Moon*, and *Journey to the Center of the Earth*. Though Verne died more than a hundred years ago, much of the technology that he described, unknown at the time, exists today. Verne imagined a future world with airplanes, helicopters, televisions, computers, automobiles, air conditioning, and motion pictures. Verne also described trips to the moon, elaborate skyscrapers built of glass and steel, and submarines that could travel miles below the ocean. He even predicted the discovery of the South Pole, which occurred in 1911, six years after his death. Jules Verne's 1865 novel *From the Earth to the Moon*, remarkably, or strangely, describes a space flight to the moon that would actually take place a little more than a hundred years later. In the book, three astronauts are sent out into outer space from a town in central Florida. This turned out to be not far from NASA's actual launching site at Cape Canaveral, Florida. Also in the book, Verne's spacecraft lands just 3 miles from the place where *Apollo 11* actually landed on its return from the moon in 1969. Neil Armstrong, the first person to walk on the moon, has claimed that Jules Verne's books had a great influence on him. Other famous inventors and scientists have mentioned that Jules Verne was their inspiration.

It is quite possible that many of our technological accomplishments actually come from the world of science fiction. Perhaps many scientists are inspired by the imaginations of fiction writers. Jules Verne himself once said, "Whatever one man is capable of imagining, other men will prove themselves capable of realizing." Think of his reaction to the world of today, which in some ways closely resembles his own imagination. Today, of course, plenty of other things that science fiction writers have imagined have not come true. These include control over the weather, communication with aliens, invisibility machines, floating vacation cities, and antigravity machines. But, pay attention to science fiction. You never know what the future may actually bring! **4** **End**

4 **Make Connections**
What books or movies have you seen that show futuristic technologies? Do you think those technologies will become reality?

Writer/Author

Covering a remote war for a prominent newspaper. Writing the next hit series of science fiction books. Describing the ins and outs of the latest video game. These are some of the assignments that writers accept.

Do you think it takes years of graduate school to become a writer? Think again. Although some writers do spend a lot of time honing their craft, this work does not always take place at a college or university. Often, real-world experience and raw talent are just as important as formal education to a writer's success.

There are two types of writers. Authors develop original texts like books, magazine articles, textbooks, or screenplays. Technical writers take technical information, such as how to operate a computer program, and write reader-friendly instructions and descriptions. Editors often work alongside writers in the word-crafting business. Editors are not considered writers, but they are partners in the work—revising, shaping ideas, and ensuring accuracy.

A day in the life of an author or technical writer could include many activities. A writer may spend time creating different kinds of writing and literature, such as a poem, comic book dialogue, or a technical manual for an appliance. Writers also may spend time researching what they will write about. This research could involve exploring a community, like visiting a remote tribe in a South American rain forest; doing research by engaging in an activity like scuba diving; or accompanying a platoon of soldiers into

---

The Future of Our Past

war. It also could involve reading other people's writing. Additionally, some writers spend time promoting themselves and their work to publishers or directly to readers. And, of course, writing can often be revised, so writers spend a lot of time improving their work.

Even though media are changing and books are giving way to the Internet, there will always be a demand for writers. After all, everything you read on the Internet was written by someone. The job prospects look best for technical writers and writers who have specialized training. The median annual earnings for salaried writers and authors in 2006 was $48,640. An author whose work becomes famous can earn significantly more than that. J.K. Rowling, the author of the extraordinarily successful *Harry Potter* series, is a billionaire!

Being a writer or author often is not easy. Many writers work as freelance writers or contract writers; they are self-employed, so their income depends on continually seeking and securing work. This kind of work can be exciting and flexible, but there is no guarantee of a monthly paycheck or benefits like health insurance.

Writers start young, often with a passion and a flair for expressing themselves in words. Save the blog you write now, the stories you think of when you are daydreaming, or your work for the school newspaper. In a few years, you may revise these pieces, and they may represent the start of a fulfilling career of words and ideas.

Star Wars clones

The Cloning Revolution

Cloning. Merely mention the word and what comes to mind? **Typically**, it's a lifeless robotic hatchling from a strange, futuristic experiment. But, a clone is simply one living thing made from another, resulting in two organisms with the same set of genes. **1** You might not believe it, but they aren't always created by scientists in a laboratory. They can be created naturally with the same DNA, or genetic makeup.

A more **deliberate** look at the natural world turns up even more clone-like surprises. Take flatworms, for example. Atypical of most beings, when they're cut in half, they can **replicate** the missing parts of their bodies, resulting in two clones of the same worm. Marine animals, such as starfish and crayfish, are also able to regenerate lost pieces of themselves. It almost seems like they can clone another arm when needed. In fact, certain species of starfish can regrow their whole body from one of their arms!

Cloning is quite prevalent among plants too. The strawberry plant shoots out a stem that grows new plants wherever it takes root, and each new plant is a clone of the original plant. This type of cloning

Starfish can regrow missing parts.

Vocabulary

typically (adv) *how things usually are; generally*

deliberate (adj) *planned or intended*

replicate (v) *make a copy of; duplicate*

1 Make Connections
If you could make an exact replica of one person, who would it be?

In the early 1900s, salamander embryos were divided—starting a revolution in cloning.

also occurs in grass, potatoes, and onions. Certain trees duplicate themselves by spreading their roots to sprout new trees. Believe it or not, entire forests can be made of trees that originated from one single plant.

Prehistoric humans used stem cuttings to clone their hardiest plants. This led to stronger crops and more fruitful harvests. These plants benefited humans by harnessing, or making use of, nature's cloning ability.

Milestones in Cloning

Scientists have long been fascinated by the concept of cloning. Over the last century, a new approach to reproductive cloning was developed—genetic engineering. With the help of this technology, scientists began to crack the code to cloning animals. Like many scientific breakthroughs, the work done by early scientists laid the foundation for today's researchers.

Hans Spemann, a German scientist, made one such achievement in 1902. He

deliberately divided a salamander embryo in half and found that the resulting two cells each grew into a normal adult salamander! This discovery showed that each embryo cell carries all the genetic information needed to create a new organism. In 1928, Spemann took another important step toward cloning when he successfully transferred the nucleus of a cell from a frog embryo to a cell of a second frog.

Later in his career, Spemann dreamed of a "fantastical experiment" for cloning higher organisms. He imagined extracting the nucleus of an older differentiated, or specialized, cell and inserting it into a fertilized egg without a nucleus. He didn't know how to do it, but he believed this method of "nuclear transfer" was the key to reproductive cloning in the future.

In 1952, a tiny tadpole made history as the first cloned animal. Two American scientists, Robert Briggs and Thomas King, took the prize for this achievement. Eventually, they cloned 27 identical tadpoles using the nuclear transfer method that Spemann had imagined 14 years earlier. Their accomplishment inspired a long period of **intense** interest in cloning research.

Another major cloning milestone occurred in 1962. At this turning point, a British scientist named John Gurdon claimed to have cloned frogs from adult cells. **2**
What was his method? He used

The world was captivated when scientists cloned Dolly.

Vocabulary

differentiate (v)
show a difference between two things

generated (v)
produced; created

nuclear transfer. This was the first demonstration that showed that the nucleus of a differentiated cell could develop into all types of cells. Gurdon's experiments set the stage for the next cloning breakthrough— the cloning of mammals.

Cloning Mammals— Hello, Dolly!

By the 1980s, scientists had refined, or improved, the process of cloning using embryo cells. Animals such as mice, cows, and sheep had been successfully cloned using this method. The next giant leap for cloning came with the birth of a cloning superstar—a sheep named Dolly. In 1996, Dolly became the first animal to be cloned using an adult animal cell.

Ian Wilmut, the scientist who cloned Dolly, learned from the earlier experiments of Gurdon, Briggs, Thomas, and Spemann. Many well-respected scientists said it couldn't be done. But, he proved that a cell taken from a body part could replicate a whole new individual animal.

Even though you couldn't **differentiate** Dolly from other sheep of her breed, she was unlike any other mammal that ever lived. **Generated** from an adult female cell, she had the identical physical traits of her mother but had no father. In spite of this, Dolly was deliberately bred and produced six lambs during her lifetime.

The birth of Dolly caused a sensation around the world. For the scientific community, her arrival shattered a widespread belief that cells from an adult mammal could not regenerate a whole animal. Now scientists thought of cloning as divided into two periods: Before Dolly and After Dolly.

A normal sheep has a life expectancy of about 12 years. Yet, at the age of 6 years, Dolly developed lung cancer and died. Lung disease is common for sheep kept indoors, as Dolly was. Yet, her death caused an intense debate about the safety of cloning. Despite this controversy, researchers went on to clone other animals including horses, mules, bulls, goats, pigs, rabbits, and cats. What or who would be next? **3**

3 Summarize

In your own words, summarize this section.

Cloned Pets

American Bernann McKinney was crushed when her beloved pit bull, Booger, died. So, the devastated woman paid a South Korean laboratory a whopping $50,000 to keep the memory of her deceased pet alive. The result was the world's first commercially cloned dogs. Now these five pit bull puppies have helped start a new cloning revolution—the cloning of pets.

The Korean lab cloned the puppies using the same technology used to clone Dolly. The procedure has a high risk of stillbirth. For animals that do survive, there is potential for ill health and premature death due to disease. Even so, McKinney was delighted with her genetic copies of Booger. Born in 2008, the puppies have the same physical traits as their mother, right down to the white spots below their necks.

Not everyone is excited about the puppy clones, however. Many animal activists believe it's selfish to clone a pet when so many animals in the world are in need of a good home. Besides, they maintain, there's more to an animal than its DNA. You might be able to replicate the unique physical traits of a dog, but its special personality also depends on its life experiences and environment.

Reproductive Cloning—The Next Frontier

The birth of Dolly improved scientists' ability not only to reproduce animals, but also to better understand the causes and mechanisms of animal disease. Yet, this cutting-edge technology holds the promise of other possible benefits.

Farmers and ranchers, for example, always search for ways to improve the quality of their livestock. Could cloning their prized animals help? Around the world, endangered animals teeter on the brink of extinction because of loss of habitat and excessive hunting. Could they be preserved through cloning? Many rare animals have already succumbed, or given in, to extinction. Could cloning re-create an extinct species?

Reproductive cloning presents a brave new world for scientists and citizens alike. It's hard to predict what direction the future of cloning will take. Here is a warning to those debating its merits, or worth: The science of cloning is progressing rapidly. The human thirst for discovery and invention is pushing the frontiers further. Like a tidal wave, it might be impossible to stop. **4** **End**

4 **Visualize**

If humans could be cloned, what would the world look like?

Microchipping Humans

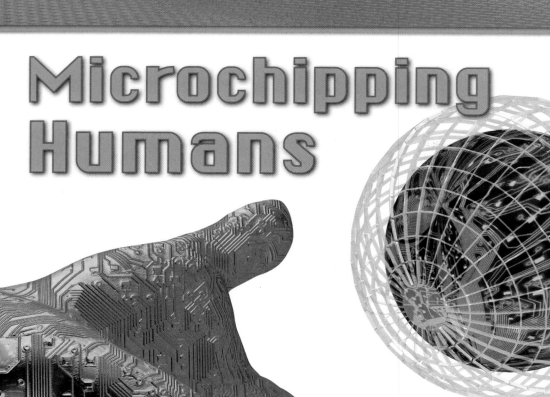

Vocabulary

convenience (n)
something that is useful and easy to use

You and some friends are leaving a store. An alarm sounds. You look up and a cop is staring down at you. He takes out a wand and waves it across your wrist. He now knows your address, phone number, parents' names, and any prior criminal activity you have been accused of. Then you wake up. Good thing it was a dream... or was it? Look at any product on a store shelf, and you are likely to see a bar code. When you buy that product, the bar code is scanned to record your purchase. That bar code is a special identifying tool that marks a specific product.

Some products have ID codes that are even more sophisticated. These complex codes are called Radio Frequency Identifications, or RFIDs for short. An RFID can be tracked throughout a product's life cycle—from manufacture, to distribution to a store, to purchase.

Identifying a nonliving product such as a bar of soap or a bag of potato chips is a modern **convenience** that is not new or

Vocabulary

debate (v) *discuss something*

conform (v) *act in an expected way*

standards (n) *rules or models used to judge how good something is*

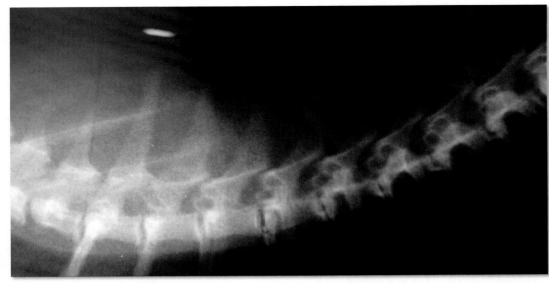

Pet microchipping: An X-ray of a cat's spine with a microchip implanted under the cat's skin between its shoulder blades

1 Main Idea

What is the stated main idea of this paragraph?

controversial. However, living things also can be identified through a technology like a bar code. That technology is called a microchip.

You may have heard about microchipping pets by inserting a tiny microchip into an animal's body. The chip, which is smaller than a grain of rice, is usually placed under the skin. If the animal is lost and brought to a shelter, a special scanner can read the microchip and discover identifying information.

If, however, you think microchipping human beings is something from a science fiction novel, think again. Microchipping is already here, and many people think it will become even more prevalent. Many people **debate** whether the good points about microchipping exceed, or outweigh, the bad points. Is microchipping a convenient form of identification, or is it a dangerous way to force people to **conform** to government **standards**? Let's take a look at the debate.

Keeping Track

Many people think microchipping is a great idea. Microchip identification could help us in many practical ways.

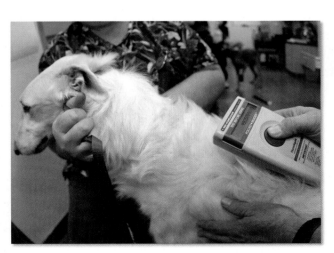

A veterinarian uses a scanner to check the microchip placed in the back of a 4-year-old Borzoi named Glaze as the dog is held by its owner.

A microchip could track a person's medical history. A frail or ill person entering the hospital may not be able to tell doctors his or her current medications and illnesses. Or, a person could be injured in an accident, unconscious, or unable to communicate with emergency medical staff. Not knowing a person's medical information can make it difficult for doctors to treat patients. A microchip could prevent dangerous drug interactions; allergic reactions; and other medical catastrophes, or disasters. **1**

The small size of a microchip makes it easy to conceal under the skin.

Microchips could also be used to identify criminals, terrorists, and other dangerous members of society. A violent person or someone with a criminal past might need to be restricted from certain areas, such as government buildings, airports, or schools. A scanner could check each person entering these areas and set off an alarm if a person's microchip is identified as restricted. On a more tragic note, a microchip also could identify a victim's body and help investigators solve deadly crimes.

Moore's Law and Microchips

Microchips are at the heart of almost all modern electronic equipment. They can be found not only inside mobile phones, MP3 players, and computers, but also in washers and dryers, automobiles, and even talking greeting cards. This widespread use of microchips (also called *integrated circuits*) can be attributed to their steady performance improvements and cost reductions during the last 50 years.

These improvements are tied directly to that of the basic building block of the microchip—the transistor. As manufacturing technology has improved over the decades, transistors have become smaller and smaller, which makes them less expensive to build. More of them also can be built into a given area, resulting in much greater processing capability. Additionally, these smaller transistors require less power to run than their predecessors, allowing them to be used in small, battery-powered applications.

In April 1965, Gordon Moore, who cofounded the computer company Intel, wrote an article. In it, he stated that the number of transistors per square inch in an integrated circuit would double every year. Though transistors have become significantly smaller, the rate of growth hasn't quite met Moore's prediction. Recently, it has taken about 18 months for the number of transistors to double. Moore's observation is known as Moore's Law. Figure 1-1 shows the rate of "growth" of the number of transistors per square inch in recent years.

Fig. 1-1

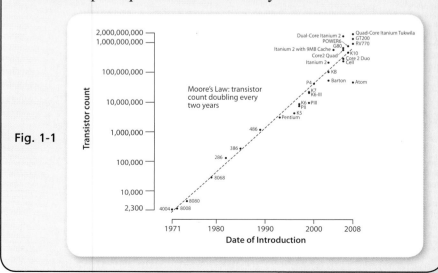

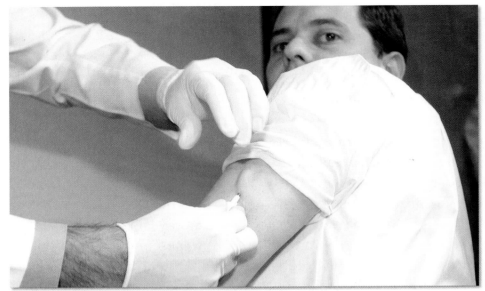

A man in Mexico is implanted with a microchip that is used to confirm everything from health history to identity. Is this technology coming to the United States?

Many people think children should be microchipped. A young child might get lost and be unable to tell anyone his or her name or family phone number. Scanning a microchip would provide all that information in a few seconds and help reunite the child with his or her family. Or, parents could follow their child's movements using a handheld computer that receives a signal from the microchip in the child's body. **2**

Scan and Shop

There are many applications for microchips in commerce. Instead of swiping a credit card to buy something, a customer could be scanned for a microchip, which would provide all the information needed to access his or her bank account.

People who enjoy the convenience of shopping or banking from home using the Internet could scan their microchip instead of typing their vital information into a form. This could be a secure way of transmitting identifying information to make a purchase or access money or financial records. It would no longer be necessary to carry identification, credit cards, ATM cards, transit cards, or the many other pieces of identification that we use in our daily lives because information could be sent wherever it needs to go with one quick scan.

The Dangers of Microchipping

Microchipping humans might sound like a great idea, but many people want to take a more **cautious** approach. They think there is a great probability that microchipping will lead to a terrible loss of privacy and individuality, as well as force people to conform to government standards or requests.

2 Make Connections
If your little sister were lost, would you feel better if you knew she had a microchip that could be used to identify her?

People who are against microchipping say that it is no one's business what you buy, where you go, or how much money you have. Many people are cautious about sharing this information, and they usually have the legal right to keep such information private. Being microchipped could take that right away. Many people do not think it's fair for someone to be able to scan their body and find out everything about them. **3**

Then there is the idea of being watched. Some people use the saying "Big Brother is watching you" as a warning that the government is aware of every move a person makes. This phrase comes from the novel *1984* by George Orwell, which is set in a society where the government, known as Big Brother, watches and **regulates** its citizens. Some people think

microchipping would allow Big Brother to know everything about us. Many people are uncomfortable thinking that the government—or any other powerful organization— could access all the information about our personal lives. Some people fear that microchipping could lead people to conform to a certain standard of behavior to stay out of trouble. For example, people might buy a certain product because it was recommended by the government or have their attendance recorded at an event to gain favor with the group that sponsored it.

Another issue is identity theft. It could be possible for a criminal to manipulate a chip or a scanner to allow the chip to provide false information. We have already seen a rise in identity theft because of electronic money transfers and people sharing identifying details

Vocabulary

regulates (v) *controls or manages*

3 Make Connections
What do you think about microchipping? Do the pros outweigh the cons?

A man unlocks a locked door with a microchip implant in his arm.

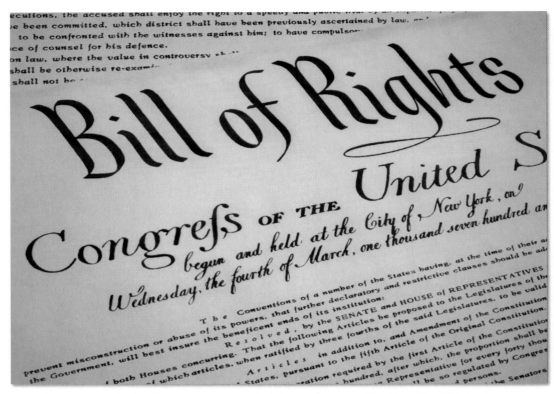

Would microchipping violate your personal rights guaranteed in the Bill of Rights?

4 Make Connections

Think about what you just read. Does it change your understanding or what you think about the excerpt from *1984* you read earlier?

over the Internet. It usually doesn't take long for a new technology to be abused, and there is a high probability that a clever criminal will find a way to abuse microchipping. **4**

Microchipping: Good or Bad?

Microchipping raises many questions. Would a person have to give permission to be scanned? Who would regulate when, where, and how a person might be scanned? These issues and the idea of losing privacy are the biggest reasons that microchipping is not becoming more widespread more quickly.

Other people dismiss worries about the lack of privacy. They say that if they have nothing to hide,

there is nothing to fear from being microchipped. They also point out that we already have given up a great deal of our privacy with cell phone triangulation that can track our movements, credit cards that record what we buy, and security cameras that record what we do in public and private places.

Microchipping would need to be heavily regulated to be accepted. People and organizations will proceed cautiously with this technology to keep the debate from getting too violent. In all probability, microchipping will become standard in the next generation or two. However, there are many obstacles that will have to be overcome, or conquered, if this new technology is to be accepted. **End**

Embryologist:
Under the Microscope

Some years ago, Jackson, a high school student, read in the papers about scientists in Scotland who successfully cloned an animal, a sheep they named Dolly. As a young man interested in science, Jackson found embryology—the study of the formation and development of life—interesting. Searching for a specialty to which he could devote his professional life, Jackson researched the training, schooling, and skills that were needed by workers in this field. Before long, Jackson decided that an embryologist career was the job for him. Perhaps, after learning about this career, you may feel the same.

An embryologist is a scientist who studies how living organisms are formed and develop. Some embryologists work with plants, experimenting with how they fertilize and grow. Other embryologists work with mammals other than humans—exploring how animals, such as sheep, form and develop.

A third kind of embryologist works with humans. Many are employed in fertility clinics. At the clinics, scientists meet with couples who cannot conceive a baby naturally. In their lab, embryologists may combine the man's sperm with the woman's egg and reimplant the egg in the woman. If all goes

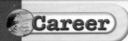

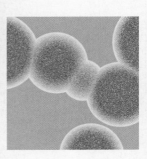

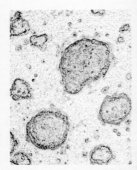

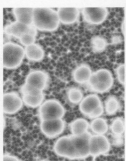

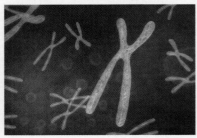

detail and are methodical and well organized. They need good eye-hand coordination and have the patience to study small objects under a microscope. Because many embryologists perform and record experiments and write reports, journal articles, and books, good communication skills are vital. Computer skills are also a must.

In cloning, scientists working in a lab produce an organism that is genetically identical to its parent. These scientists recognize that their area of specialization is controversial. But, the scientists are committed to using technology to achieve medical benefits for people. These scientists believe that experiments in cloning will one day lead to an understanding of genetic diseases, those passed down from one generation to the next. Despite debate about this field, these scientists are dedicated to finding what causes genetic conditions and producing treatments for those conditions.

Embryologists generally are compensated with professional salaries. An entry-level embryologist completing a bachelor's degree can expect to earn around $45,000 a year but can expect that salary to rise quickly. The average mid-level embryologist earns around $75,000 a year, but many earn much more, especially those who have trained and have earned several graduate school degrees.

Many embryologists report that their work is demanding but rewarding. Though the workweek is long, as creative scientists, they are thrilled when there is a breakthrough, discovery, or helpful drug that improves the quality of people's lives. If the demands on an embryologist seem reasonable and the rewards fulfilling, then the job of embryologist may be right for you.

well, an egg matures into a fetus, and the woman gives birth to a baby.

While some embryologists work in clinics, others work in labs, hospitals, or pharmacies, or other drug-making settings. Embryologists perform experiments to see why abnormalities arise in human fetuses. Or, they try to understand how chromosome abnormalities, like those that occur in Down's syndrome, develop, and search for preventive measures. Other embryologists research diseases such as Parkinson's or diabetes, searching for medical solutions.

No matter where or in what specialty an embryologist works, all scientists in the field share similar schooling. They take high school and college courses in biology, chemistry, microbiology, and genetics. Many go on to get a Ph.D. in embryology or biology.

Just as dancers need physical dexterity to do their art well, embryologists need a special set of skills to work at top form. Like all scientists, they need an inquiring mind—always raising questions, exploring new ideas and searching for answers to medical mysteries. They show attention to

Fashionistas

- **Which fashions are really new and which have been recycled from previous generations?**

- **What are the pros and cons of school uniforms?**

- **How does brand influence the clothes you purchase?**

179

Boomerang Fashion

1 **Make Inferences**
What did women in the early 1900s value in their fashion? How do you know?

Scarlett is getting dressed for a dance. The year is 1902. Although Scarlett is old enough to dress herself, she needs her sister's help to tighten her stiff, lace-up corset. This large undergarment allows her to cinch her waist to a mere 20 inches. "Exhale," her sister orders as she tugs on the crossed laces, "and don't breathe!" Over the corset, Scarlett slips a gown with a full skirt and off-the-shoulder top. Dresses with tight-fitting top parts,

A corset was worn under dresses.

snugly pulled waists, and huge skirts were the popular style during the early 1900s. **1**

Some 70 years later, Tim considers himself stylish enough to be the height of 1970s **fashion**. He has just wriggled into an incredibly tight pair of navy blue **synthetic** polyester pants that are flared at the bottom. His shirt, with a huge butterfly collar, is purple with scattered scarlet blossoms that will **coordinate** with the pants. Tim's four-inch platform shoes are shiny powder blue.

You might think "trendy" fashions like these are found only in the past because people today choose sensible, **practical** clothes. But, what about the boot-cut, or flared, pants you see on men and women today? They're a recycled fashion statement from the 1970s called "bell-bottoms" that began even earlier. They're not exactly practical either. How sensible is it to carry an extra yard of cloth at the bottom of your pants? Bell-bottom pants are a fashion trend that can get caught in an escalator or trip the wearer.

Although most people think of bell-bottom pants as a fashion statement from the 1970s, this seemingly impractical fashion actually has it roots in the military, where practicality is highly valued. The exact timeline of how and who started wearing bell-bottoms in the navy is a little unclear, but we do know that by the early 1800s they were part of the uniform. These pants could be removed and used as flotation devices if the sailor found himself off the ship in the water. Other theories for why sailors liked these pants were that the big leg could be turned up over the thigh so the pants wouldn't get wet when sailors scrubbed the deck, and the big cuffs kept the often barefoot sailors' feet warm. Sailors today, however, no longer wear the once-popular bell-bottoms. **2**

Many fashions or trends we

Bell-bottoms go from practical to fashionable.

think were just someone's wild idea have their roots in some useful, easily explained purpose. However, some are simply the idea of a designer wanting to try something new. One such fashion is the miniskirt. This **modern** trend, popularized by an English designer named Mary Quant, really is rather impractical.

To address this, some girls today have adopted fashions from dance, coordinating tights or leggings, made of stretchy, synthetic spandex. The miniskirt itself was introduced in the 1960s, causing uproar in the fashion industry. At the time, more than one news article linked fashion to declining morality and other problems of young adults behaving inappropriately.

2 Summarize
What were some ways bell-bottom pants were useful to sailors?

Think about jeans. Modern? Hip? Trendy? Well, yes, if they're low-rise with a designer label. But, the first blue jeans were a practical solution created by Levi Strauss in 1873 for gold miners whose pants would not hold up to the rough work. Through the decades, designers have created loose jeans, tight jeans, fit-and-flare jeans, black jeans, acid-washed jeans, crinkled jeans, cotton jeans, synthetic jeans, striped jeans, jeweled jeans, and jeans with rips and holes everywhere. **3** Trendy jeans might be cut off at the ankle, mid-calf, knee, or shorter.

With ever-changing fashion trends, a person might wonder why people like to buy the latest fashion. There are many reasons someone would buy modern clothes only to stop wearing them when a new design comes into style. Maybe someone's friends all had shoes with big, clunky heels. Maybe a teenager wanted to be the first girl at school with a poodle skirt. Perhaps certain people liked the colorful design of a cotton tie-dyed T-shirt or the swish of a synthetic bowling shirt. Moreover, the fashion business dictates changing and recycling trends (as long as the cycles are long enough).

Are fashion trends, then, a waste of money—a way to suggest you are part of a group or really "in the know"? **4** Or, do they give people choices to express themselves? Each person decides how to react to fashion trends. Tim's grandson may pick up that brightly flowered shirt because Hawaiian shirts have become popular again. Scarlett's great-great-granddaughter may coordinate one of Scarlett's corsets with a cute shirt, making the old-fashioned feel modern. **End**

3 Visualize

When reading a passage with descriptions, it is helpful to picture the things being described.

4 Language

The phrase "in the know" means being aware of the latest news.

Are You What You Wear?

Personal Encounter

It's fairly late in the afternoon as a grandmother walks home. She works part-time at the library just a block from her house. Ahead on one corner she sees a teenage girl dressed in tight black leather pants with thick chains hanging from her belt. Her black leather jacket is decorated with a huge red skull and crossbones. Her heavy leather boots have pointed toes and silver rivets. Her hair is brilliant orange, standing straight up in long, pointy spikes.

On the other corner across the street, a teenage boy in a neat white shirt, striped tie, and khaki pants stands at a bus stop, with a magazine rolled underneath his arm. His brown hair, cut short and wavy, just shows under his ball cap, which has a local team's logo.

The woman has to walk by one person or the other. Does it make a difference to her which person she passes? Many people would make a quick **judgment** about the "tough" girl and the "well-dressed" boy. They might conclude the girl's **behavior** is antisocial, and the boy's behavior is friendly. The woman might avoid passing the girl. But, are judgments based on clothing appropriate or even **accurate**?

2 Context Clues

How do context clues help you define *characteristics* in this sentence?

3 Word Reading

You may need to reread this sentence because *rebel* is pronounced differently as a noun or a verb. How is it used here?

Profiling and Fashion

Profiling is making judgments about people based on characteristics, or features, that can be seen. **2** A profile of someone is a description of personality and most likely behavior patterns based on visible characteristics. When people profile another person, they may note the person's age and project certain ways of thinking and behaving onto that person because the person is 15, or 50, or 80. A large part of profiling also involves fashion. People will almost always observe and judge the way a person is dressed. They may allow what the person wears to represent a full range of accompanying beliefs and behaviors that may not be what the person is really like.

Moreover, these judgments are often made without any real thought—they often are subconscious. Before someone even speaks a word, another person may classify him or her as "a nice young man" or "an angry rebel." They affiliate their clothes with the kind of person they believe them to be. In the personal encounter example, profiling the people on the street corner probably would not have any serious consequences. But, in other circumstances, profiling may result in extreme reactions and even cause people to **discriminate** against others who dress differently from themselves.

Are Baggy Pants Criminal?

Let's look at the fashion of wearing baggy pants, the ones that hang low enough to expose underwear. Young people, especially young men, claim that this is a "hip" fashion. Like many trends of the young, baggy pants defy, or rebel against, what most adults consider to be appropriate and fashionable—the fashion profile for young people that adults hold. **3** The controversy of baggy pants has become so heated that some states have proposed laws to outlaw baggy pants, claiming they don't want to see other people's underwear. This strong reaction to a fashion fad might be hiding a deeper meaning that is linked to profiling.

The style of baggy pants originated in prison among such offenders as petty criminals and drug dealers. These baggy pants, with large T-shirts, were then adopted by hip-hop and rap artists of the 1990s, some of whom were former criminals. The profile created by the fashion includes the behavioral characteristic "criminal." So, a young person wearing these low-hanging baggy pants may be more likely to be suspected of wrongful behavior or questioned by the police because of the profile.

From Profiling to Outright Prejudice

Another recent controversy involves retail stores that may have a certain profile for their most-sought-after customer. You've probably noticed the fashion advertising that consists of huge photographs of attractive young men and women dressed in the latest styles of the store. But, have you paid attention to whether all these models fit a

certain profile? Are they of a variety of ethnic backgrounds, for example, or just one?

Whichever is true, this way of advertising isn't ideal, but is it damaging? **4** Consider this true-to-life situation. A particular store has an image in mind such as "all-American clothes." This store features models with a particular profile the store owners feel best fits their fashions. They slant their sales pitch directly to that group. The young men in the store's posters and printed on the shopping bags are tall, thin, blond-haired, athletic, and Caucasian. They are wearing neat

logo T-shirts and fashionable, fitted jeans. The women in the advertising all have long, straight, blond hair and blue eyes. They are wearing low-cut blouses, incredibly short shorts, and high-heeled shoes. Like

4 **Ask Questions**
Pause to consider how this way of advertising could be damaging. As you read, see when the question is answered.

Vocabulary

portray (v) *make a picture or mental image of*

the men, they are Caucasian. The message they seem to **portray** is these are the profiled all-American customers who are really welcome to shop at the store.

When the management takes a further step toward supporting their ideal image by hiring only sales clerks who fit the profile, perhaps engaging workers of other ethnic backgrounds in the stockroom, profiling seems to have turned to fully developed discrimination based on race. In recent times, workers such as African Americans, Hispanics, and Asians have taken legal action against certain retail stores that have set up such a profile. They have accused the stores of racial discrimination.

Do You Get Profiled?

The situations portrayed here may not be part of your personal experience. So, it may not seem you are being inaccurately profiled by your fashion. But, it is happening all the time. Maybe you're a girl who is excited to go to school dressed in a new miniskirt and a sparkly blouse you found on sale at your local discount

store. A group of girls gather at the back of the cafeteria as you walk through the doors. They keep looking at you and whispering. You hope they are admiring your new outfit. But, instead they are saying your skirt "is not even real; it's just a knock-off!" They immediately decide they don't want to talk to you. Were you just negatively profiled?

Or, perhaps you're a guy, and you've just entered a business office where you want a summer job. The interviewer looks you over. He notes your wrinkled, bright red T-shirt and the holes in your jeans. But, he seems particularly interested in the piercings through your lip and eyebrow. You think he might be admiring them, but in reality he's thinking, "This one's way too rebellious for our office." You just lost your chance at the job based on his profiling, but you will probably never know that's why you didn't get the job. While some may see this is an example of discrimination, people need to understand that ultimately people do believe you are what you wear. In certain situations, it may be more beneficial to fit into the mold of what is expected of you rather than express your personal style. **5** **End**

5 **Ask Questions**

At the end of a passage, it is good to stop and think about what you read. Ask yourself, "What did I learn from this passage?"

Fashion Designer

Just Your Style

Imagine this: You're attending a fashion show, and a model wearing one of your latest designs walks onto the runway. Or, you go into a local department store, and see clothing you designed hanging on racks for sale. Perhaps you're out on the street, and a well dressed passerby is wearing one of your fashion designs. If you are willing to work hard and be patient, you could make fantasies like these come true by becoming a fashion designer.

What Makes a Good Fashion Designer?

The career of fashion designer is especially suited to the person who has creative ideas and can communicate these ideas in words and drawings. The person should be able to accept criticism. Also, the person should respond to and incorporate the ideas of other people, such as professionals in charge of the production, marketing, and sales of clothing. A fashion

designer also has to have a practical side. A designer should know how clothing patterns are drawn and cut, how clothes are sewn together, and how a particular design will fit on the human body. The ability to use math and a strong scientific knowledge of the human body support the practical aspects of fashion design. Use of the computer to model designs is also important.

Most fashion designers attend a two- or four-year college, majoring in fashion design. Many work several years as interns, junior designers, or design assistants. They gain experience and build up an individual portfolio of designs. Some designers take

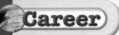

jobs in retail marketing. They see all the different styles and fashions consumers tend to purchase. Eventually, fashion designers may work for ready-to-wear apparel manufacturers, retail stores, specialty stores, or even individual customers. Others may start their own business.

What Can You Do as a Fashion Designer?

A fashion designer thinks up and creates designs for new garments. To begin, a fashion designer thinks of an idea for a new design. Then, the designer sketches it out. Usually, a designer works with one type of clothing. So the sketch may show, for example, a woman's dress, a man's suit, or a child's jacket. The designer continues to draw several sketches from different angles. Then, the designer may obtain reactions from other designers, production managers, and salespeople. The designer redraws a design that aims to satisfy a target audience. To come up with a design that appeals to today's market, a fashion designer needs to be well informed of current fashion trends. That way, the designer can use them, build on them, or even promote personal trends in fashion.

After a design is finished, the fashion designer needs organizational and technical skills. These help the designer plan how the garment will be put together, how the pieces needed to create it will be laid out, and how it can be mass-produced using modern tools and equipment. The designer draws and cuts a pattern for a sample garment. He or she creates the garment, fits it to a model, and changes it to make it perfect. The designer improves the garment's appearance and fit with suggestions from other professionals.

In the process of creating the sample garment, a fashion designer uses artistic talents, creative ideas, and relevant knowledge. These help the designer select the right kind and composition of fabric. The designer must choose fabrics with pleasing colors, textures, and patterns that work well with the design. He or she must pay attention to the details of design. Any decorations such as trims and buttons need to balance with the whole.

When a designer approves a sample garment, he or she then oversees the creation of a line of sample garments. These will be shown to the news media and potential buyers. If the design is received favorably, the designer will work with the pattern maker. The designer helps make sure the pattern is made and used correctly to avoid fabric waste. Working for a company, a fashion designer in 2009 could make an annual salary of about $36,000 to $54,000.

The process, which involves both independent designing and teamwork to design and create the best possible garment, then leads to a fine fashion product. The result of all the hard work depends on consumer response. Taking a creative idea and making it into an actual fashion is exciting, and the rewards can be great.

UNIFORMS:

Just Right or All Wrong?

Dear Editor:

I'm absolutely sick of hearing parents, teachers, and even a few students say the policy of our school to require school uniforms is a great choice. First of all, the word *choice* is totally contradictory; we students had no **personal** choice in the matter, no chance to affect the decision to have uniforms or the selection of the uniforms themselves. In this land where freedom is treasured, our freedom was crushed by those who want to **control** us. The committee of hand-picked parents, school board members, and administration chose, of all things, a bland white blouse with a **conservative** tan skirt (not even

pants!) for us girls. We can wear a light blue shirt only on Fridays. For the boys, they selected a

Vocabulary

personal (adj) *one's own; private or individual*

control (v) *be in charge of; direct*

conservative (adj) *traditional or modest*

Vocabulary

focus (v) *fix attention on something*

individual (n) *a single being or thing*

white shirt and straight-leg tan pants. The outfits they picked make almost all of us look like elementary school kids on some kind of childish outing, rather than young adults.

However, the actual appearance of the conservative clothing is not the most important issue to **focus** on. Clothes, besides being a way to cover and protect the body, are a powerful means of self-expression we students have now lost. Uniforms make students conform to a standard that takes away their right to dress as they like. Every person deserves to be an **individual**, to dress basically how he or she wants.

I agree that attention-seeking clothing should be left for personal, rather than school, use. That's why schools have conservative dress codes. But, dressing in our own individual styles helps us feel comfortable, happy, and more ready to learn. We leave home in the morning with a sense of creativity and fun, rather than feeling like inmates in a prison. **1**

A deeper issue revolves around what the use of school uniforms suggests about parents' and professionals' view of today's students. I believe requiring uniforms supports the idea that we are not mature enough to select our own clothes. It also robs us of the chance to experiment and learn to dress properly, yet in our own way, for future situations. The education we are told school provides does not focus simply on coursework, but also on values that are important in our society. Isn't learning to dress appropriately, rather than having a non-personal style forced upon us, an important skill? How can we learn such a valuable skill without practice?

Some parents and students argue that uniforms save money. Because we have to buy uniforms, rather than wear the clothes we already own, I don't see how that works. Why not make good use of the resources we already have? Why spend money and buy more clothes that will later end up in landfills? Furthermore, it is ridiculous to wear white shirts. White shirts get dirty quickly and have to be washed nearly every day, and they stain far more often than any choice I'd make for school. It makes no sense. Also, how many students

1 Recognize Bias
What support does the author give for her argument so far?

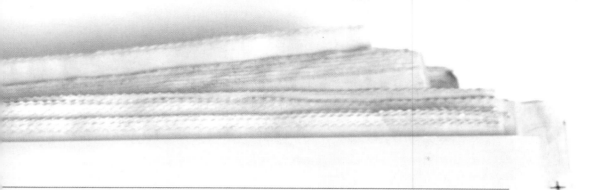

do you know who have ruined a uniform in science lab? Without proper aprons in our school, the best choice for lab days is to wear old clothes, not expensive uniforms. So, the constant washing and drying as well as the need for extras (when one uniform is waiting to be washed) and replacements result in costs that uniform supporters overlook.

In conclusion, I want to ask each student some vital questions. Is being yourself important to you? Do you want to move from the arena of being controlled into one of appropriate self-expression? Let's begin by reacting like adults and showing our maturity with a carefully planned and executed protest. Let's inform parents and administrators that we feel stifled and unhappy, stuffed into skirts or straight pants, and expressionless white shirts! **2**

Chrissy Reynolds

2 Ask Questions
Ask yourself if the author has convinced you of her point of view. Why or why not?

Dear Editor:

I am a transfer student to this school. Because of all the commotion here lately about school uniforms, I want to tell you about my experience at my previous school to help show how beneficial uniforms are for education and the school community.

I came from a school where students dress exactly as they like. One of the major problems with letting students wear individual fashion styles to school is that a lot of today's fashions can cause a distraction in the classroom. The school environment should be controlled so the focus is on learning, not fashion. More than once, I found myself embarrassed because I had been staring at the rhinestone

3 Visualize

Picture this writer in your mind. Try to put yourself in his place and understand his reasons for wanting uniforms.

design on a shirt or trying to read what was printed on the back of a T-shirt instead of listening to the teacher. I had never seen such bold and fancy clothing before.

I know some parents and students complain about the cost of uniforms. Oddly enough, I'm not sure those people complaining are really the ones who do not have much money. My family did not have money to buy me new clothes and shoes for every season of the school year. I worked part-time to pay for my school uniform. I think that taught me responsibility, and it cost far less than if I tried to buy a whole new wardrobe every year.

In my old school, several groups of students dressed pretty much alike and even seemed to share a particular style of dressing. But, my family does not have a lot of money. Because of the financial situation in my home, I often had to wear hand-me-down clothes that were old and worn looking. I could not walk down the hallway or into a classroom without glaring glances or ridiculing remarks, and sometimes other guys tried to start a fight with me. I can tell you the situation

did nothing for my education and caused me unfortunate personal suffering. **3**

Here in my new school, nobody can judge me unfairly for what I wear. I am treated with the same respect as other kids, rather than being singled out for ridicule. My experience is that uniforms bring a sense of community to the school environment. And, they make it easy to recognize who is part of the school community and who is not—an important factor in today's world. So, I feel safer as an individual and protected in the school community.

Some students feel really strongly about clothes as self-expression. But, if you have no money to buy clothes that suit you as an individual, you suffer for something over which you have no control. These students probably have not considered the situation of students like me. Now that I have shared my experiences, I hope they think twice about trying to abolish school uniforms. Let's keep the school environment fair for everyone. Fairness is clearly a more important value than individuality in dress. **4**

Roberto Alvarez **End**

4 Make Connections

How do this boy's arguments compare to the girl's arguments against uniforms? Could he add other arguments?

In the Public Eye

What Is Branding?

In the Old West, a rancher heated a metal tool to brand his cattle, marking his animals with a symbol that stood for the ranch. The brand protected the rancher from losing his cattle to thieves. The brand also let buyers know the cattle they bought were from a ranch they could trust.

Today, branding is an important economic concept used on **goods** and services, and it has spread to the world's marketplace. Yet, it shares some characteristics with the practice of branding cattle. Branding is symbolic, it represents a particular company, and it creates a certain expectation.

A brand is the mark or name a company puts on the things it makes or sells. A brand sets a product or service apart from similar products or services in the marketplace: Ford cars, Nike footwear, The North Face jackets. One brand stands apart from other brands by its name and by logos and other symbols. Marketers, people who promote and sell the product, use many types of advertising to lead the public to identify and connect with the goods their companies sell. Web sites, billboards, magazine photos, and special price events, for example, advertise products. Through effective branding, one seller's goods stand out from another's to create **loyal** customers who usually buy only the first seller's brand.

Beyond identifying products,

Vocabulary

goods (n) *things that can be bought or sold; products*

loyal (adj) *faithful to someone or something*

1 Summarize

What are the benefits of branding?

2 Ask Questions

Check your understanding by asking yourself how the Industrial Revolution caused the need for branding.

branding appeals to what people value. Branding helps create the feeling a buyer expects when purchasing a particular brand: "When I put on new Nike shoes, I expect them to fit perfectly, look fantastic, last a long time, be noticed, and make me feel like a million dollars." So, the perceptions a buyer has about a seller's goods is influenced by the brand. Branding aims to affect the feelings of the buyer. Branding tries to **bias** the buyer into choosing one brand over all others. **1**

Mass-Marketing Created Branding

The need for branding began with the Industrial Revolution in the 1800s. The invention of machinery to **manufacture** goods cheaply and rapidly in factories changed the economics of acquiring needed goods. Before that time, most families produced the goods they required, such as food, soap, and clothing. Sometimes, they bartered with neighbors, exchanging a dozen eggs for soap, for example. Or, they bought from nearby families who operated cottage industries. Cottage industries were families working at

home using all the family members to produce goods, like weaving cloth or knitting sweaters. To get people to trust non-local products, companies began to brand their products. Names such as Coca-Cola, Frye boots, Wrigley's Juicy Fruit, Stetson, and Levi's emerged in the marketplace. **2**

Over time, manufacturers and marketers learned they had to do more than just attach a name and distinctive packaging to their products. To succeed in a competitive marketplace, they needed to create a brand image that had special value to **consumers**. To attract repeat customers, they had to inspire consumer loyalty.

What's in a Name?

The brand name itself has little impact on consumers—people will buy almost any name—but all the values and ideas created in the minds of consumers by the branding are important. They allow a brand to acquire and hold a strong market presence.

For example, consider a $395 Dolce & Gabbana pair of sunglasses. The idea of D&G sunglasses with a new stylish look might easily appeal

Brand Name Item	Date	Originator
Frye boots	1863	John A. Frye
Stetson hats	1865	John B. Stetson
Levi's blue jeans	1873	Levi Strauss
Coca-Cola	1886	John Stith Pemberton
Lee jeans	1889	Henry David Lee
Wrigley's Juicy Fruit gum	1893	William Wrigley Jr.

to a young woman. But, why would this potential buyer choose the D&G sunglasses over less expensive ones? Let's examine several possible reasons:

1. The design is unique.
2. The materials and quality are exceptional.
3. Famous actresses buy D&G sunglasses.
4. People are impressed by the expensive label.

Branding is responsible for all these beliefs and experiences. D&G branding promises its sunglasses will deliver fine design, expert quality, and a product that important or trusted people approve of, wear, and notice. The potential buyer feels an emotional link with the sunglasses, created by its luxury branding.

Another manufacturer may not want to make people think of its product as a luxury. Its branding is directed to values that are important to a different group of consumers. For example, Saf Organic Cotton Clothing advertises itself as a company that uses only organic materials and does not use unfair labor practices, such as sweatshops,

in the manufacture of its line of clothing. The brand works to bias people against companies that do not follow the same practices. At the same time, it promotes Saf Organic Cotton Clothing. The branding appeals to environmentally conscious consumers. **3**

Too Many Choices

Branding in today's marketplace is particularly important because of the number of choices. Look at any simple product in the supermarket. If you had to evaluate every purchase, you'd never finish shopping. Instead, you grab your favorite brand. The clothing industry is also flooded with choices. How many brands of jeans or T-shirts can you name? When you shop, do you only consider purchasing Lucky Brand jeans or American Eagle T-shirts because you know they fit your body and your style? Branding helps you make a choice you know will work, even if it costs more than a similar item in a discount store.

3 Make Inferences
How can branding affect a buyer's emotions? What evidence from the text helps you know this?

Information or Persuasion?

A successfully branded product is one people will pay a little more for or travel farther to get. Moreover, each time consumers make a purchase, they will loyally search for the same brand. But, does that mean the product is really better? Is Prada better than Fossil? Is Hollister better than Plugg? The branding of the higher priced products tries to convince the consumer the answer is yes. Consumers who believe the message behind the branding often part with more money or time to get "exactly the right brand." But, are they really getting their money's worth? Did they base their choice on sound information, or were they persuaded by branding? **4**

No matter how much advertising a product gets, or how successfully branded it is, if you buy it and don't feel what you expected to feel, the experience is disappointing. To maintain the bias branding creates, your experience with the product must live up to your expectations. Otherwise, the company will lose your business. The company may face a reversal in the marketplace as more and more people realize the branding was, in fact, "just hype." Then, the branding that persuaded consumers to buy the company's product can turn into negative branding that reminds them not to buy. Think of that Old West cattle rancher. If his brand is no longer trusted, he might as well let his cattle roam free and start again with a new brand on another herd. **End**

4 Make Connections

Have you ever been persuaded to buy a product just because of the brand?

Retail Salesperson

Share Your Style

Are you a person who loves clothes—all kinds of clothes, new fashions, exciting combinations, ethnic styles? Do your friends always compliment you on your judgment in combining styles into outfits, saying how "together" you look? Or, do you have a particular interest in sports clothing and accessories? Do you know just which shoes and gear work well and look great? Are you sociable? Do you like to help people? If you answered yes to any of these questions, you could be a retail salesperson in a store that sells clothing.

Being a clothing store retail salesperson is not for someone who wants to roll out of bed, fall into a wrinkled T-shirt and dirty jeans, and head for work. But, if you like to dress so you look neat, knowledgeable, approachable, and friendly, being a salesperson in a retail store could be the right job for you.

The retail market is a good place to find work. Shoppers spend millions every day on retail merchandise. They depend on the salespeople to help them find what they want and make a purchase decision. Employment opportunities in retail sales are common. New employees often learn the skills on the job, learning as they earn.

As a salesperson, you won't sit behind a desk. You probably won't talk to anonymous people on the telephone. You will be in the middle of a busy store, working with customers who need help. You will share your knowledge

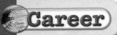
of modern clothing styles. You will use your ability to judge how things look and your expert knowledge in a sport or some other special interest with people who want your help. You must communicate your ideas clearly and tactfully so as not to insult customers or make them angry. Your job will be to create a shopping experience customers enjoy, so they make the right purchase and come back again.

As a retail sales clerk in a clothing store, for example, one of your tasks will be to know exactly what the store has in stock. Suppose a shopper wants a special pair of jeans. You will know exactly where to find the jeans to show her. You will also know which jackets, sweaters, shirts, and accessories will look perfect with the jeans. That way, you can recommend combinations. Perhaps you know that there are no jeans similar to what she wants on the floor, but a new style has just arrived in the stockroom. You get the jeans from the stockroom and show them to the customer. If you know the store has no jeans, you may show her some cargo pants. In this way, your job will involve problem-solving to help each customer make his or her purchase.

After the sale is made, you may complete the transaction at the cash register. You handle the payment, provide a receipt, and put the items purchased in a bag. Thus, you carry through all your hard work to a successful end. Your store may pay you a commission for whatever you have sold.

As a retail salesperson in a large sports store, your tasks will be similar to those of the clothing store clerk. But, you will be selling practical products related to your particular area of interest and knowledge. Perhaps a

young man is trying to find basketball shoes in the shoe department. You ask if he needs help. You direct him to the section of the department where shoes appropriate for basketball are displayed. As an informed salesperson, you know how the shoe sizes run, so you ask about his normal size and advise him on appropriate sizes to try. You may help him find a good fit. If he decides on a particular pair of shoes that are not in stock, you offer to order them for him. Or, you might recommend a similarly styled shoe you have found to be exceptionally well made for the price to see if he might be interested in changing his mind.

When the pleased young man walks out of your department to pay for a great pair of shoes he might have missed if you weren't there to help, you'll feel the satisfaction of a job well done. You might even picture him on the court, shooting hoops in the shoes you helped him find.

Animals: Heroes and Scholars

- How does animal intelligence differ from human intelligence?
- What jobs can animals perform better than humans?
- How do animals learn?

199

Right for the Job

Vocabulary

officials (n) *people who hold important positions in an organization*

evaluate (v) *decide the condition or value of someone or something after thinking carefully about it*

In the midst of a raging battle, a general must get a written message to troops behind enemy lines. The general hands this message to Roger, who slips into enemy territory to find the stranded troops.

At a large international airport, **officials** in charge have been warned that passengers are attempting to transport cocaine and other illegal drugs. Officials order Missy to **evaluate** travelers and determine whether they are carrying drugs, while they direct Clark to check all baggage for signs of illegal substances.

Dog handler at work with her dog in a minefield near Visoko, central Bosnia

Vocabulary

domestic (adj) *to do with the home; not wild*

acute (adj) *sharp*

discern (v) *recognize or identify*

Cars zip through a busy intersection as Ms. Gomez waits to cross. When the traffic pauses, Sam leads Ms. Gomez across the intersection.

What do Roger, Missy, Clark, and Sam have in common? They are dogs—and they were all just right for the job.

A Dog's Resume

What are a dog's credentials for work? A dog's physical shape and size make it right for certain tasks. For example, a small dog can squeeze somewhere humans cannot fit. In general, people think of dogs as **domestic** animals, so a dog can walk by without rousing, or attracting, suspicion.

What special characteristics do dogs possess that help with work? For one thing, because dogs have been domesticated, they can be trained easily. Most domestic dogs are obedient and follow through on their masters'

commands. **1** But, it is their **acute** senses of smell, sight, and hearing that make them so valuable. Dogs have almost 220 million smell-detecting cells, which is more than 40 times more than humans have, so they are able to **discern** smells easily. Dogs also have eyes that are more sensitive to light and motion than human eyes. Their sense of hearing is sharp, so they can hear a larger range of sounds and also move their ears to locate the source.

Mine Finders

Some working dogs use their skills to detect unexploded land mines, such as in Sri Lanka, where land that was fought over in the 1980s remained riddled with mines. Land mines were planted throughout the land to destroy enemy artillery. When the fighting ended, the mines became a danger to playing children and other civilians. The mines sometimes exploded, killing anyone nearby. A team of four dogs and their handlers arrived

1 Context Clues
Using the context clues, what is the definition of *obedient*?

2 Ask Questions

Think about what
you just read. Was
there a part that was
confusing? Stop and
ask your own question
about that part. Then
look for an answer in
the text.

A member of an urban search-and-rescue team works with his dog in the effort to uncover victims after the attack on the World Trade Center in New York City.

in 1999 to find the mines. In pairs, the dogs acutely sniffed the ground to pick up the smell of explosives and other chemicals that leak from the mines. The dogs' sense of smell allowed the mines to be marked and safely removed.

Disaster Dogs

The United States has about 200 official government-certified rescue dogs that have been trained to help during emergencies. The dogs use their acute sense of smell and ability to scramble through places humans cannot to discern the whereabouts of disaster victims. Rescue dogs searched for survivors in homes flooded by hurricane Katrina, and after 9/11, rescue dogs wearing search-and-rescue vests dug through the smoking rubble of bricks and stones to find survivors. **2**

Witnesses for the Prosecution

Given a dog's sense of smell, it is easy to understand how dogs can find things. But, how could a dog give evidence in a court case, and would the evidence be usable in court? In September 2008, a French dog nicknamed Scooby became the first domestic dog called as a witness. The dog's owner was found dead in her apartment. The woman's family claimed she had been murdered and wanted a thorough **inquiry**. A hearing was held. A veterinarian led the dog to the witness box, and a suspect was escorted into the courtroom. Reports say the dog was able to discern the smell of the murderer and "barked furiously," which convinced officials to hold the requested murder inquiry.

Questions about Working Dogs

The use of dogs in these and other ways brings up certain questions. Is it really right to use dogs in perilous situations, exposing them to land mines, disasters, and dangerous chemicals and people? How dependable is a dog's skill, or a dog's evidence? If using dogs is right, in which ways can they continue to help us? Which future jobs will be just right for dogs? **End**

Animal Intelligence

Beyond Instincts

A crow fashioning a hook? A parrot talking with you and sorting buttons by size? Two dolphins planning their own trick? These may sound like scenes from a fantasy movie, but psychologists who study animal cognition, or intelligence, are proving these are facts. **1**

We understand that every animal knows how to survive. When an animal is born, it knows what it must do to live. Without being taught, a newborn reptile knows how to find food. Without being taught, a butterfly migrates to the exact region it needs to move to. Each of these is an example of an animal **instinct**. Hibernation is an instinct of bears. A bear seeks shelter, remains inactive, and has a lower body temperature. Hibernation allows a bear to survive when little food is available. No one teaches a bear to hibernate—the bear just does.

How do baby birds know how to find food?

We also know that animals can learn. Young animals learn **complex** survival skills from their parents, such as a jaguar cub learning how to catch a turtle. But, people teach animals well beyond survival skills. For example, they train dogs to round up cattle, and birds to say "hello." Cognitive psychologists have been experimenting with animals to learn what kind of intelligence they have. Psychologists want to know what and how animals learn. **2**

Pavlov's Salivating Dogs

An early experimenter on animal intelligence was a Russian named Ivan Pavlov. In the 1890s and 1900s, Pavlov carried out experiments on the **conditioned** responses of dogs. A conditioned response is a response that is

How can we teach birds to ride bicycles?

3 Make Connections

Can you relate to Pavlov's dogs or Skinner's pigeons? For example, if you see your favorite food do you suddenly feel hungry?

Professor B. F. Skinner conducted psychological experiments with pigeons in which they were to match a colored light with a corresponding colored panel in order to receive food.

learned from previous experience. In Pavlov's study, the response was salivating at the sight or smell of food. The food was a **stimulus** that caused the response. Pavlov conditioned his subject dogs to salivate, or drool, at the sound of a nonfood stimulus, such as a bell. So, Pavlov took the instinctual behavior of salivating in the presence of food and made it into the learned behavior of salivating when a signal those dogs had learned to **associate** with food was sounded. His experiments proved that animals could react to a learned stimulus.

Skinner's "Dancing" Pigeons

Pavlov was concerned with controlling the stimulus—the sound that brought about the dog's response. American psychologist B. F. Skinner experimented to learn if he could train pigeons to realize that a certain action they performed brought about the response they

wanted: food. Skinner's experiments in the 1950s and 1960s showed that pigeons could learn to associate whatever behavior they were performing when they received food with the food itself. Thus, a conditioned behavior developed. The pigeons would repeat the movement they associated with the food. Whether it was pecking the cage roof or spinning twice counterclockwise, whenever they wanted food, they repeated their "dance." Skinner's behavioral conditioning could be used to teach animals to repeat certain actions. **3**

A Deeper Understanding

In recent studies, psychologists have come to realize that animal intelligence extends far deeper than the simple stimulus-response conditioning of Pavlov or the behavioral conditioning of Skinner. Animals have performed complex actions and activities that people associate with higher intelligence. For example, some animals

Chimpanzees use a stick to remove termites from a nest.

A crow uses a hook that it created from wire.

think creatively, solve problems, communicate, and express emotions—all things many people believe are reserved for the human species only.

Tool-Making Crows

The use and creation of tools is an intellectual achievement humans often claim as their own. Today, stories abound of monkeys using tools, such as sticks to probe, or explore, termite nests. Alex Kacelnik, who studies bird behavior, has discovered that crows not only use tools they pick up from nature, but also make hooks and probes from sticks and stems of leaves to poke into trees to find grubs. Kacelnik studied tool-making crows to determine if the behavior was instinctual or learned. He found that even if crows never observed other crows using tools, they still used tools to reach food. **4**

Kacelnik also set up tests to challenge crows to come up with solutions to new problems, ones he was sure the crows had not experienced. One crow, Betty, was tested multiple times in a situation where a hook was needed to secure food. Each time, whatever was left

for her to work with—bits of wire, flat pieces of metal—she fashioned it with her beak into a hook the right size and shape to obtain the food.

Chatting with a Parrot

Chimpanzees and gorillas have been the subject of numerous studies of animal-human communication. These primates have learned to use sign language taught to them by trainers. Some have even combined signs and symbols they learned in order to communicate something new, something from their own thinking. But, primates are often considered to be higher-order animals. What about lower-order animals?

Irene Pepperberg wanted to learn if birds could communicate out loud with humans. In 1977, she chose the parrot as her subject because parrots have the inborn ability to form words. Pepperberg learned that in the wild, parrots need to put things

Irene Pepperberg works with Alex the parrot.

4 Main Idea
What is the implicit main idea of this paragraph?

Animals: Heroes and Scholars

into useful groups, or classify them. For example, they need to know what is food and what isn't; they need to know which shapes represent predators and which don't. Pepperberg believed that instinct was not enough to explain these very complex understandings. To test her theory, she set about teaching her ordinary parrot Alex names he could say out loud to group different objects, actions, colors, numbers, and even materials. Alex learned more than 100 words with which he communicated with Pepperberg. Alex demonstrated an ability to classify, **exhibited** math skills, and learned the sounds of letters. **5**

Signing with Bottlenose Dolphins

In the 1970s to 1980s, psychologist Louis Herman experimented with dolphins. Herman and his team created a language of arm and hand signals that was based on a simple grammar in which the order of the signals would affect the meaning of the phrases. Dolphins that learned the signals could perform the exact series correctly, in whatever order was requested, the first time.

Herman even made up a signal to command dolphins to "create," and they would make up their own series of behaviors. One time, Herman signaled two dolphins to create a trick to perform together. The dolphins dove underwater and circled for 10 seconds. The two dolphins then leaped up at the same time with a clockwise spin, spitting water out of their mouths. Not only had Herman communicated to the dolphins, but the dolphins had communicated with each other! The dolphins exhibited intelligence.

Beyond the Ordinary

These and countless other experiments with animals have allowed psychologists to prove that animals have abilities and intelligence far beyond what was once assumed. Yet, because each species is unique, the degree to which an animal understands, thinks, communicates, and feels is still difficult to determine. The truth may lie somewhere between the concept that a pig acts only from instinct to the idea that a pet cat understands everything its owner says. Psychologists continue to search for answers. **End**

5 Make Connections

Have you ever taught an animal something? What did you teach it?

Animal Trainer

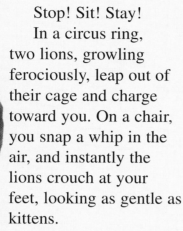

Stop! Sit! Stay! In a circus ring, two lions, growling ferociously, leap out of their cage and charge toward you. On a chair, you snap a whip in the air, and instantly the lions crouch at your feet, looking as gentle as kittens.

In a large aquarium, you blow your whistle, and three dolphins jump high out of the water, each one spinning until they all splash together under the surface.

When people talk about animal trainers, places like circuses, zoos, and aquariums often come to mind: elephants standing on stools, seals catching balls, rabbits jumping out of hats—all at a trainer's command. These are exciting jobs if you love to perform and work with animals. But, there are other types of jobs for people who have the skills to train animals. For example, you might train animals to help people with disabilities. A guide dog, which is not a domestic pet, gives a sightless person the freedom to walk through the city. A trained monkey helps pick up things for a person whose movement is impaired.

Or, maybe you're looking for a particularly exciting way to help others? You might be interested in training dogs to do dangerous work. With patience, determination, understanding, and love, you can train a dog to work in an official capacity for the police, crisis rescue services, or even the United Nations.

What would you do to train a dog? Let's look at one example: training dogs to find unexploded land mines. These dogs go into countries where land mines and other explosives were planted during war. Using their acute sense of smell, dogs sniff out the land mines so that mine locations can be mapped. Then the areas can be cleared of mines and become safe again for people to use. The training of these dogs is specific to the task. Yet, the methods are similar in all kinds of animal training, and the qualities required of the trainer are the same.

Animal training involves conditioning an animal to respond in a particular way to a set of commands or another stimulus. An animal trainer needs to exhibit patience because the animal must learn in small steps and practice to learn the skill well. At the right

Toby, a capuchin monkey, adjusts trainer Alison Payne's eyeglasses at Monkey College. The monkeys begin school when they are 5 years old and are trained for 2 years.

Police officer Li Wei trains a police dog to jump through a fire loop.

moment, the trainer needs to give positive reinforcement—a treat, praise, a pat on the head, a toy—to condition the dog to correctly perform all the steps needed to do the job.

Some trainers are specialized and work to teach a specific skill, such as mine detection. To train mine detection dogs, or MDDs, you would need to know which substances in these mines a dog can detect, and which ones can be smelled in the air or the ground. You would use conditioning to teach the dog to respond to up to 10 of these target odors. At first, the dog's task might be presented as a game, just like a pet owner might play "find the ball" with a pet dog. As the dog's detection skills develop, training might move to an experimental cage. After teaching the dog what to do, the trainer gives the command signal for the dog to start. The dog sniffs a cylinder containing an odor, the stimulus. The dog then presses the correct lever to indicate whether the smell was clean air or a target odor. When the dog is right, you reward it so it associates a correct answer with a positive outcome.

As an MDD trainer, you repeat the same training over and over. You wouldn't want any mistakes when the dog is in a minefield! You train your dog to be obedient and accurate because the dog's survival and the life of others depend on its skills. You demand the dog's complete attention when it works, and teach it to sit without moving to signal it has sensed a land mine.

Though very important, the work of an animal trainer does not necessarily require years of education. Most animal trainers do have a high school diploma. Many take special training courses to learn more about how to train animals, especially for official jobs. Animal trainers typically make from $16,000 to $48,000 a year. If you love animals and enjoy working with them, a good place to start is with a job at a veterinary clinic or an animal adoption agency or as a pet sitter—actually, any job that gives you more experience with animals. You might even teach your old dog new tricks.

FROM
WHITE FANG

BY JACK LONDON

PART V: THE TAME

CHAPTER 5
THE SLEEPING WOLF
PART 1

It was about this time that the newspapers were full of the daring escape of a convict from San Quentin prison. He was a ferocious man. He had been ill-made in the making. He had not been born right, and he had not been helped any by the molding he had received at the hands of society. The hands of society are harsh, and this man was a striking sample of its handiwork. He was a beast—a human beast, it is true, but nevertheless so terrible a beast that he can best be **characterized** as carnivorous.

In San Quentin prison he had proved **incorrigible**. Punishment failed to break his spirit. He could die dumb-mad and fighting to the last, but he could not live and be beaten. The more fiercely he fought, the more harshly society handled him, and the only effect of harshness was to make him fiercer. Straight-jackets to restrain him, starvation, and beatings and clubbings were the wrong treatment for Jim Hall; but it was the treatment he received. It was the treatment he had received from the time he was a little pulpy, shapeable boy in a San Francisco slum—soft clay in the hands of society and ready to be formed into something.

It was during Jim Hall's third term in prison that he encountered a guard that was almost as great a beast as he. The guard treated him unfairly, lied

---

Animals: Heroes and Scholars

about him to the warden, lost his credits, and **persecuted** him. The difference between them was that the guard carried a bunch of keys and a gun. Jim Hall had only his naked hands and his teeth. But he sprang upon the guard one day and used his teeth on the other's throat just like any jungle animal.

After this, Jim Hall went to live in the incorrigible cell. He lived there three years. The cell was of iron, the floor, the walls, the roof. He never left this cell. He never saw the sky nor the sunshine. Day was a barely noticeable twilight and night was a black silence. He was in an iron tomb, buried alive. **1** He saw no human face, spoke to no human thing. When his food was shoved in to him, he growled like a wild animal. He hated all things. For days and nights he bellowed his rage loudly at the universe. Then, for weeks and months he never made a sound, in the black silence eating his very soul. He was a man and a monstrosity, as fearful a thing of fear as ever imagined in the visions of a maddened brain.

And then, one night, he escaped. The warders said it was impossible, but nevertheless the cell was empty, and half in half out of it lay the body of a slain guard. Two other dead guards marked his trail through the prison to the outer walls, and he had killed with his hands to avoid noise.

He was armed with the weapons of the slain guards—a live arsenal that fled through the hills pursued by the organized might of society. A heavy price of gold was upon his head. Greedy farmers hunted him with shotguns. His blood might pay off a loan or send a son to college. Public-spirited citizens took down their rifles and went out after him. A pack of bloodhounds followed the way of his bleeding feet. And the sleuth-hounds of the law, the paid fighting animals of society, with telephone, and telegraph, and special train, clung to his trail night and day.

Sometimes they came upon him, and men faced him like heroes, or stampeded through barbed-wire fences to the delight of the people reading the account at the breakfast table. It was after such encounters that the dead and wounded were carted back to the towns, and their places filled by men eager for the manhunt.

And then Jim Hall disappeared. The bloodhounds **vainly** quested, or searched, for him on the lost trail. Inoffensive, ordinary ranchers in remote valleys were held up by armed men and **compelled** to identify themselves. While the remains of Jim Hall were discovered on a dozen mountainsides by greedy claimants for blood-money.

In the meantime the newspapers were read at Sierra Vista, not so much with interest as with anxiety, or worry. The women were afraid. Judge Scott pooh-poohed and laughed, but not with reason, for it was in his last days on the bench that Jim Hall had stood before him and received sentence. And in open court-room, before all men, Jim Hall had proclaimed that the day would come when he would wreak, or bring about, vengeance on the Judge that sentenced him.

For once, Jim Hall was right. He was innocent of the crime for which he was sentenced. It was a case, in the language of thieves and police, of "railroading." Jim Hall was being "railroaded" to prison for a crime he had not committed. **2** Because of the two prior convictions against him, Judge Scott imposed upon him a sentence of fifty years.

Judge Scott did not know all things, and he did not know that he was party to a police conspiracy, that the evidence was hatched and falsified, that Jim Hall was guiltless of the crime charged. And Jim Hall, on the other hand, did not know that Judge Scott was merely ignorant. Jim Hall believed that the judge knew all about it and was hand in glove with the police in the promotion of the monstrous injustice. So it was, when the doom of fifty years of living death was uttered by Judge Scott, that Jim Hall, hating all things in the society that misused him, rose up and raged in the courtroom until dragged down by half a dozen of his blue-coated enemies. To him, Judge Scott was the keystone in the arch of injustice, and upon Judge Scott he emptied the vials of his wrath and hurled the angry threats of his revenge yet to come. Then Jim Hall went to his living death . . . and escaped.

Of all this White Fang knew nothing. But between him and Alice, the master's wife, there existed a secret. Each night, after Sierra Vista had gone to bed, she rose and let in White Fang to sleep in the big hall. Now White Fang was not a house dog, nor was he permitted to sleep in the house; so each morning, early, she slipped down and let him out before the family was awake.

On one such night, while all the house slept, White Fang awoke and lay

vainly (adv) *unsuccessfully; futilely*

compelled (v) *made someone do something by giving him or her orders or using force*

2 Context Clues
Using the sentences before and after, and the context within the sentence, what do you think *railroading* means?

very quietly. And very quietly he smelled the air and read the message it bore of a strange god's presence. And to his ears came sounds of the strange god's movements. White Fang burst into no furious outcry. It was not his way. The strange god walked softly, but more softly walked White Fang, for he had no clothes to rub against the flesh of his body. He followed silently. In the Wild he had hunted live meat that was **infinitely** timid, and he knew the advantage of surprise.

The strange god paused at the foot of the great staircase and listened, and White Fang was as dead, so without movement was he as he watched and waited. Up that staircase the way led to the love-master and to the love-master's dearest possessions. White Fang bristled, but waited. The strange god's foot lifted. He was beginning the ascent. **3**

Then it was that White Fang struck. He gave no warning, with no snarl anticipated his own action. Into the air he lifted his body in the spring that landed him on the strange god's back. White Fang clung with his forepaws to the man's shoulders, at the same time burying his fangs into the back of the man's neck. He clung on for a moment, long enough to drag the god over backward. Together they crashed to the floor. White Fang leaped clear, and, as the man struggled to rise, was in again with the slashing fangs. **4** **End**

3 **Visualize**
Picture in your mind
the scene described.
What do you see?

4 **Make a Prediction**
Who do you think will
win the fight? Why?

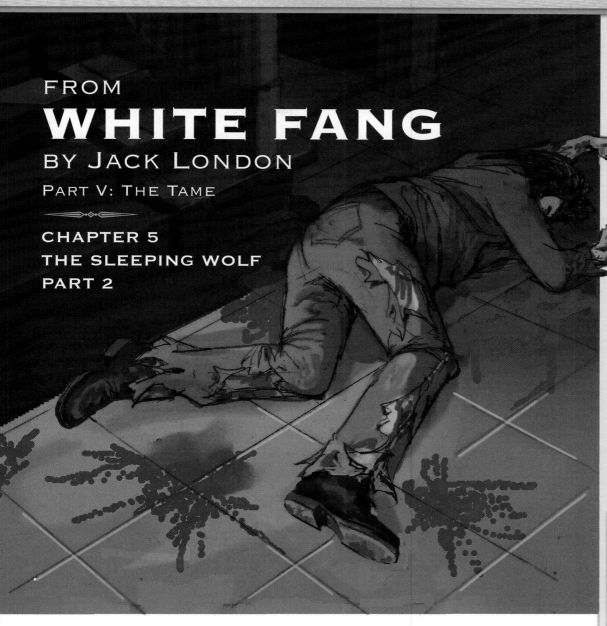

FROM
WHITE FANG
BY JACK LONDON
PART V: THE TAME

CHAPTER 5
THE SLEEPING WOLF
PART 2

Vocabulary

fiends (n) *evil or cruel people*

commotion (n) *a lot of noisy, excited activity*

abyss (n) *a very deep hole that seems to have no bottom*

Sierra Vista awoke in alarm. The noise from downstairs was as that of twenty battling **fiends**. There were revolver shots. A man's voice screamed once in horror and anguish, or pain. There was a great snarling and growling, and over all arose a smashing and crashing of furniture and glass.

But almost as quickly as it had arisen, the **commotion** died away. The struggle had not lasted more than three minutes. The frightened household clustered at the top of the stairway. From below, as from out of an **abyss** of blackness, came up a gurgling sound, as of air bubbling through water. Sometimes this gurgle became a hiss, almost a whistle. But this, too, quickly died down and ceased. **1** Then naught, absolutely nothing, came up out of the blackness but a heavy panting of some creature struggling sorely for air.

Weedon Scott pressed a button, and light flooded the staircase and downstairs hall. Then he and Judge Scott, guns in hand, cautiously descended the stairs. There was no need for this caution. White Fang had done his work. In the midst of the wreckage of overthrown and smashed

1 Context Clues
Look at the words before *ceased*. What do you think *ceased* means?

Animals: Heroes and Scholars

213

furniture, partly on his side, his face hidden by an arm, lay a man. Weedon Scott bent over the man in the middle of the debris, moved the arm and turned the man's face upward. A gaping throat explained the manner of his death.

"Jim Hall," said Judge Scott, and father and son looked thoughtfully at each other.

Then they turned to White Fang. He, too, was lying on his side. His eyes were closed, but the lids slightly lifted in an effort to look at them as they bent over him, and his tail was **perceptibly** agitated in a vain effort to wag. Weedon Scott patted him, and his throat rumbled an acknowledging growl. But it was a weak growl at best, and it quickly ceased. His eyelids drooped and went shut, and his whole body seemed to relax and flatten out on the floor. **2**

"He's all in, poor devil," muttered the master.

"We'll see about that," asserted the Judge, as he started for the telephone.

"Frankly, he has one chance in a thousand," the surgeon plainly announced, after he had worked an hour and a half on White Fang.

Dawn was breaking through the windows and dimming the electric lights. With the exception of the children, the whole family was gathered about the surgeon to hear his verdict.

"One broken hind-leg," he went on. "Three broken ribs, one at least of

2 Visualize

Think about what you have read. What pictures did you have in your mind as the fight scene was described?

which has pierced the lungs. He has lost nearly all the blood in his body. There is a large likelihood of internal injuries. He must have been jumped upon. To say nothing of three bullet holes clear through him. One chance in a thousand is really optimistic. He hasn't a chance in ten thousand."

"But he mustn't lose any chance that might be of help to him," Judge Scott exclaimed. "Never-mind expense. Put him under the X-ray—anything. Weedon, telegraph at once to San Francisco for

Doctor Nichols. No reflection on you, doctor, you understand, but he must have the advantage of every chance."

The surgeon smiled indulgently. "Of course I understand. He deserves all that can be done for him. He must be nursed as you would nurse a human being, a sick child. And don't forget what I told you about temperature. I'll be back at ten o'clock again."

White Fang received the nursing. Judge Scott's suggestion of a trained nurse was angrily protested by the girls, who themselves undertook the task. And White Fang won out on the one chance in ten thousand denied him by the surgeon.

The surgeon was not to be criticized for his misjudgment. All his life he had tended and operated on the soft humans of civilization, who lived sheltered lives and had descended out of many sheltered generations. **3**
Compared with White Fang, they were frail and flabby, and clutched life without any strength in their grip. White Fang had come straight from the Wild, where the weak perish early and shelter is granted to none. In neither his father nor his mother was there any weakness, nor in the generations before them. A physique of iron and the vitality of the Wild were White Fang's

3 **Context Clues**
Using context clues, what does the word *descended* mean?

Vocabulary

tenacity (n) *the quality of holding on firmly to something*

venture (v) *put oneself at risk by doing something daring or dangerous*

4 **Inference**
Why was White Fang able to recover from his injuries? What in the text helps you make your inference?

inheritance, and he clung to life, the whole of him and every part of him, in spirit and in flesh, with the **tenacity** that of old belonged to all creatures. **4**

Bound down a prisoner, denied even movement by the plaster casts and bandages, White Fang lingered out the weeks. He slept long hours and dreamed much, and through his mind passed an unending display of Northland visions. All the ghosts of the past arose and were with him. Once again he lived in the lair with Kiche, crept trembling to the knees of Gray Beaver to show his allegiance, ran for his life before Lip-lip and all the howling commotion of the puppy-pack.

He ran again through the silence, hunting his living food through the months of famine; and again he ran at the head of the team, the gut-whips of Mit-sah and Gray Beaver snapping behind, their voices crying "Ra! Raa!" when they came to a narrow passage and the team closed together like a fan to go through. He lived again all his days with Beauty Smith and the fights he had fought. At such times he whimpered and snarled in his sleep, and they that looked on said that his dreams were bad.

But there was one particular nightmare from which he suffered— the clanking, clanging monsters of electric cars that were to him colossal screaming lynxes. He would lie in a screen of bushes, watching for a squirrel to **venture** far enough out on the ground from its tree-refuge. Then, when he sprang out upon it, it would transform itself into an electric car, menacing and terrible, towering over him like a mountain, screaming and clanging and spitting fire at him. It was the same when he challenged the hawk down out of the sky. Down out

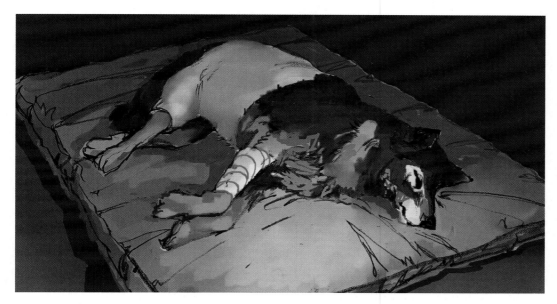

of the blue it would rush, as it dropped upon him changing itself into the prevalent electric car. Or again, he would be in the pen of Beauty Smith. Outside the pen, men would be gathering, and he knew that a fight was on. He watched the door for his enemy to enter. The door would open, and thrust in upon him would come the awful electric car. A thousand times this occurred, and each time the terror it inspired was as vivid and great as ever.

Then came the day when the last bandage and the last plaster cast were taken off. It was a festive day. All Sierra Vista was gathered around. The master rubbed his ears, and he crooned his love-growl. The master's wife called him the "Blessed Wolf," which name was taken up with acclaim, and all the women called him the Blessed Wolf.

He tried to rise to his feet, and after several attempts fell down from weakness. He had lain so long that his muscles had lost their cunning and all the strength had gone out of them. He felt a little shame because of his weakness and loss of finesse, as though, indeed, he were failing the gods in the service he owed them. Because of this he made heroic efforts to arise, and at last he stood on his four legs, tottering and swaying back and forth.

"The Blessed Wolf!" chorused the women.

Judge Scott surveyed them triumphantly.

"Out of your own mouths be it," he said. "Just as I contended right along. No mere dog could have done what he did. He's a wolf."

"A Blessed Wolf," amended the Judge's wife.

"Yes, Blessed Wolf," agreed the Judge. "And henceforth that shall be my name for him."

"He'll have to learn to walk again," said the surgeon, "so he might as well start in right now. It won't hurt him. Take him outside."

And outside he went, like a king, with all Sierra Vista about him and tending on him. **5** He was very weak, and when he reached the lawn he lay down and rested for a while.

5 **Figurative Language**
White Fang is described "like a king." What do you think that means?

Animals: Heroes and Scholars

Then the procession started on, little spurts of strength coming into White Fang's muscles as he used them and the blood began to surge through them. The stables were reached, and there in the doorway lay Collie, a half-dozen pudgy puppies playing about her in the sun.

White Fang looked on with a wondering eye. Collie snarled warningly at him, and he was careful to keep his distance. The master with his toe helped one sprawling puppy toward him. He bristled suspiciously, but the master warned him that all was well. Collie, clasped in the arms of one of the women, watched him jealously and with a snarl warned him that all was not well.

The puppy sprawled in front of him. He cocked his ears and watched it curiously. Then their noses touched, and he felt the warm little tongue of the puppy on his neck. White Fang's tongue went out, he knew not why, and he licked the puppy's face.

6 Ask Questions

Stop and ask questions as you read to help you understand confusing parts of the story. Why does the author call humans "gods" throughout the story?

Hand-clapping and pleased cries from the gods greeted the performance. **6** He was surprised, and looked at them in a puzzled way. Then his weakness asserted itself, and he lay down, his ears cocked, his head on one side, as he watched the puppy. The other puppies came sprawling toward him, to Collie's great disgust, and he gravely permitted them to climb and tumble over him. At first, amid the applause of the gods, he betrayed a little of his old self-consciousness and awkwardness. This passed away as the puppies' antics and mauling continued, and he lay with half-shut patient eyes, drowsing in the sun. **End**

Veterinarian
Animal Technician
Animal Service Worker

A family's pet cat dashes across a busy street to get home. A car swerves to miss the cat, but just hits the cat's back leg as the cat pauses, terrified. Tenants rush out of their apartments to see what the commotion is about. Thankfully, the cat is alive, but it is vainly trying to get out of the street, dragging an injured leg. The worried owners carefully lift the cat into a travel crate, get the crate into their car, and drive quickly to a veterinary clinic. Would you like to be the person who treats this injured cat and helps it recover? If so, you might want to be a veterinarian.

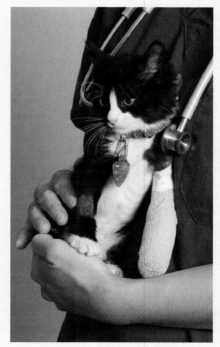

If you are thinking of a job as a veterinarian, or vet, you must love animals. You also need a strong interest in science and medicine. A vet is a doctor who provides care to sick and injured animals. A vet examines animals, diagnoses diseases, sets broken bones, performs surgery, and administers tests. A vet needs a keen eye to perceive visual clues about an animal's condition. A vet needs to be very aware of normal animal behavior in order to detect, for example, a barely perceptible change in behavior that indicates an injury or illness.

To become a veterinarian, you would attend a four-year college. Your main classes would include biology, chemistry, nutrition, and other areas of science that relate to your work. You would also study English for communication skills and math for analysis. After graduating from college, you would go on to a veterinary school for four years. There, you would get hands-on experience in animal care, such as surgery, diagnosis, and reading test results. Finally, you would be required to take a test to get a license to practice veterinary

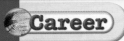

medicine. A veterinarian earns about $44,000 to $135,000 a year.

Once out of school, you might set up your own business. You could have a clinic in your home to treat small animals such as dogs, cats, and gerbils. Or, you might set up your workspace in a traveling truck if you love large animals such as horses or sheep. That way, you can travel to your patients. You

might get a job in an animal clinic with other vets, or in a large or small animal hospital. Universities and research organizations offer jobs in laboratories where vets can work on gaining new knowledge or developing new treatments. You could get a job at a company that makes animal food. There, your knowledge of nutrition would be valuable to make a better food for cats or dogs. At a zoo, your veterinarian job might involve keeping snakes, sharks, bears, and tigers healthy with the right foods, the right inoculations, and the right treatments. As a vet, you could also work for the government. You might become an army vet who treats animals of service members or helps diagnose illnesses and prevent diseases in wild animals

all over the world.

If you love animals but are not interested in going to veterinary school, you still could get a job working with animals in a vet's practice. Most vets today hire veterinary technicians. After a two- to four-year veterinary technician program, you could become an animal technician who acts as a sort of nurse to a vet, performing routine examinations and tests. Your likely salary would be $19,000 to $40,000, much less than a vet's salary. Or you could get a job as an animal service worker, earning from about $7.00 to $15.00 per hour. At an animal clinic, you might be responsible for taking care of hospitalized or abandoned animals. Your job might involve anything from cleaning and disinfecting cages to holding a bird when it gets a shot to playing with someone's lost dog. You might be asked to train, feed, water, bathe, groom, or exercise an animal. In all of these jobs you would be helping animals have infinitely better and healthier lives.

Before launching into a career with animals, you should consider the risks. Frightened or injured animals can behave very aggressively. They may bite or scratch whoever is handling them. Seeing animals that have been injured or abused can be upsetting to many people. Would your reaction in such situations be characterized by anger, fear, or depression? Or would you just want to help the animal?

If you answered yes to the second question, you could be a candidate for a job as a veterinarian, an animal technician, or an animal service worker.

Going Green

- How can our individual actions affect our environment?

- Why should we care about the state of resources a hundred years from now?

- What are some things you presently do to positively impact the environment?

Smaller Steps, Better Impact

Vocabulary

prohibit (v) *forbid by law or by an order*

hybrid (n) *something that has two different parts performing essentially the same function*

efficient (adj) *bringing about the wanted result using the least amount of time, materials, or effort*

response (n) *something that is said or done in answer; a reply*

accumulation (n) *the process of piling up, collecting, or gathering over a period of time*

A massive Hummer rumbles by with large tires, a big engine, a tall body, and a grand chrome grille. In its wake, this imposing vehicle leaves a trail of carbon dioxide from burning gasoline; it gets 14 miles per gallon. Is it a gas-guzzling, air-polluting giant that state laws should **prohibit**?

A small, quiet Prius **hybrid** zips past. This hybrid has an **efficient** engine-and-battery system that gets 48 miles per gallon. The car was developed as a **response** to large vehicles. Obviously, a Prius will consume less gas in its lifetime than a Hummer, saving resources and decreasing the **accumulation** of

environmental pollutants. But, is a Prius a better choice for Earth?

What Is a Carbon Footprint?

A carbon footprint is the total carbon dioxide given off during the life of an object, from creation through disposal. Reducing the size of carbon footprints helps reduce the amount of pollution in our world. All gasoline-burning vehicles release carbon dioxide that accumulates in the atmosphere in the form of pollution. Carbon dioxide also is released by factories, such as automobile factories, and by power plants providing energy to

Vocabulary

significant (adj) *very important*

those factories. Any object, such as a car, has a carbon footprint. **1**

Different factors add up to a larger, more damaging carbon footprint, and one of these factors is a vehicle's fuel efficiency. All the materials that go into a vehicle also add to the carbon footprint, so smaller vehicles usually have a smaller contribution in that area. The planning, designing, and manufacturing of vehicles take energy, which means that the simpler the vehicle, the smaller the size of its carbon footprint. **2**

Studies now reveal the size of carbon footprints of automobiles. These studies are **significant** because they can be used to find ways to reduce the size of carbon footprints, which is a responsible way to ensure our survival. Chemicals that we allow to

accumulate in the environment can be harmful not only to us, but to future generations around the world.

Hummer vs. Prius

Does a hybrid or a traditional vehicle have a smaller overall environmental impact? One 2005 study by a leading marketing research firm suggested that large sport utility vehicles (SUVs), like Hummers, are actually more energy efficient per mile than hybrid vehicles. The report considered the energy it takes to produce the car, then dispose of it, as well as its fuel economy. Energy efficiency affects the carbon footprint. If it takes more energy to manufacture an energy-efficient car than a big SUV, then the overall carbon footprint of both cars would be large.

Other studies, done in response to this one, came to opposite conclusions, though. They claimed that the research firm made assumptions that were not facts. One of these statements they supposed to be true was contradicted by leading scientific research firms. However, the car's manufacturer did evaluate how the Prius is manufactured and made improvements. In 2008, the

1 Main Idea
What is the main idea of this paragraph?

2 Inference
Think about the information in this paragraph. Why would a simpler vehicle have a smaller carbon footprint than a more complicated vehicle?

marketing firm reported that the Prius no longer was less energy efficient because the way the car was manufactured had been changed to a more "eco-friendly" process.

One significant difference between the two vehicles is that the Prius is designed with many efficiencies, whereas the Hummer is not. Even if the Hummer were more energy efficient in the long run, that doesn't mean everyone should buy one. More efficient, smaller gasoline cars have neither the complexity of a hybrid nor the wastefulness of a Hummer. Driving a vehicle only as large as you need makes sense. Biking or walking more often could reduce the carbon footprint in another way. A more constructive, or useful, solution would be a nationwide campaign for environmental responsibility.

Earth's Future

A car's carbon footprint affects not only us but our neighbors as well. The impact even reaches into the future. Being mindful of the impact of our carbon footprints and attempting to reduce their size could preserve our planet. **3 End**

3 Inference

According to the information in this passage, how do our carbon footprints affect our future?

The Greener Life

Dear Readers:

Imagine you are on a spacecraft traveling through a solar system much like our own. You land on a planet, the third one from the system's sun. The air is smog-filled and so polluted it is nearly unbreathable. Garbage is piled so high, the waste material is toppling over onto barren ground and is left where it falls. Trees are sticks of wood, and bushes are broken, splintered branches. The whole world is utterly silent. **1**

This image is science fiction, but unless people work together to solve Earth's problems now, our environment could suffer like this imaginary planet. We could use up all of our **resources**. **2** We could ruin the **ecology**. We could find our planet overwhelmed by waste.

The good news—and it is very good news—is that individuals and groups of people have begun to take steps to **preserve** and protect Earth. You might have heard people talk about "going green." The phrase indicates a new way to look at one's needs, one's life, and the life of the planet as a whole. People who go green are concerned with preserving and improving the **environment**. They are not satisfied with old ways that don't consider the whole of Earth: the ecological balance, other human lives, and future generations. They refuse to live a lifestyle that is in any way **negligent** of Earth's future.

So what kinds of activities are suggested by going green? Recycling waste, like paper and plastic, is a green activity because

Vocabulary

resources (n) *things that are available to take care of a need*

ecology (n) *the balance between people's lifestyles and the living things on Earth*

preserve (v) *protect from harm or damage; keep in a certain condition*

environment (n) *all the conditions surrounding plants, animals, and people that affect the health, growth, and development of those living things*

negligent (adj) *being careless*

1 Visualize
Try to see this scene in your mind.

2 Make Connections
Think of some resources on Earth that we might use up.

it preserves resources and keeps trash out of landfills. Making new goods from old ones is a responsible choice for the planet, saving resources and energy.

Ending overconsumption is another ecologically positive choice. If we buy only what we need and as much as we need, we will have enough. Buying a smaller car or one television instead of two, for example, lowers consumption and leaves less waste to be disposed of later.

An example of excessive consumption is the use of layers of packaging by manufacturers and food-processing businesses. Have you ever opened a package of crackers with multiple layers of wrapping? The crackers are grouped in sealed packages of six crackers each; these are all inside a cardboard box that is wrapped in cellophane. By the time you get to the crackers, you have a stack of waste material. People who go green will buy snacks that do not have these excessive layers of packaging.

Reusing goods is another way to go green. Instead of throwing out or even recycling a plastic food container, we can wash it to store more food or other items. When carpenters remove wood and nails from one structure, they can use them to build a new structure.

Another way of reusing goods that helps limit consumption and waste disposal is sharing goods. Perhaps you and a group of neighbors can share a rake or a ladder. The item is used more often, rather than sitting around neglected; and when it's time to dispose of it, there is just one to recycle, not more.

All of these choices—recycling, reducing consumption, reusing, and sharing—help the environment and are ecologically sound. But, they require a whole new way of looking at your life and your property. **3** Let's take a peek at how people who are making these and other positive choices are changing the outlook for our future. We can look at a few specific examples, but the movement is really happening in homes and neighborhoods everywhere.

In 2006, in California, 10 friends planned a year without purchasing anything new, except food and a few

3 Summarize

Based on what you have read, how can recycling, reducing consumption, reusing, and sharing help the environment?

necessities for health and safety, such as toilet paper and brake fluid. To get everything else they needed during the year, they bought from secondhand stores, borrowed from within the group or from other people they knew, or they would barter. Bartering is trading or swapping one thing for another. For example, one person may offer to fix a neighbor's fence in return for an extra sofa that has been sitting in the neighbor's garage; no money would be exchanged. The group took advantage of thrift shops and consignment stores. They also used Internet sites, such as craigslist.com and The Freecycle Network, that now exist to help people effectively exchange goods. Some of these sites have more than 4,600 groups dedicated to the concept of reusing.

Another group of environmentally conscious people call themselves "freegans." The name combines the word *free* with the word *vegan*. A vegan is a person who does not use or eat any products from animals or that are tested on animals. Vegans do not want their life activities to harm animals. The freegan way is to step totally outside of the normal economic system, which they feel has a negative impact and has been negligent of the environment, human rights, and animal rights. **4**

The main strategies that freegans follow involve the reclaiming and limiting of waste. One activity they use to reclaim goods is "urban foraging" or "Dumpster diving." In the garbage of homes, businesses, and industries, freegans find goods that are clean, safe, and usable. Many items are as good as new because people throw away a lot of useful goods including books, clothing, furniture, toys, and unopened foods. Sometimes individuals seek out things for themselves. Sometimes groups work together to recover items that can be used to help the homeless. After noticing the many useful items that

4 **Ask Questions**
A good question to ask yourself at this point is "How do freegans carry out their lifestyle?" Keep reading to see if your question is answered.

people discard, freegans became concerned about limiting waste. They strongly support recycling, composting organic matter, and repairing rather than discarding broken goods.

Like many other groups, freegans try to avoid using automobiles. They consider the total ecological impact of automobile travel, from air pollution to environmental destruction caused by the building of roads. The choices that freegans make may seem radical to some, but they are not neglectful of Earth and its living things.

the freegan lifestyle for 30 days, felt the most valuable awareness she gained was to consider where everything she buys comes from and where it will go when it's no longer needed. If we look at our purchases that closely, we can make informed decisions that will benefit our environment.

Many people who are going green are doing it quite literally by growing their own food. Growing one's own food means you avoid packaging and have less wasted food because you can pick only what you need. Your food is fresh, and you will have goods to barter or share with others. Establishing gardens in vacant lots or other unused areas changes neglected land to land rich with resources. The process also brings people back to their connection with Earth, a planet that will continue to support generations to come if we become less negligent and take responsible actions. **6**

The Editor **End**

Some people who have tried to live the freegan lifestyle have found it difficult. **5** But, that doesn't mean we can't learn from it—to limit what we buy, to reuse and recycle, to share. Raina Kelley, who experimented with

5 **Inference**

What might people find difficult about the freegan lifestyle? What text evidence supports your inference?

6 **Ask Questions**

Do you have additional questions about the information in this passage? Discuss them with your partner or group.

Refuse Worker

Reduce and Reuse

In the 1960s, the average person created approximately 2.7 pounds of garbage each day. By 2007, that number had almost doubled to 4.6 pounds of garbage each day. For the United States as a whole, that adds up to 254.1 million tons per year. The average car only weighs about a ton, so 254 million cars would have to be thrown away to equal the amount of solid waste or garbage we throw away each year in the United States. Some of that waste is recycled.

Have you ever given any thought to what happens to your garbage and recycling once you put it out? Sure, you know that huge trucks roll by. Suddenly the waste material is gone, and empty trash barrels and recycling containers remain on the sidewalk or along the street. But, who is responsible for the waste material's disappearing act? It is the person commonly called the garbage collector or refuse collector.

As we create more and more waste, we need to find ways to recycle more effectively. There are many careers associated with waste management and recycling. Some of the careers, such as environmental engineer, require a college degree. Other jobs, such as recycle technician or refuse collector, require a high school diploma or a vocational degree. As an environmental engineer, you could do many things from evaluating a city's recycling program to inspecting waste water treatment plants and identifying problems. As a recycle technician, you will do some of the same tasks that a solid waste or garbage collector would. You may ride on a truck collecting recyclables from homes and businesses, or you may work at the facility where the materials are recycled.

The work of a refuse or recycling collector can be physically hard with long hours lifting and hauling other people's garbage. However, if you want to contribute to keeping Earth clean and you don't mind

getting dirty, you might like one of these jobs. Doing this job, you could work almost anywhere around the world.

As a refuse collector, you must be in good health and may be required to provide a doctor's certificate. Physical strength is important, as are stamina and a lot of energy. Obviously, you should not be too sensitive to smells because garbage naturally produces odors as it decays. The pay of a refuse worker is about $14 per hour as a garbage collector, but with five years of experience, a refuse worker can make up to $42,000 a year.

With experience and a commercial driver's license (CDL), you may drive a 25-ton truck with 4-foot tires and a cab that looks down on even large SUVs. You would collect garbage and recycling from homes, industries, or other businesses. You would haul it to landfills or recycling centers and drive back again for another load. You also may learn to drive a forklift or operate compacting equipment. You could drive a front-loading truck that empties Dumpsters. Or, you might drive a grapple truck that picks up large waste. You would operate a device

called a grapple that is like a large clamshell with jaws on the end of a long mechanical arm to pick up the trash.

With experience, you could become a refuse worker who supervises other workers, operates incinerators that burn trash, or oversees landfill sites. You could help design and launch recycling programs. You might even help plan landfill areas that are better for the habitat or help develop new theories of waste disposal. However, as systems for reusing, reducing, and recycling garbage become more common, you may find yourself in a specific new role in which you could get an even larger salary.

Global Warming and Global Climate Change

Earth's Big Greenhouse

Have you been in a greenhouse? If you have, you may have noticed that the air inside is much hotter than the air outside. This effect of captured heat is known as the "greenhouse effect." The glass of the greenhouse allows sunlight to enter. In the greenhouse, much of the light changes to heat energy, which the glass traps inside.

The atmosphere around the **globe** acts like the glass of a greenhouse, holding in heat. This heat energy creates a planet in which people, animals, and plants can live. The atmosphere keeps temperatures within an acceptable range. Why is that important?

Nature can be greatly affected by temperature changes. The complicated **system** of weather and the **habitat** of animals have a lot of delicate factors. These factors must stay in balance to make Earth livable. The concentration of oxygen, the heat at Earth's surface, the amounts of water and patterns of rainfall, for example, are all important. If these factors were much different, places that were once lush and green with plants might dry into deserts, and coastal cities might become submerged under the ocean. Because the greenhouse effect can cause large temperature changes, as it does inside greenhouses, an increase in this effect could alter Earth's climate dramatically. **1**

Role of Carbon Dioxide in Global Warming

The **theory** of global warming is based on the greenhouse effect. One of the gases that **contributes** to this effect is carbon dioxide. Carbon dioxide collects in the atmosphere and traps heat energy from the sun, warming Earth's

Vocabulary

globe (n) *Earth*

nature (n) *everything in the physical world that is not made by human beings*

system (n) *a group of things or parts working together or connected in such a way as to form a whole*

habitat (n) *place where an animal or plant is normally found*

theory (n) *an explanation of how or why something happens*

contributes (v) *has a part in bringing about*

1 Ask Questions
After reading this section, could you describe the greenhouse effect? What questions do you still have about the greenhouse effect?

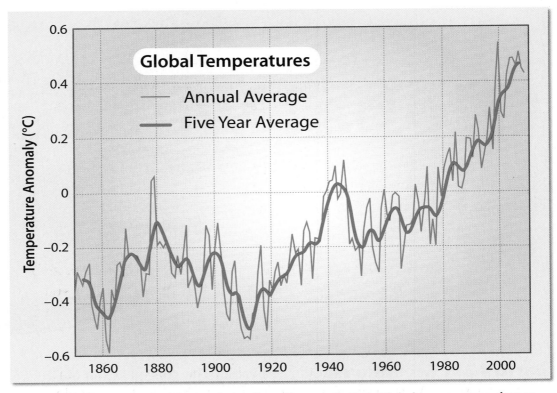

Global Temperatures

— Annual Average

— Five Year Average

Temperature Anomaly (°C)

Adapted and reproduced with permission from Hansen, J, et al. Global temperature change. PNAS 103(39), September 26, 2006. Copyright 2006 National Academy of Sciences, U.S.A.

surface. Factories, cars, and other human activities are main contributors to the emission, or release, of carbon dioxide.

Since the late 1700s, when the Industrial Revolution began, greater amounts of carbon dioxide have entered the atmosphere because factories stopped relying on natural power, like rivers, and started to burn coal. This time period coincides, or occurs at the same time, with the beginning of a fairly rapid increase in yearly temperatures around the globe. The average yearly temperature rose about 0.7 degrees Celsius in the 20th century.

This rise in temperature is not all the fault of humanity. Year-to-year temperature variations and long-term climate cycles, from warming periods to ice ages, are natural. They have occurred throughout the planet's history. But, tracking recent temperature increases provides data to show how widespread the changes in habitat and ecological systems might become. Some scientists interpret the data to mean that we could be heading for an abrupt temperature change they believe has the potential to cause great damage. Other scientists, however, note that the changes follow the natural patterns seen in the past. **2**

Effects Now and in the Future

Scientists believe that in the past great rises in temperature caused ice ages through complex climatic

2 Main Idea

What is the main idea of this section?

interactions. That is, melting polar ice caps and glaciers of Greenland may have caused cold freshwater to flow into the northern Atlantic. This shut down the Gulf Stream, which kept Europe and northeastern North America warm. But, another ice age is not likely to occur in the near future. The more immediate results of the current warming period are reduced polar ice, habitat loss, and extreme weather conditions.

Melting polar ice could remove the main habitat for certain animals, such as polar bears. Glaciers are also melting due to the rising temperatures. The glaciers and ice caps store enough water to raise the sea levels by many feet if they were all to melt. This is why some scientists believe that ocean water would cover many Pacific islands, flood the levees in the Netherlands, and sink all or part of many of the major coastal cities. New York, Boston, and San Francisco would be at risk.

The rising temperatures also contribute to larger deserts in Africa and elsewhere. This decreases the habitat available for nondesert animals. The death of these species reduces Earth's biodiversity. **3** Sometimes animals and plants that are important to the climate die off. The increase of desert also threatens the survival of humans in those regions. Agriculture becomes difficult or impossible. Also, global warming results in more carbon dioxide dissolved in ocean water, making the water more acidic. This changes the ecosystems in the oceans, and some animals and plants might not be adaptable. Algae photosynthesize a lot of carbon dioxide. This means the algae take in the carbon dioxide and, through a process called photosynthesis, change it to oxygen. Therefore, algae is an important force in controlling

3 **Word Reading**
Use what you know about the prefix *bio-* and the word *diversity* to determine the meaning of *biodiversity*.

carbon dioxide. But, algae can die in an acidic ocean.

Collected data suggest that during the past 30 years, weather has become more severe. Some scientists believe global warming is fueling these extreme events. Others believe it is not global warming, but rather a natural cycle of warming. In general, heat waves have become hotter, more frequent, and widespread. Heavier rainfalls have caused severe flooding, and hurricanes and other tropical storms have increased in intensity and duration. **4**

Denial vs. Doomsday

There is great debate as to whether the current warming trend is caused by humanity and global warming or is simply part of Earth's natural cycle. Some claim that the warming will be small and harmless. These people do not believe that Earth is in danger. They do not feel they need to make what they believe are extreme changes in their lifestyles.

On the other hand, some people may be too worried about global warming. They predict dire consequences, such as the evaporation of Earth's water and the starvation of all of humanity.

It is important to remember that the concept of global warming is a theory, and theories should not be accepted without question. However, it is possible that our species has contributed to the warming. The greater issue becomes not whether climate change is occurring, but what might be done to prevent further damage.

A More Balanced View

The systems of the globe are very complicated, with many interacting factors. For example, the contents of the atmosphere change as plants absorb carbon dioxide during the growing season because gases are slowly incorporated into the ocean and into life-forms, while other gases are released from volcanoes and human activities. The systems are so complicated and so poorly understood that our ability to predict the future is limited and may be inaccurate. It may be that some little-understood system will start absorbing a lot of carbon dioxide and rebalance global temperatures in the next few decades. But, our computer models cannot predict such a surprising change. Plus, if we continue to destroy habitats, we may very well destroy the little-understood system that would have balanced out the global warming.

Just because we do not fully understand the climate does not mean people should allow the world to warm by man-made carbon dioxide emissions. Because the consequences of global warming could be damaging, taking action now makes sense. Right now, for one thing, we can at least reduce the severity of any climatic changes by reducing carbon dioxide emissions. If we wait any longer, we are taking unnecessary risks. **5** **End**

4 **Summarize**
What are the effects of global warming?

5 **Inference**
Based on the information in this passage, what is the best response to the problem of global warming?

OCTOBER 2008

Renew Earth

GREEN SOLUTIONS FOR THE FUTURE

Good-Bye, Fossil Fuels

by I. M. Greene

Scientists say that within a few hundred years, fossil fuels except coal will be **depleted**. What does that mean to us? Having no more fossil fuels could cause a **crisis**. It could mean, for example, no more gasoline for cars, no more oil or natural gas for heating, and no more electricity—for lights, computers, and televisions.

Fossil fuels—petroleum, natural gas, and coal—are natural resources we burn to produce **energy**. Fossil fuels formed over a long period of time from tiny plants and animals trapped in layers of rock. But, fossil fuels are nonrenewable. They cannot be replaced if depleted because we burn fossil fuels much faster than they form. The burning of fossil fuels also adds pollutants like carbon dioxide to the air. If we want to avoid a crisis and have fuels that produce clean energy, we need **alternative** solutions. **1**

Vocabulary

depleted (v) *reduced in number or quantity so as to endanger the ability to function*

crisis (n) *a time of great danger or difficulty; anxiety about the future*

energy (n) *the power of certain forces in nature to do work*

alternative (adj) *allowing a choice between two or more things*

---

1 Main Idea

What is the main idea of the first two paragraphs?

Dams produce energy for hydroelectricity.

Hello, Alternative Energy

The idea of obtaining energy from the forces of nature, such as sun, wind, and water, is not new. Think about a **design** of the past, such as a waterwheel to operate machines and a windmill to grind grain. Waterwheels used the running water of a river to turn the wheel, operating a machine connected to it. Windmills did the same thing with wind. As wind turned the windmill, parts of the machinery inside would begin to turn. Today, however, wind and water most often are used not as the energy to operate machines directly, but as the mechanical energy used to generate electricity. **2**

Using Moving Water

A hydroelectric power plant is designed to use the energy of running water to create electricity.

Hydroelectric power plants, however, require dams on fast-moving rivers. The water used to produce electricity is not depleted, and the process creates little pollution. However, the dam changes the flow of water and affects the environment. Vegetation is killed when the flow of water around it is changed.

Tidal power plants use the regular movement of ocean tides. Tidal plants produce clean, dependable energy, but they need to be located on or near the coast. The plants also can impact the coastal environment. Underwater "windmills" take advantage of ocean currents without a visible effect on the environment. Like other tidal plants, they work well for coastal areas that have little wind or sunlight. But, they may harm underwater life.

Geothermal power plants use heated water from deep inside Earth. These plants must be located where access to heat from below Earth's crust is possible. Once established, they can produce energy continuously from the internal heat of Earth. **3**

Gathering Sunlight

Sunlight is an important, clean, renewable source of energy. Solar cells that collect energy from sunlight can be used anywhere the sun shines. Houses can have solar collectors that gather energy to heat water or provide electricity. Large solar collectors create enough energy to power cities, but they require a lot of sunlight and a lot of space.

Breaking Atoms Apart

A drawback of the previous alternatives is that each must be located in a particular type of place. Nuclear power plants, which create electricity from the structure of matter, can be located in a variety of places along rivers and coastlines. These power plants create energy from nuclear reactions. Nuclear reactions happen when atoms are split.

An atom is the smallest piece of matter, even smaller than a molecule. Atoms of uranium, a simple mineral found in rocks, are used to create nuclear reactions. When the nucleus, or center, of the atom is broken apart, it emits huge amounts of energy, which can be converted to

3 Summarize

What are one advantage and one disadvantage of hydroelectric, tidal, and geothermal power plants?

Solar panels on a home

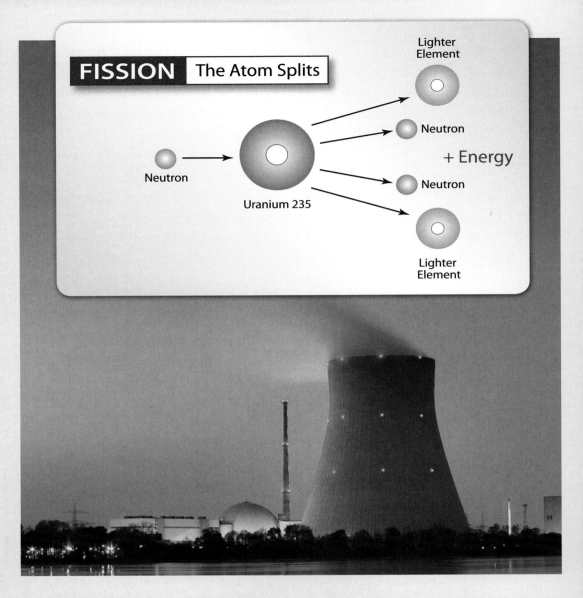

FISSION The Atom Splits

Neutron

Uranium 235

Lighter Element

Neutron

+ Energy

Neutron

Lighter Element

4 **Summarize**

This paragraph contains difficult concepts. Reread it to make sure you understand these concepts: What is an atom? What is a nucleus? How does a nuclear reaction produce energy? If you wanted a deeper understanding of nuclear reactions, where could you go for information?

electricity. (See the diagram.) But, this nuclear reaction also produces radioactive waste that is dangerous to people, causing a problem of safe disposal. Accidents that can occur at nuclear power plants can be life threatening. **4**

Catching the Wind

Perhaps wind energy could be the real problem-solver for renewable, clean energy. Wind energy can be collected anywhere the wind blows moderately. The design is simple: Huge wind turbines consist of a spinning blade atop a tall tower that turns when the wind blows. This mechanical energy is used to generate electricity.

Wind turbines can be located on land in places where the wind is steady. They also can be located along seashores, where breezes provide an almost continuous supply of wind. However, a wind plant has a limitation that a fossil fuel or nuclear plant does not: wind power cannot be turned on without wind. To solve this problem, scientists are developing a battery that stores energy and allows a steady flow of electricity from wind turbines. Researchers have calculated that wind power plants could generate about 70 times the amount of energy produced by all power plants in the United States. These estimates were based on the current 80-meter height of most wind turbines. If new designs could catch winds higher in the atmosphere, where wind speed increases, electrical production would increase greatly. Current scientific research focuses on new technologies, such as wind kites that could fly higher to catch the wind's energy.

Fuels from Foods and Wastes

The depletion of fossil fuels could also result in a crisis for travel, home heating, and other things that depend on petroleum products. Biofuels, fuels made from living matter, are being studied to meet these energy demands. The burning of biofuels recycles carbon rather than adding pollutants to the air. Because they are made from plant materials, biofuels are a renewable resource.

Ethanol is a modern biofuel made mostly from corn. The process to produce ethanol, however, requires so much energy that it may not save fuel. Making ethanol also requires huge amounts of corn. Many farmers who grow corn for humans or livestock would need to convert their fields to biofuel-corn.

Other alternative biofuels, such as biodiesel fuel, use vegetable oils from seeds such as safflower and sunflower. Again, the impact is that the food products become more expensive and less available. A solution being studied is to use algae as a nonfood source for the production of biodiesel fuel. **5**

Another solution might be to use waste materials. The United States produces about 1.4 billion tons of organic waste, or biomass, a year. The cellulose in the waste could be converted to sugar, then into ethanol. As yet, this process has not achieved the desired results. However, researchers have discovered that any organic matter can be turned into a gas, which can be changed to a liquid fuel. This would allow ethanol to be made totally out of organic waste. **6**

5 Make Connections
Based on what you read previously about algae in "Global Warming and Global Climate Change," what problems do you foresee in using algae as a source for biodiesel fuel?

6 Context Clues
Reread this section. What does *converted* mean? What clues helped you figure out its meaning?

Fuel Cells

A fuel cell is a technology that can be used to produce electricity and to power machines, such as automobile engines. A fuel cell produces energy through a chemical reaction. The energy is stored in a battery until it is needed. Some types of fuel cells work well in large stationary power plants, whereas others can power small appliances or automobiles. However, for fuel cells to be effective, issues such as how much they cost, how well they operate, how long they last, and how much energy they store still need to be solved. **7**

A Hopeful Future

The many possibilities for creating alternative energy and fuels suggest that a future without fossil fuels does not have to be grim. Using some of these alternatives provides cleaner air and decreases the problem of waste disposal. Scientists have just begun to look at possibilities. Other answers may be just around the corner for scientists who can design new types of power plants and energy-production processes. **End**

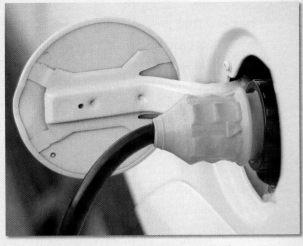

With fuel cell technology, instead of gasoline pumps you need an electric power plug.

This Ford automobile is powered by fuel cell technology.

7 Main Idea

Find the main idea sentence in this paragraph. What details support it?

Farmer

A Down-to-Earth Job

It's 4:00 a.m., the sun hasn't risen, and you're rolling out of bed to go to work. Do you have a long commute to a city job? No, you're a farmer. You work outside, tending to crops and livestock, driving the tractor or using it to pull a plow. You may own a small farm, selling fresh produce at a local vegetable stand, or you may run a huge corporate farm with hundreds of employees.

If you like to work outside, perform physical tasks, and take care of gardens or animals, consider a career in farming. As a farmer, you would provide important natural resources such as food or cotton. You would determine what crops or animals would thrive in your area without harming the surrounding lands. The practices you use could have a significant positive impact on ecology.

One of the different types of farming might be right for the region where you live, as well as your interests and personality. A farmer with a relatively small farm may grow many fruits and vegetables and sell these crops, as well as goods made from them, at the farm's own market. You would probably work in the fields—seeding, planting, and harvesting. You might experiment, growing new foods to respond to your customers' needs. You might know your customers by name.

Farmers with larger landholdings and businesses may grow one or more cash crops such as grains or hybrid corn. On a sizeable farm, you would use large, efficient machines to till the soil, apply fertilizer, plant seeds, and harvest crops. For help, you might employ a farm manager, year-round workers,

or part-time workers for the busiest seasons.

Some types of farmers focus on raising animals. As a livestock farmer, or rancher, you could raise cattle or sheep. As a dairy farmer, you would have cows that produce milk, which you might sell at a farm stand, local store, or supermarket. As a poultry farmer, you might breed, raise, and sell chickens or turkeys. You would have to care for your animals, keep their pens clean, and never be negligent of their health.

If your environment has a coastal or lakes region, you might practice aquaculture: the raising of fish, or aquatic plants such as kelp or seaweed. Your job would be stocking and caring for the animals by protecting the ecology of the farm ponds, preserving the surrounding environment, and maintaining the nets that keep your "farm animals" on the farm.

If you'd rather not work outside and you don't have good farmland, you could work at hydroponics. Using hydroponics, you would grow vegetables such as lettuce and peppers in huge greenhouses. The plants would grow in water with nutrients, not soil.

Whichever choice you make, farming is hard work with a lot of responsibilities. During the busy seasons, usually planting and harvesting, you might actually work from sunrise to sunset. Every day, you would have physical work to accomplish. The choices you make as a farmer or farm manager are important to the environment and to the people who depend on the quality of your food. You may decide to grow organic foods, without harmful pesticides that pollute the earth and make the foods less healthy. You might feed livestock organic feeds and allow them to roam.

Farming doesn't require a college education. Some people become farmers because they learned the skills growing up or working on farms, or through organizations such as 4-H. However, you should take classes in math, biology, other life sciences, and business and economics. Some farmers earn a college degree in agriculture or their special field of interest because operating a modern farm is complex.

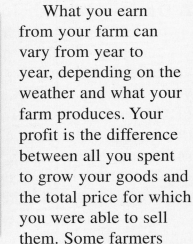

What you earn from your farm can vary from year to year, depending on the weather and what your farm produces. Your profit is the difference between all you spent to grow your goods and the total price for which you were able to sell them. Some farmers receive money from the government to help with the cost of farming. A farm manager who works for a farmer may make a steady wage of about $50,000 a year. Farming used to be a family business. Some of these still exist; however, today corporate farms have turned simple farming into big business.

Just for the Sport of It

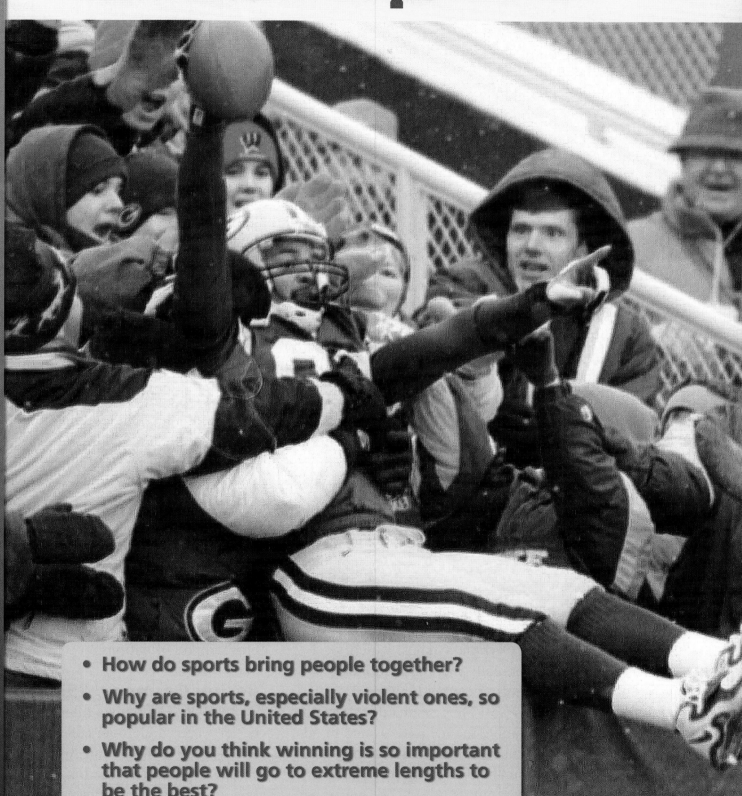

- **How do sports bring people together?**

- **Why are sports, especially violent ones, so popular in the United States?**

- **Why do you think winning is so important that people will go to extreme lengths to be the best?**

The Real Winner
Doesn't Always Get the Gold

Vocabulary

assembled (v) *gathered together in one place*

symbol (n) *an object that represents something else*

compete (v) *try hard to outdo others in a contest*

tolerance (n) *acceptance and respect of others and their beliefs*

expert (adj) *very skilled at something*

ideal (adj) *perfect; very suitable*

1 Inference

Why do you think two groups of people that had been at war would come together to compete against each other in a different manner?

Olympic History

In 776 B.C., a Greek athlete sprints across the finish line of a 200-yard dash while the crowd **assembled** in the valley of Olympia cheers. He is crowned with an olive wreath, a **symbol** of victory. He is among the first Olympic athletes competing in the first Olympic Games, which were held after two warring city-states signed a peace treaty, or agreement. **1**

Olympic Games, which eventually incorporated more events, were held in Greece until 394 A.D. They resumed in 1896 to promote the idea of a sound mind in a sound body. Diverse nations assembled to **compete** in games where brotherhood and **tolerance** flourished, or grew.

The Ideal Olympian

An Olympic athlete is an **expert** athlete. Today, the range of sports has expanded to include cycling, gymnastics, swimming, and skating, just to name a few. Who is the **ideal** Olympian? The easy answer is one who wins a gold, silver, or bronze medal, today's symbols of victory. But, the real winners of the Olympics are those whose actions show tolerance and friendship in the brotherhood of nations.

Berlin, Germany, 1936

In 1936, Germany's ruler, Adolf Hitler, ordered German athletes not to associate with African American competitors. During the long jump, U.S. competitor Jesse Owens, an African American, had fouled twice;

German champion Luz Long and U.S. champion Jesse Owens chat together in the Berlin stadium during the 1936 Olympic Games.

one more mistake would disqualify him. **2** At the risk of punishment by Hitler, expert German jumper Carl Ludwig "Luz" Long showed his tolerance by giving Owens advice that helped him make his third jump, winning the gold medal. Long won the silver medal and faced Hitler's wrath.

During the same Olympics, two Japanese pole-vaulters, Shuhei Nishida and Sueo Oe, tied for second place. Rather than hold a jump-off, Oe accepted the bronze, allowing Nishida to take the silver. Back in Japan, the two agreed to cut the medals and fuse them together into two combination medals, half silver and half bronze. These became the "Medals of Friendship," symbols of friendly teamwork.

Innsbruck, Austria, 1964

Eugenio Monti, an Italian bobsled racer, came to the rescue of the British two-man bobsled team, led by Anthony Nash. The British sled had a broken bolt, so Monti removed a bolt from his bobsled to allow the British team to compete. The British team won the gold medal, while Monti's team won the bronze. When people commented on his helping the British to victory, Monti replied, "Nash didn't win because I gave him the bolt. He won because he had the fastest run."

Seoul, South Korea, 1988

Occasionally, an act of brotherhood saves lives. During a sailing race, Canadian Lawrence Lemieux controlled his boat

2 Context Clues
Using clues around the word, what does *fouled* mean?

Eugenio Monti and Anthony Nash

Beckie Scott and Sara Renner of Canada celebrate winning the silver medal in the women's cross-country skiing team sprint.

3 Visualize
Picture the scene in your mind. How do you think the Singaporean sailors felt when they saw Lemieux?

expertly in suddenly rough water, holding second place. Two sailors from Singapore, competing in a different race, cried out as their boat capsized. One clung to the overturned boat in the high waves, as the other was being swept away. Lemieux sailed out of his race to reach both sailors and pull them onto his boat. **3** He waited for the rescue boats, an act that left him in the bottom half of finishers.

Sydney, Australia, 2000

Over the years, war and unrest have resulted in canceled games and boycotts in which certain countries refused to compete. Since the 1950–53 Korean War, North and South Korea have remained separated, intolerant of each other politically. During the opening ceremonies in Sydney, the teams of the two countries marched together under one flag, temporarily setting aside differences to demonstrate the spirit of brotherhood.

Turin, Italy, 2006

Sometimes, the ideal Olympian isn't an athlete. In the cross-country skiing competition, a young Canadian skier, Sara Renner, broke a pole during her team's event. Without equipment, she would have to drop out. But, Norwegian cross-country coach Bjørnar Håkensmoen handed her an extra ski pole. Sara's team won the silver medal, while the Norwegian team placed fourth.

Olympic Winners

The examples you just read about are a few of the ideal Olympic heroes. These Olympians enriched the lives of people from diverse countries, people they would not have met except for coming together in brotherhood at the Olympic Games. **End**

From Peach Baskets to Hoops to Hoopla

Basketball is one of the most popular sports in the world. The National Basketball Association (NBA) is nearly as popular in faraway places like Japan as it is in the United States. You don't have to look hard to find players from many nationalities playing in the NBA.

James Naismith invented the game of basketball.

Duck on a Rock Changes Form

When you watch or play basketball, do you think about how the game started? James Naismith, who was born in Canada, is known as the inventor of basketball. When Naismith was growing up, he played games, just as most young children do. One game of choice for Naismith and his friends was called *duck on a rock*. One person was "it." He put his rock on top of a large rock. One or two other kids did the same. These kids then tried to retrieve their rocks without being tagged by "it." Other players were trying to knock "its" rock off. So, he had to protect his rock and make sure that the other players weren't able to retrieve their rocks. If "its" rock was knocked off, it had to replace the rock before tagging anyone.

Naismith grew up and attended college and all but forgot about this game until 1891 when he became director of the Young Men's Christian Association (YMCA) training school in Springfield, Massachusetts. Naismith needed a sport that would **benefit** students' physical health and one that could be played inside during the cold, snowy New England winter. He wanted a game that emphasized skill rather than strength. Perhaps thinking about his joy playing duck on a rock, Naismith set two peach baskets as goals into which a soccer ball could be thrown; the goals sat at either side of the court, or playing area.

The game was not complicated, and it could be played inside in a small area. The rules of this new game, called basketball, were easy to learn. Two teams of players **opposed** each other on the court, and each team had nine players—a goalkeeper, two guards, three centers, two wings, and a home man. The ball was kept in **motion**, thrown or batted from player to player, but without using the fist. Players were not allowed to run with the ball.  Contact was discouraged, fouls could lead to disqualification or points for the other team, and the winner was the team that made the most baskets in two 15-minute periods, with a 5-minute break between. Best of all, with the constant motion on the

Hull House team Chicago Tri-Chis in 1908

court, the players benefited from the physical activity.

Over time, a few changes improved basketball. In 1892, Lew Allen, of Hartford, Connecticut, made a wire basket to replace the wooden peach-basket goals. In 1894, a basketball replaced the soccer ball. Some rules were changed and added, a five-person team became standard, and the **transition** from Naismith's basketball to today's game was complete.

Basketball Encircles the Globe

At first, Naismith's game of basketball spread from Springfield to other YMCAs across the country. The appeal, or attraction, of the game broadened quickly. In 1892, at Smith College in Northampton, Massachusetts, the first women's basketball game took place. In 1895, several girls' high schools began basketball programs, and soon other schools and organizations formed teams and

1 Visualize
Picture a basketball game in which there was no dribbling and players either played offense or defense—not both. How different would the game be?

began competitions. During the following years, high schools, colleges, civic organizations, and even businesses established basketball teams and held internal competitions as well as external contests against outside groups. **2**

Basketball's transition to a professional sport came in the mid-1900s. The first long-lasting professional basketball league, having 11 teams, began as the BAA (Basketball Association of America) in 1946 and became the NBA in 1949. The NBA consisted of 17 teams in three divisions. Professional players grabbed the attention of the **media**, and over the following years, some became celebrities, including Bob Cousy, Wilt Chamberlain, Bill Russell, Kareem Abdul-Jabbar, Larry Bird, Earvin "Magic" Johnson, and

Michael Jordan.

While basketball grew in popularity in the United States, the game also became an internationally known sport. In 1932, eight countries formed the International Basketball Federation, and in 1936, basketball was introduced at the Berlin Olympics. **3**

Basketball on the Streets and the Screen

Basketball, almost the way Naismith invented it, is still a popular high school, college, and professional sport. But, a new surge of players has taken the game to **urban** playgrounds and gyms around the world. Following most of basketball's conventional, or standard, rules, basketball has transitioned, or developed into, streetball. In streetball, however, besides the usual 5-player teams, the run, or game, can be played with two people as opponents—called one-on-one—using one basket and half the standard basketball court.

For amateur streetball, usually anyone who shows up at a court can play a pickup game; players just have to wait their turn. But, in the same way that basketball transitioned into a casual sport for everyone, streetball now has professional teams as well.

Some people suggest the Harlem Globetrotters were the model for modern streetball. The Globetrotters, who began playing in 1927, are known for their skillful

Kobe Bryant flies high above his opponent.

2 Context Clues
What clues in this sentence help you determine the meaning of *internal* and *external*?

3 Inference
Why do you think the sport of basketball spread so quickly?

4 Make Connections
Have you ever watched streetball performers display their skills? Do you think it is more entertaining than watching the NBA?

and flashy court antics. In 2001, the Street Basketball Association (SBA), became a way for skilled streetball players to gain recognition and media attention. Games were played in front of live audiences and televised.

The transition of streetball continues, as teams have set themselves up as traveling media shows. One such publicity-seeking group is the AND 1 team, which travels around the country challenging local teams. The play, instead of focusing on the traditional skills, highlights individual players. The players display flashy moves and ball-handling skills, acrobatic stunts, slam dunks, and alley-oops. Trash-talking is one of the standard features of the game.

Videos of the AND 1 team highlight these showy plays and players, causing some critics to say the team is not about basketball, but about showmanship. Even some of the players' nicknames support this negative viewpoint: Kenny "Bad Santa" Brunner, John "Helicopter" Humphrey, Tony "Go Get It" Jones, and Jerry "The Assassin" Dupree.

Though nicknames for players are not new, one could argue that in the past, they emerged more naturally—like Wilt "the Stilt" Chamberlain—rather than being applied for effect. **4**

What about Basketball's Goals?

What would James Naismith say about how his sport has changed? Whether basketball or streetball, amateur or professional, players still physically benefit from continual motion as they run, jump, spin, and glide to the hoop. In that sense, the game is still reaching its goal. Whatever the showplace—a high school gymnasium, a professional arena, or a DVD—spectators enjoy the skill, excitement, and style of players in motion. Moreover, no matter how many professional teams exist, young people in gymnasiums and vacant lots, in rural and urban areas, enjoy Naismith's cold-weather creation. **End**

The Dyckman Basketball Tournament features some of the best street basketball in New York City.

Physical Therapy

Working It Out

With the score tied, forward Matt Carlson steals the puck and skates toward the goal. He slams the puck at the net. Reggie Marshall, the opposing goalie, blocks the shot. The puck bounces away, and the players scramble. Suddenly, Carlson is down on the ice. Play pauses. Teammates help the injured Carlson off the ice. The media report that Carlson has sprained his ankle.

If you were a physical therapist, you might help Carlson recover, regain a full range of motion in his ankle, and return to team play. A physical therapist is a professional who works with people who have sustained injuries or have diseases that impair motion. Some therapists treat diverse conditions. Others specialize in a particular field, such as

sports medicine or neurology, the treatment of nerve disorders. Still others only treat patients in a certain age group, such as pediatric therapists, who work with children.

For example, a physical therapist may treat a sports injury, such as one that affects the ankles, legs, arms, or neck. The therapist works to lessen pain and improve the movement in the injured area. A physical therapist also may help people after an automobile or bicycle accident. These patients may have fractured or broken bones or head and neck injuries. A therapist may work with a person who has a disabling disease, such as cerebral palsy. The therapist helps that person make the transition to a more healthful life. Whatever situation brings a patient to physical therapy, the therapist focuses on the

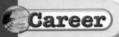
recovery of motion and health. The overall goal is to prevent, or at least lessen, permanent limitations of movement.

To begin treatment, a physical therapist examines the patient's medical records. The therapist learns the recorded causes and effects of the physical problem as reported by a physician. The therapist may have the patient perform certain actions. These tests may show the strength, range of movement, balance, motor function, and breathing of the patient. The therapist plans a program for the patient's benefit. Treatment may be performed with the therapist in the facility or by the patient at home. The therapist may use electric stimulation, delivering small electrical currents to an injured area to promote motion and healing. Treatments also may include ultrasound, delivering high-frequency sound waves that help lessen swelling and pain. Hot or cold packs, deep-tissue massage, and traction may be part of the healing program. The patient may receive a beneficial personal program of exercise or stretching.

What kind of person makes a good physical therapist? A therapist should have expert knowledge of the body and a desire to help people. Most physical therapists work in hospitals, clinics, and specially equipped offices. Some visit homes or schools. Because they work closely with patients and with other professionals, such as doctors and nurses, therapists should enjoy working with people. They need good communication skills. Therapists may need to kneel to help a patient

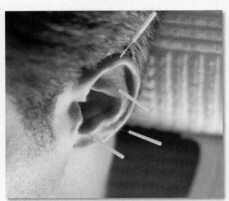

move an ankle, or stoop to exercise a patient's knee, so they should be in good physical condition. The work also may require lifting heavy training equipment or fully supporting a patient's weight.

To gain the skills to work in physical therapy, students study general and specialized science, such as biology, chemistry, and biomechanics, and also learn how to examine and test patients. Students must receive a master's or doctoral degree in a physical therapy program, which requires two to four years beyond a bachelor's degree. To practice, a therapist must pass national and state tests to obtain licenses. The benefits of this hard work are the reward of helping people, the promise of employment opportunities, and a good salary with an average range from about $55,000 to $71,000 per year.

If you like the idea of helping people with injuries, but don't feel physically strong enough to be a therapist, you might become an acupuncturist or a chiropractor. An acupuncturist is trained in the Chinese medical practice of reading pulses and placing needles or applying electric stimulation at certain points to help heal and balance the patient's body. A chiropractor uses the hands to adjust and align bones and muscles expertly. Both these positions require a strong knowledge of the structure and health of the body, years of specialized training, and a license to practice. However, the earning potential for these positions may exceed $85,000 per year.

Steroids and Health

Many steroids can be detected in urine. Why can some drugs only be detected in blood?

Lance Armstrong has never tested positive for performance-enhancing drugs.

Winning by Drugs or Determination?

On July 24, 2005, Lance Armstrong pedaled toward the finish of the Tour de France, on the Champs-Élysées, in Paris, France. He knew every second would count and rode as fast as he could. Sweating and grimacing, Armstrong crossed the finish line, completing a feat of strength and endurance in this cycling race that began 2,500 miles and 3 weeks before. With this victory, Armstrong became the first cyclist to win the Tour de France seven times in a row.

How Armstrong managed to stay at the top of his sport for so long has been the subject of great controversy. Some people **speculate** he has used illegal ways to win. They have accused him of

cheating—specifically, of using performance-enhancing **chemicals** banned, or outlawed, by the sporting organization. Claiming to be "the most tested athlete in the world," Armstrong has proven himself innocent of the charges. **1** But, each year of the Tour de France, many cyclists are disqualified for taking performance-enhancing drugs, such as steroids. The use of steroids has become a major issue for all professional sports. Moreover, the possibility of using these drugs has filtered down to high school athletes.

Steroid Composition, Structure, and Effects

Steroids are **organic** chemicals. An organic chemical is a substance containing carbon, usually found in living things. Steroids are

Vocabulary

speculate (v) *wonder or guess about something without knowing all the facts*

chemicals (n) *substances formed when two or more other substances act upon one another*

organic (adj) *made using only natural products*

1 Make Connections
Have you ever been unfairly accused of something you didn't do? How did that make you feel?

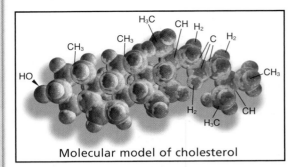
synthesized, made in and by cells of the human body. Many steroids are necessary for the body's proper functioning. One example is cholesterol, which keeps cell walls fluid. Steroids are lipids, or fat molecules. Therefore, they are not highly **soluble** in water. All steroids have a characteristic shape consisting of four connected rings of carbon atoms, plus multiple arms.

Steroids make up one group of chemicals that athletes use to get an illegal advantage over their opponents. The class of steroids used to increase performance is anabolic steroids. These steroids are related to testosterone, the male sex hormone. Some performance-enhancing chemicals are made from organic molecules found in the human body, while others are not. They are, however, similar enough to such molecules that they act in the same way. Both types can be synthesized artificially in laboratories and made into pills or injections. To make a fluid for injection, the steroid is put into a liquid in which the steroid is soluble.

Anabolic steroids have various **effects** on the human body. Exposure to high levels of these chemicals can cause an increase in the growth of body hair and a lengthening of the vocal cords, which deepens the voice. Also, these organic substances can impair, or damage, fertility in males. **2**

None of these effects is particularly useful to athletes. But, athletes are interested because anabolic steroids also increase muscle mass and strength. This can be quite beneficial to performance in many sports.

Early Performance-Enhancing Drug Use

The idea of using drugs to gain an edge over opponents is not new. Before the 20th century, athletes took cocaine or other stimulants, which are drugs that increase alertness, to try to improve performance. These often caused death from overexertion and dehydration, or loss of water.

Steroids were first used in medicine in 1931, when Adolf Butenandt isolated the male hormone androsterone from urine. After it had been set apart from other substances, chemists were able to synthesize this hormone artificially.

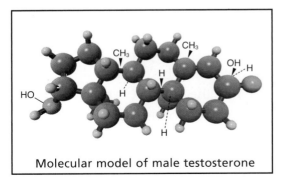

Molecular model of male testosterone

By 1934, Butenandt and others had artificially synthesized testosterone. The first human trials of the chemical began as early as 1937. There is speculation that during World War II, Nazi Germany experimented on soldiers, using the hormone to increase their aggression. Steroid programs were effective in athlete training programs for bodybuilders in the Soviet Union and Eastern Europe in the 1940s and 1950s, and widespread use across the world followed. The performance effects were so extreme that athletes who did not take the drugs found it difficult to win, a fact that greatly encouraged the use of the substances.

Defensive end Lyle Alzado, who died at age 43, blamed his fatal brain cancer on steroids and human growth hormone. Has cancer been linked to steroid use?

Health Problems

Using steroids can produce a variety of health problems. Steroids often cause muscles to outgrow and injure the tendons and ligaments that attach them to the bone—leaving an athlete unable to compete. Also, steroids have to be broken down by the body, particularly by the liver. Steroid tablets can cause liver damage if

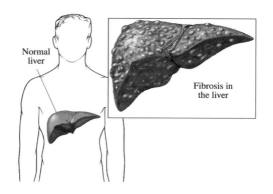

Normal liver

Fibrosis in the liver

used at high dosages over a long time. Steroids also can cause enlargement and thickening of the left ventricle of the heart, leading to various heart problems. Because

athletes' hearts work hard during exercise, they can be especially susceptible to such problems during competition. Steroids also have been linked to high blood pressure, baldness, kidney problems, acne, mood swings, and lowered immunity to disease. **3**

With the obvious factor of unfairness in competitions, these health risks have led the governing organizations of every major sporting event to ban steroids. Most Western governments also have made nonmedical uses of steroids illegal. Using steroids or other performance enhancers to win is not only unhealthy, and sometimes deadly, but it defeats the purpose of sport. Winning should be about honor, skill, and hard work, not about who can take the most effective chemicals to gain an unnatural edge.

Detecting Steroid Use

With steroids banned from competitions, detection has become a major issue. Various steroids react

3 Summarize
What are four health problems linked to steroid use?

differently in the body and can be detected through different methods. The easiest type of test is a urine test. Molecules that aren't broken down pass from the body in urine. Chemical analysis of the urine can detect these compounds. Blood tests also can be used to detect these chemicals in the bloodstream. They are harder to administer than urine tests, but they can detect chemicals that urine tests cannot. Today's athletes have to submit to numerous tests to compete in events.

When steroid use is discovered, athletes can be punished in accordance with the rules set by the sport's governing organization and the country where the competition takes place. Penalties can include deduction of points from a person's score, disqualification, fines, exclusion from future events, or even imprisonment. Yet, some athletes continue to use steroids, and get caught and punished for it. This is a testament to the performance benefits of these chemicals—proof that despite the risks, people continue to use them. As new artificial steroids are developed, new tests have to be created to detect them.

Many athletes in professional baseball, football, and track and

U.S. sprinter Marion Jones won five medals at the 2000 Olympics but has since agreed to forfeit all medals and prizes after admitting that she took performance-enhancing drugs.

field have been the focus of steroid speculation in the past. Fortunately, the use of steroids overall is probably decreasing in professional athletics. Penalties have become stricter as governing organizations realize that steroid doping is widespread. However, the organizations still have to allow for medical exemptions because steroids that are used to treat certain diseases and conditions are excusable. One such example is cortisone, a common steroid in anti-itch cream that is used to treat inflammation. This complicates the issue of regulation because acceptable use must be defined and enforced. Also, athletes could fake medical problems to get compounds otherwise prohibited.

Steroids are fat-soluble organic substances that have a variety of effects within the body. These steroids can be healthy in small quantities; for example, testosterone and estrogen are necessary for reproductive development. However, when steroids are used to boost athletic performance, they often can cause serious side effects and sometimes death. Not only is the use of steroids to boost athletic performance ethically wrong, but it causes an unnecessary health risk. **End**

Mixed Martial Arts: Sport and Media Show

Vocabulary

competent (adj) *having the skill or ability to do something well*

endeavors (v) *tries very hard to do something*

Ted "Slammer" Rosewood kicks A.J. Henson into a corner. Rosewood grabs Henson in a clinch, strong-arming Henson to the floor and overpowering him. Henson, known as a **competent** fighter, is surprised by Rosewood's strength. Rosewood is pounding Henson with a series of right jabs and left strikes, smashing fists against Henson's skull and ribs. It looks as if Rosewood has pressed Henson into the ground and **endeavors** to keep him there. He's using all his weight to keep him down. Henson can't get a hit off. The buzzer signals the end of the match. The judges declare Rosewood the winner.

MMA: From Start to Finish

For people who don't know the modern sport, the name *mixed martial arts* evokes, or brings to

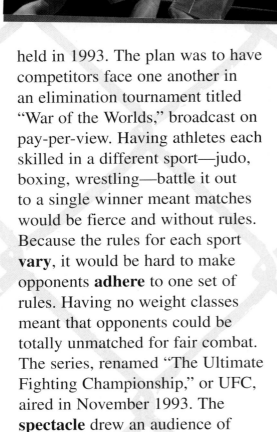

mind, images of Eastern practices: white uniforms, black belts, and graceful bows before and after combat. The **maneuvers** in most martial arts—though they can be fierce or even life-threatening in a sport such as jujitsu, or graceful yet effectively defensive in aikido— have dignity and beauty.

Mixed martial arts (MMA) is a different sport from traditional martial arts. The sport began as a full-contact, combat sport with an anything-can-go attitude. Participants use a broad range of techniques and maneuvers. These are taken from traditional martial arts and other sports (boxing, wrestling, and kickboxing, for example). Striking, grappling, kicking, elbowing, and kneeing occur as opponents circle in constant movement around the ring. A clinch hold is a maneuver that keeps an opponent close for takedowns and throws. On the ground, players press, punch, and slide, while trying to knock out or gain a submission hold on the opponent.

The first modern competition that set the stage for MMA was held in 1993. The plan was to have competitors face one another in an elimination tournament titled "War of the Worlds," broadcast on pay-per-view. Having athletes each skilled in a different sport—judo, boxing, wrestling—battle it out to a single winner meant matches would be fierce and without rules. Because the rules for each sport **vary**, it would be hard to make opponents **adhere** to one set of rules. Having no weight classes meant that opponents could be totally unmatched for fair combat. The series, renamed "The Ultimate Fighting Championship," or UFC, aired in November 1993. The **spectacle** drew an audience of almost 87,000 paying viewers.

These first competitions were extremely brutal and dangerous, although the stated goal was to find the best fighters, whatever the style. With few rules—such as no hair pulling or eye gouging—and limited adherence to the rules, people criticized the UFC for promoting violence. Political pressure eventually forced the group underground, away from media coverage and the public eye. **1** But, by the late 1990s, with new rules, new sponsors, and new publicity, MMA emerged as an accepted sport—not just a spectacle. Matches were limited to three to five 5-minute rounds. Weight divisions were set. A list of about 30 rules prohibited the most obviously harmful actions. Victory could be gained when the opponent submitted, by knockout (loss of consciousness), technical knockout (the referee, a doctor, or the corner man stops the fight because of injuries observed), or by the judges' decision.

The sport has grown so popular that in 2006, MMA competitions brought in more profit through their pay-per-view broadcasts than any other programming ever in a single year. Various leagues in the United States hold competitions on a regular basis. Shows featuring MMA continue to be broadcast and earn profits. But, exactly why are viewers so intrigued by the spectacle of MMA? Are they interested in the players' skills? Or, are they watching to see someone writhing, or twisting in pain, with a wrenched shoulder or bleeding from a bashed head? Many people seem to be drawn to violence. People watch boxing, war footage, and now MMA. Is it a primal urge, or is it something learned? **2**

Injuries in MMA

The sport of MMA has decreased in brutality since its beginnings. But, players still can face serious injury and sometimes death. Participants often suffer a broad range of injuries. These include broken bones, knee and shoulder tears, shoulder and ankle sprains, cuts, bruises, and infections that can set in during the healing process. Like in other contact sports, such as boxing and football, head injuries are common. A single blow to the head, or a series of blows, can damage the brain, which can result in death. Because MMA uses full-body movements from wrestling and various martial arts, such as arm bars and leg locks, the risk of head injury is somewhat lessened.

In 2006, Johns Hopkins University did a study on the injuries sustained in professional MMA competition for 3 years from September 2001 to December 2004. The study included 171 matches; in 69 of those matches, either one or both participants sustained, or suffered, injuries, resulting in 96 recorded injuries to 78 players. The most frequently recorded medical problem was cuts to the face, which made up about 48 percent of the

1 Context Clues
What clues from the text can help you understand the meaning of *underground*?

2 Make Connections
Have you ever watched a fight? Why did you watch it?

injuries. Injuries to the eyes, nose, shoulders, and hands were also common. The conclusion reached in the study was that MMA was dangerous but did not pose a higher threat of injury than other combat sports, such as boxing—provided fighters adhere to the rules. The fact that a player could "tap out" of competition—that is, strike the mat with a hand to let referees know he had had enough—was seen as a positive way of limiting injuries.

3 Inference

How could *tapping out* limit injuries?

However, since the Johns Hopkins study, in a sanctioned, or official, MMA match, a participant died, presumably from being knocked out by his opponent. Vince Libardi endeavored to knock out Sam Vasquez in an October 20, 2007, match in Houston, Texas. Vasquez collapsed, was hospitalized, and had brain surgery to remove blood clots. He died after a second operation. Although some people have questioned whether Vasquez had a pre-existing medical condition, as an official participant he had completed medical screening before he was given his license to take part in MMA competitions.

Vasquez may be the only "official" fatality. But, with the popularity of the sport established by professionals, other MMA competitors with little or no medical screening and less qualified medical help at the ring have been killed during MMA matches. Two examples are Douglas Dredge, in an unsanctioned match in 1998, and a man in South Korea in 2005. Critics of MMA suggest that given its short history and the limited number of matches compared with other sports such as boxing, the risks of serious injury and death in MMA competitions could be quite high.

Is MMA Worth the Risks?

In one sense, MMA is no different from any other sport. The risk of injury or death is present in any athletic endeavor, from diving to football to track. But, statistics suggest that more injuries, and sometimes more serious injuries, occur in high-contact sports. MMA has about as much contact as a sport can have. Any sport in which competitors use high-velocity strikes has an increased risk of injury. In fact, about 40 percent of the time, an MMA match ends in injury of one or both competitors. Yet, competitors seem to enjoy the challenge of making strategic and competent attacks against opponents whose main skill may lie in a different sport. Viewers obviously love the excitement of the one-on-one combat. **End**

Athletic Trainer/ Athletic Coach

On the Team, Off the Playing Field

Would you like to be a valuable part of an athletic team without the stress of playing on the team? Maybe you could be an athletic trainer.

In that position, you would have a broad range of duties. You would be part coach, part physical therapist, part nurse, and part adviser.

As a trainer, you would be responsible for the health of an athletic team. You would analyze the physical condition of the team's athletes, and work with each one to bring the player into top condition for athletic competition. You would plan a workout schedule to develop and strengthen muscles, focusing on exercises especially needed for the particular sport. Your goal would be to make each player ready for any maneuver in the sport, so that the player performs well and avoids injury. You would also plan a diet for athletes that maintains a healthy weight and provides the right nutrition. An overweight athlete has a greater risk of injury or disease.

Watching the health of your team, you would try to ensure that none of your athletes are using illegal or harmful drugs, such as steroids or other dangerous chemicals. Athletes might be tempted to use drugs because their effects could enhance performance or mask pain. But, as their trainer, you must ensure that players stay healthy and naturally strong. You should prevent them from doing anything to put their careers in danger.

Your job would also include first aid for injuries—such as cuts, bruises, sprains, or strains—experienced during games, meets, or practices. You also would perform routine treatments, such as massage or gentle movement

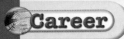
of injured areas, to relieve muscle or joint tightness or pain. You would use your expert knowledge of the body's muscles, joints, and ligaments to wrap injured fingers, wrists, or ankles for added support. You might apply thermal therapy, using heat or cold to bring down swelling or relieve pain. In emergencies, you might use CPR (cardiopulmonary resuscitation) to revive a player who has been seriously injured during play. Additionally, you could decide to call in a physician for an examination or additional treatment.

Not all trainers work for athletic teams. You might work as a personal trainer, helping an athlete, a celebrity, or an ordinary person. In that position, you would still be likely to perform many, if not all, of the tasks of a team trainer. But, your focus would be just on your individual clients. Some companies and businesses hire trainers for their employees. In that position, you would likely be working with ordinary people, helping them stay in good shape despite sedentary jobs, in which little movement is required, such as jobs at desks or machines. You would help employees strike a balance between their sedentary work and their need for exercise. Schools and colleges also hire athletic trainers to work with students and student teams.

A certified trainer needs a degree from a college and is required to pass an exam. With a certificate, your pay expectations for a job at a company could range from about $30,000 to $45,000 a year. As a head trainer for a college, your salary could be around $60,000 a year. As a personal trainer, your salary could depend on how many clients you have, and how well known you are. But, if you were a competent athletic trainer for a major professional team, your salary might rise far higher.

Perhaps instead of filling the broad range

of roles an athletic trainer has, you want to focus on the sport itself. Another job you could have with a team is as a coach. If you are interested in a particular sport and willing to go to college, you might coach a professional or amateur team. As a coach, your main concern would be the performance of the team: what moves they make, how they make them, how well they play, and how they can improve. Coaches set up practices, teach techniques, and instruct players on the best form to use to succeed and to avoid injury. During games or meets, coaches decide who will play, so that the team's performance will be the best it can be.

A coach's average salary range is about $40,000 to $80,000 in high school. And, if you were a coach for a successful professional or college team, you could earn far more than the average. Many coaches have million-dollar salaries like the athletes themselves.

Giving Your All

- How can you overcome obstacles that could make it difficult to obtain your goals?

- Who in your life would help you overcome a great difficulty? Why did you choose that person?

- Why do some people in emergency situations have great strength or courage?

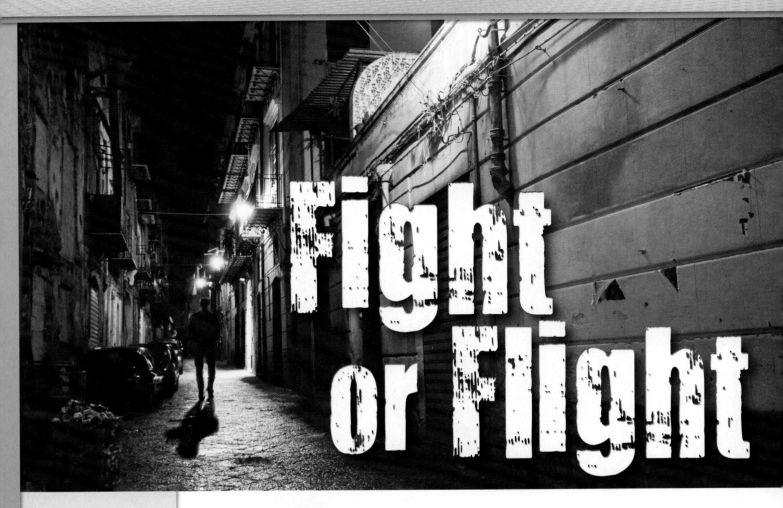

Fight or Flight

Vocabulary

situation (n)
condition or state of affairs

instances (n)
occurrences or things that happen

affect (v) *bring about a change*

Suppose you are taking your trash outside to a dark alley. Suddenly, the trash barrels ahead rattle, and someone leaps out from behind them. For a second, you freeze, observing the **situation** as the person comes toward you. Then, without thinking, you will probably do one of two things: prepare to fight off this possible attacker or turn and race out of the alley.

The Instinctual Response

In 1915, psychologist Walter Cannon introduced the phrase "fight or flight" to describe the response of animals and humans to threatening situations. To understand how people respond in such **instances**, it's important to look at how the brain can **affect** the body. ■

The nervous system consists of the brain, spinal cord, and nerves, and controls how a person responds to the world. A stimulus, such as the sudden appearance of a stranger, reaches the brain through sense organs—the eyes. The brain sends the information throughout the nervous system as electrical signals that cause the body to respond to the stimulus.

When a person is not in a stressful situation, the brain processes the information differently, and the person decides how to act based on past experiences. Under extreme threat, the signals go directly from the brain to parts of the nervous system that cause a person to take immediate action. An instinctual

■ Main Idea
What is the main idea of this paragraph?

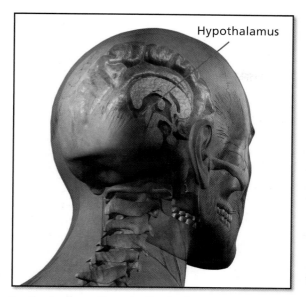

Hypothalamus

Instinctual reactions in the brain cause you to pull away from touching something hot.

reaction—one that is inborn and requires no conscious thought—occurs. This is the same response that happens, for instance, when a person touches something hot. The instinctual reaction is to pull the hand away; the person does not pause to consider the choices. The action of fight or flight is an instinctual response. **2**

Biological Changes that Affect the Response

After the stimulus of a threat, the response to act depends on biological changes. The hypothalamus, located at the base of the brain, communicates through nerve cells to the whole nervous system and to the endocrine system, the body's glands. Responding to a threat, the hypothalamus automatically signals nerve cells that affect all parts of the body including glands, the body parts that synthesize certain hormones. For example, the hypothalamus sends nerve signals to the adrenal glands, which produce the hormone adrenaline. The release of adrenaline into the blood affects the body, resulting in physical changes that prepare the body to attack or run: heartbeat and breathing quicken, senses sharpen, pain sensitivity lowers, digestion slows, and more blood flows to muscles. **3**

2 Ask Questions
After reading this section, you might ask yourself how the brain affects the body.

3 Make Connections
Have you ever felt threatened or scared? Which of the symptoms mentioned here did you experience?

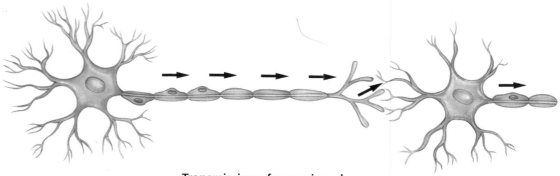

Transmission of nerve impulse

Watchful lioness protecting her kill

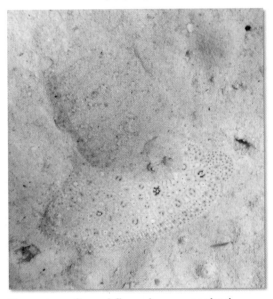

Two camouflaged flounders on seabed

4 Ask Questions

At this point, you may be asking what dangers this instinct could possibly cause. Keep this question in mind as you continue reading.

Beyond Simple Fight or Flight

Let's look at a simple instance of fight or flight: a lioness makes a kill, and a hyena appears, growling. Will the lioness defend her kill (fight) or run off (flight)?

The fight-or-flight response doesn't, however, mean that attacking or running away are the only possible reactions. Some animals use instinctual escape methods that do not involve running but have the same effect as flight: A threatened fish changes color to blend into its background; a bird plays dead to avoid being hunted.

High School Lockdowns and Fight or Flight

The fight-or-flight instinct can result in great danger in certain situations. **4** Recently, many high schools have initiated a lockdown policy that is enforced if administrators believe students are threatened, such as by a disturbed person. Classrooms are locked to help protect students from the threat, a practice that lowers the risk in dangerous situations and also avoids the instinctual response of fight or flight, which could easily result in harm to innocent students. Students attempting to fight an attacker are likely to be injured and could be killed; masses of students exiting the building could become easy targets.

Threats in Today's World

Life today seems to include many fearful situations, and unfortunately, people feel threatened, or stressed, so frequently that the body often releases the fight-or-flight hormones when they are not needed, causing physical symptoms. Often, people overreact to perceived instances of threat, becoming angry or irritated when the body puts them into the fight-or-flight mode, but neither action is appropriate. People can sometimes prevent such overreactions by maintaining a careful awareness of their surroundings and staying alert to sudden changes in situations. **5**

Remember the person in the dark alley? After you carefully observe the situation, you realize it's only your neighbor. He was taking his trash out too, and now he's coming over just to chat. **End**

5 Summarize

What problems are caused by our natural fight-or-flight instinct in today's society?

People react to the sight of the collapsing World Trade Center towers in New York after they were struck by hijacked airplanes on September 11, 2001.

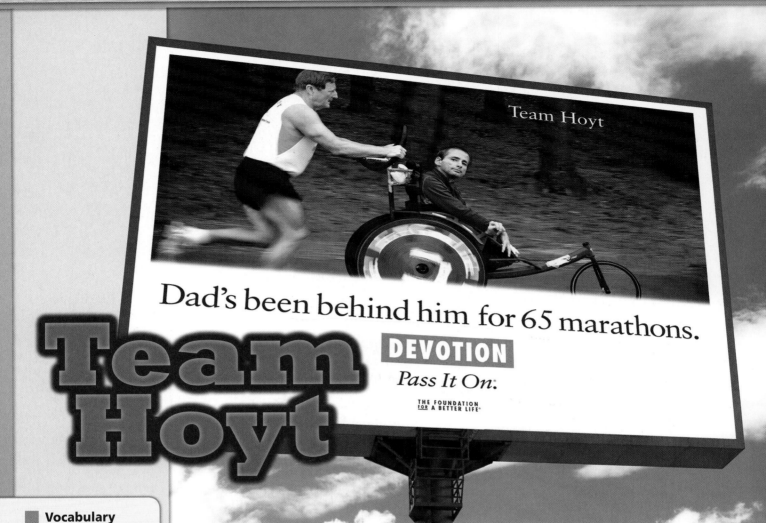

Dad's been behind him for 65 marathons.

DEVOTION

Pass It On.

THE FOUNDATION
FOR A BETTER LIFE®

Team Hoyt

1 Visualize
Picture this scene in your mind. What do you see?

Racing beyond Disability

Cheered by the spectators lining the race route, Team Hoyt approaches the finish line of the Boston Marathon, a 26.2-mile race held yearly in Massachusetts. Exhausted runners pass by this father-and-son team, patting them on the back and offering words of encouragement, as Dick Hoyt pushes the wheelchair holding his son, Rick, over the finish line to complete another marathon for Team Hoyt. **1** In this race, Dick is 67 years old, and his son 46; but the **inspiring** story of what this father-son team can **achieve** through great effort began 46 years ago.

A terrible situation occurred at Rick's birth in 1962. The umbilical cord, the cord connecting the unborn baby to his mother, became wrapped around Rick's neck. Oxygen could not reach his brain, resulting in cerebral palsy. Doctors told Dick and his wife, Judy, that their son was permanently disabled, and no amount of effort would allow Rick a normal life. But, Rick's parents were unwilling to accept the diagnosis of the doctors. They wanted their son to live as normal a life as possible, in spite of his many **disabilities**. The only movements he could make were a slight tilting of the head and bending of the knees.

Everywhere they turned, the family faced challenges. In 1972, Rick's parents asked engineers at Tufts University to create a computer Rick could use to communicate, since Rick could not talk. The engineers at first refused, claiming that Rick would not understand. Dick told them to tell his son a joke, and when Rick laughed, the engineers agreed to develop a system for Rick. **2**

That year, the Boston Bruins hockey team was in the finals. The first words Rick formed, by moving his head to click a switch to type a displayed letter were, "Go, Bruins." Rick's parents then knew their son loved sports, but they had no idea where this would lead.

For years, the family struggled to get Rick into public school. They finally succeeded in 1975. Two years later, Rick expressed a desire to run in a benefit race for a lacrosse player who had been paralyzed in an accident. Rick's father was not a runner, but he was so inspired by his son's request, they took part—Dick pushing Rick in a wheelchair. The race's organizers believed Dick and Rick would drop out, but father and son managed to cross the finish line. Rick's response, typed on his computer, was inspiring: The effort and achievement made him feel more like an athlete, less like a disabled person.

Soon Rick and his father participated as Team Hoyt in more

races. During these first years of racing, organizers discouraged Team Hoyt's participation, and competitors stayed as far away as possible from Rick and his father. **3**

Ignoring these responses, Dick and Rick signed up for their first marathon, the Boston Marathon of 1981. To the amazement of organizers and spectators, Dick pushed his son to finish in the top quarter of a field made up of about 20,000 runners. People gained a new perspective on Team Hoyt.

Team Hoyt continued to run in the Boston Marathon and also began participating in other racing events. In 1985, father and son took

2 Ask Questions
Think about Rick's disabilities. What questions do you have about how he functioned? As you continue to read, see if your questions are answered.

3 Make Connections
What would you have done if you were Rick's father?

4 Context Clues

Based on this sentence, what is a triathlon?

5 Make Inferences

Why did race organizers and racers change their opinions about Team Hoyt?

part in their first triathlon, an endurance sporting event that includes three parts: running, biking, and swimming. **4** For biking, Dick had a special bicycle with a seat in front for Rick. For swimming, Dick pulled a boat. In Ironman Triathlons, Team Hoyt swam 2.4 miles, biked 112 miles, and ran the standard 26.2-mile marathon. By May 2008, Team Hoyt's list of accomplishments included 65 marathons—26 in Boston—and 224 triathlons.

The response of spectators and competitors has changed since their first races. Cheers of encouragement and appreciation have replaced words of discouragement and uneasy silence. Team Hoyt continues, through actions and words, to encourage people to follow their dreams, in spite of challenges. The Hoyts receive letter after letter telling them how much their achievement has inspired others to accomplish their own dreams. **5 End**

Liz Murray

Overcoming the Obstacles

The winter evening is cold and windy, with crisp-looking stars shining over Bronx, New York. Liz Murray, just 12 years old, doesn't want to go home because her parents are doing drugs again. She is walking the streets, alone, headed for the home of a friend. She knocks on an apartment door, hoping to spend the night on the sofa in her friend's parents' apartment. Maybe she'll go home to check on her mother in the morning, or maybe she'll go to school.

What will the future life be for a child who lives like this? Could the result of such a life—begun in a **background** of parental drug addiction and **poverty**—be education at a famous university and public success? That outcome was unlikely, but Liz Murray made it possible.

Vocabulary

background (n) *a person's training and experience*

poverty (n) *condition of being poor; lack of money*

Born into Poverty

Liz Murray was born in 1980 to parents who lived in a shabby apartment in the Bronx. Liz's parents were addicted to drugs and lived on welfare checks they spent mostly to feed their addictions; the remaining $30 a month was all there was left to spend on food.

When Liz was growing up, she missed a lot of school because she took care of her mother. She loved her parents and did not realize the lifestyle she was living was different from that of many children. As a young girl, Liz did not even realize that most people go to work each day to earn money to live.

Death Brings Realization

When Liz's mother was diagnosed with HIV, her father moved to a shelter for the homeless. Liz was sent to a group home, but conditions at the home were so bad that Liz soon ran away. On the streets of New York, she found food in garbage bins and shelter in friends' homes or on

subway trains. When Liz was 16, her mother died of AIDS, and Liz began to think seriously about overcoming her background of poverty and improving her life with education. The sudden realization that she was truly on her own, and that she could rise out of her background only by her own effort, pushed her forward.

Getting an Education

At 17, Liz enrolled in an alternative high school. Because she was intelligent and motivated, or willing to try hard, she found **academic** study easy. **2** She graduated in two years instead of the usual four, even though she was still homeless, sleeping out on the streets sometimes and working at odd jobs to earn money. Then something fantastic occurred: She was one of six students who received a *New York Times* scholarship for needy students. She applied and was accepted at Harvard University, a respected Ivy League university in Massachusetts known

1 Summarize
What made Liz think about her education?

2 Context Clues
What clues in this sentence help you understand the meaning of *motivated*?

A New Direction

In New York, Liz attended Columbia University for a while, but exciting changes in her life brought unexpected opportunities. The *New York Times* published a story about her scholarship, the television show *20/20* told her story, and Oprah Winfrey interviewed her. In 2003, a television movie about Liz's life was made.

Liz realized that her story might have the power to help others. But, even better, her experiences and her knowledge might allow her to create strategies, or ways, to help people cope with hardships and move beyond them to a meaningful life. Liz returned to Harvard in May 2008 to complete her degree. Today, Liz lectures to groups throughout the country, encouraging others to rise to their own dreams, whatever the dreams are, whatever background they come from, however hard they need to work. She should know! **4** **End**

for academic excellence.

Liz enrolled at Harvard University in the fall of 2000 and completed several semesters of academic study before, in 2003, she returned to New York to take care of her father, who had become sick with AIDS. **3**

Liz with her father in New York City

3 **Main Idea**
What is the main idea of this section?

4 **Summarize**
What events in Liz's life led her to where she is today?

Josh Hamilton

From High School to Heroin to Hero

Texas Rangers center fielder Josh Hamilton was the winner of the American League Player of the Month award for May 2008, the second month in a row. Josh looked pleased to be honored for his performance. But, one could also sense a deeper feeling of gratitude in Josh because he almost missed the chance of success in the sport he believes he was meant to play.

High School Honors

For Josh Hamilton, the road to success was not a straight line. He began his career as a strong baseball player in Raleigh, North Carolina. On his high school team, Josh looked as if he were heading straight for baseball stardom. At the end of his senior year, Baseball America named Josh the High School Player of the Year. In 1999, he was **nominated** for and received USA Baseball's Amateur Player of the Year. After high school in 1999, Josh signed with the Princeton Devil Rays, a minor league team linked to the Tampa Bay Devil Rays for $3.96 million. He played successfully for that team and several other minor league teams for the next two years.

Vocabulary

nominated (v) *named as a candidate for election*

Addicted to Drugs

Josh's parents quit their jobs to go everywhere their son played. Before the 2001 season, Josh and his mother were injured in an automobile accident in Florida. His mother returned to Raleigh with his dad to recover from her injuries. Josh was alone. He began hanging out with people who used drugs. As he says, "When I first got into drinking and using drugs, it was because of where I was hanging out, it was who I was hanging out with. You might not do it at first, but eventually, if you keep hanging around long enough, you're going to start doing what they're doing." He began experimenting with heroin and other drugs. He became addicted. Several times over the next years, he tried to improve his life and overcome his growing

abuse of drugs and alcohol. Each time, his attempt at rehabilitation failed, and he returned to using drugs. By the 2003 season, he was missing practices. He eventually took the remainder of the season off.

Josh hoped to return to play in 2004, but his efforts at rehabilitation continued to fail, and the Major League Baseball (MLB) organization **enforced** a 30-day suspension and a fine for his drug use. Josh was suspended several times because of drug use; between 2004 and 2006, he was prohibited from playing baseball. He made an attempt in 2005 to play with a minor league team during one of his rehabilitation periods, but the MLB continued to enforce the suspension. **1**

Vocabulary

enforced (v) *made to obey*

1 Make Connections
Have you or someone you know ever been suspended from a game or activity because of low grades? How did it feel?

Giving Your All

Vocabulary

blunders (n) *ideas, answers, or acts that are wrong; mistakes*

Getting Back on the Right Road

Josh describes this period in his career—and life—as a dark period, a time when his dreams filled with nightmares. He sometimes woke up not knowing where he was. He was separated from his wife and family, spending his money on drugs and alcohol. One night in October 2005, he collapsed at his grandmother's home, weak and disturbed after heavy heroin use. Josh moved in with his grandmother, Mary Holt. After having a disturbing nightmare associated with his drug use, Josh sought his grandmother's advice. She encouraged him to use the faith in which he was raised to confront his drug habit. Josh began to improve, making a complete effort to rehabilitate himself and show that he could move beyond drug and alcohol abuse and enforced suspensions. The **blunders** he had made in his life began to fall away, and he was on the road to success again, after a long, painful detour.

In December 2006, the Chicago Cubs drafted Josh, then sold him to the Cincinnati Reds for the 2007 season. Finally, he had made it into the major league, an accomplishment that had been expected of him soon after graduation from high school. He was traded in 2007 to the Texas Rangers, for whom he played the 2008 season, cheered on by excited fans. He took second place in the 2008 Major League Baseball Home Run Derby.

Teaching through Success

What does Josh say about overcoming the blunders of his past? He says, "It's a God thing," meaning his personal faith keeps him going. To demonstrate that he has totally improved his life, he stays on the baseball diamond, playing hard and encouraging rookies not to follow the difficult route he followed. Rather than hiding his past mistakes in shame, Josh tells his story to those who will listen. They learn that drugs and alcohol can make people risk losing the right and the ability to do what they were meant to do. For Josh Hamilton, he believes playing baseball was his destiny and his way to save himself and others. **2 End**

2 Ask Questions

Try explaining to a friend what caused Josh's downfall and how he recovered. Do you find you have questions? Reread to help you understand.

Aron Ralston: Trapped in the Canyon

Aron Ralston set out for a hike near the remote Maze District of Canyonlands National Park, south of Moab, Utah. Aron loved the **solitude** of hiking in the desert, away from other trails and other hikers, so alone that self-sufficiency was a necessary quality. During the day, the sun highlighted the range of colors of the canyon landscape, with isolated red stone mesas and buttes, and wispy clouds dotted the blue sky.

On this Saturday in April 2003, the 27-year-old left his truck in Horseshoe Canyon, then rode his mountain bike 15 miles to isolated Bluejohn Canyon. He planned to climb down this remote slot canyon. A slot canyon has a very narrow passageway through which a hiker must canyoneer, the process of using ropes and other rock-climbing gear to travel through the canyon. Aron had successfully completed most of the routes, rappelling—climbing down on a fixed rope—so that he had only one more section to rappel to reach the bottom. He climbed carefully atop a huge boulder that wedged between the narrow canyon. As he made his way carefully down the other side of the boulder, a **disastrous** event occurred: The boulder slipped, and Aron's arm became pinned under the 800-pound rock.

Aron was trapped with the weight of the rock crushing his right hand and lower arm. The situation was **desperate**, and Aron panicked, thrashing around to escape. Finally,

Vocabulary

solitude (n) *being alone*

disastrous (adj) *causing great distress or injury*

desperate (adj) *very serious with little or no hope*

1 Make Connections

What would you have done if you were Aron?

he calmed down and carefully considered his options. Although it was very unlikely, he hoped that maybe someone would find him. But, he knew he couldn't count on that. He had to think about what he could do to save himself. Moving the boulder or chipping it away were his first thoughts. If those things didn't work, the only option left would be to cut off his arm. **1**

He first tried to chip the rock away, but after hours of chipping he had made no progress. The temperature dropped to 30° Fahrenheit at night, and the canyon remained cold and sunless most of the following day. Two

Dried blood streaks mark the place where a boulder trapped Aron's hand. The local sheriff's department and Park Rangers from nearby Canyonlands later moved the boulder and removed the hand, which was cremated and given to Aron.

Aron appears on CBS's *The Late, Late Show* with Craig Ferguson.

days passed without escape, and by Tuesday, Aron's backpack was empty of food and water.

By Wednesday, Aron was forced to drink his own urine. Desperate, he recorded a good-bye message to his parents on his video camera, and scraped his name, birth date, and what he assumed was his date of death into the canyon wall. The disastrous accident had defeated him, and he felt certain he would soon die.

On Thursday morning, he was motivated to try one more time to free himself. According to Aron's account of his struggle, he had a dream that gave him hope for his future. He had to do something to save himself. Aron broke his arm so he could wriggle it loose enough to amputate it below his elbow with a multiuse tool. Leaving his hand trapped under the boulder, he began the hard work of rappelling down and out of the canyon. **2** Using a self-made sling over his shoulder, he walked toward Horseshoe Canyon, where a family heard him cry out for help. The mother and son agreed to go get help while the father stayed with Aron. The mother and son waved down a helicopter that was flying over the region trying to locate the missing hiker. The helicopter picked up Aron and flew him to a hospital in Moab, where Aron walked into the emergency room.

Before the disaster, Aron Ralston had a plan to hike more mountains and desert canyons. Rather than allow the loss of his arm to deter him, he has continued hiking in the solitude of the western deserts and mountains. He has recounted his story in a book and had numerous television interviews. Aron is an inspiration to all, demonstrating the amazing power of the will to survive a desperate situation. **3** **End**

2 Inference
Why didn't Aron wait a little longer to take such drastic action? What in the text supports your reason?

3 Make Connections
Think about what you read in "Fight or Flight." How would the response of Aron's brain to his self-inflicted surgery have helped him survive?

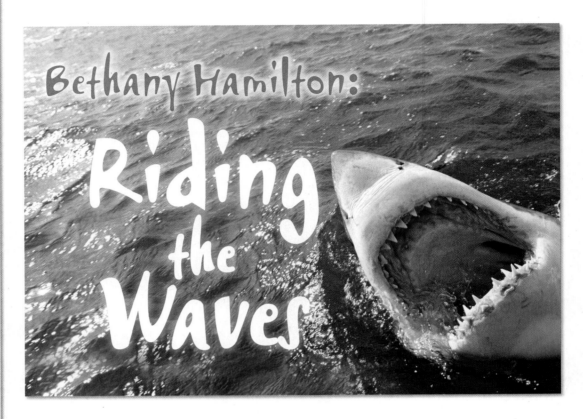

Bethany Hamilton: Riding the Waves

A Dangerous Gray Shadow

The early morning sun sparkled in the Hawaiian sky, making October 31, 2003, seem like a peaceful day. At Tunnels Beach, Kauai, champion surfer Bethany Hamilton was surfing with best friend Alana, Alana's brother Byron, and Alana's father, Holt. Bethany enjoyed the refreshing feel of the clear ocean water when she paddled out. She loved each surfing experience because every ride to shore was different.

Thirteen-year-old Bethany had ridden several waves, paddled out, and was lying on her board resting, with her left arm hanging in the water. Suddenly, a huge gray shadow flashed beside her, and she felt herself tugged back and forth. In seconds, her attacker let go, but chunks of her board had been bitten off, and her left arm had been **severed** near the shoulder by a **ferocious** shark. She called out, "I got attacked by a shark." Bethany's friends were shocked when the ocean around her became red with blood as she paddled toward Holt.

Life before the Shadow

Bethany was born on February 8, 1990, the daughter of parents who

Vocabulary

impair (v) *weaken or damage*

had moved to Hawaii for better surfing. Bethany's parents had their daughter on a surfboard from the time she was about 3 years old. At 5, Bethany won first place in a Quicksilver Push 'n' Surf contest. In a Push 'n' Surf contest, one person pushes the young surfer into the waves on a surfboard and another catches the surfer. At 8, she took part in her first major competition, winning first place in both the shortboard and longboard divisions. Everyone, including Bethany, believed this was the beginning of a long, successful surfing career.

Bethany kept practicing and competing, coming in first in the 1999 Haleiwa Menehune Contest, and first and second in different divisions of the Volcom Pufferfish Surf Series. She began participating regularly in the National Scholastic Surfing Association (NSSA) competitions. She believed nothing could **impair** her plans to become a professional surfer, earning a living from the sport she loved.

Encountering the Shadow

What happened after the attack of the 15-foot tiger shark on October 31, 2003? Holt and Byron reached the injured Bethany and began pulling her to shore, a 20-minute paddle, as Bethany held onto them with her right hand. Holt tied his rash guard around the wound so Bethany would not bleed so much as they paddled. On shore, he tied a surfboard leash around Bethany's wounded arm to stop the bleeding.

An ambulance carried her 30 minutes to the hospital, where her father was about to have a knee operation. His doctor left him in the operating room to check on the emergency, and when Bethany's father heard a surfer had been attacked, he feared the worst. Bethany took her father's place on the operating table. **1**

1 Make Connections
How is this story similar to that of Aron Ralston? How is it different?

Giving Your All

Reaching beyond the Shadow

Recovering from surgery, Bethany feared that her ability to surf had been permanently impaired—how could she surf with one arm? Soon her personal faith and love for her sport roused her determination. About three weeks after the ferocious attack, Bethany carried a surfboard into the ocean to experience surfing with just one arm. Her only request was that no one help her catch a wave the first time she tried.

Bethany continued not only to surf, but to compete and to win awards for her competent surfing. In 2004, she won the Best Comeback Athlete of the Year award and a Teen Choice Award for special courage. In 2005, Bethany won first place in the NSSA National Championships, a goal she had set for herself before the shark attack. In 2008, she began participating in international competitions, placing third that year among the world's best women surfers. **2**

Besides surfing, Bethany has appeared on television and written a book, discussing how she survived the difficulties brought about by the ferocious tiger shark. She does not hesitate to tell people about her faith. She believes her impairment has given her the chance to help other people overcome adversity and live with life's difficult challenges. **End**

2 **Inference**

What does winning all these awards tell you about Bethany's character?

9/11: Terror from the Sky

At 8:45 a.m. (EDT) on September 11, 2001, the first hijacked airliner slammed into the north tower of the World Trade Center, ripping a huge hole in the building, setting fires, and sending shock waves of horror around the world. At 9:03 a.m., a second hijacked airliner struck the south tower, exploding into flames. At 10:05 a.m., the south tower **collapsed**, sending piles of burning debris into the New York City streets. At 10:28 a.m., the north tower plummeted to the ground, adding more debris, smoke, and tons of dust. During those 103 minutes, from impact to total collapse, about 2,700 people died, including more than 400 rescue workers. Ordinary citizens became extraordinary in their struggle to survive and to help others survive. For every story of what a person did, hundreds of **heroic** stories remain untold. Each individual story is both a tale of personal courage and a symbol of the courage of all who experienced 9/11.

Jan Demczur
Window Cleaner

Jan Demczur arrived from Poland in 1980 and in 1991 began working at the World Trade Center, where he was a window cleaner. On September 11, he was riding in an elevator in the north tower with several other men, strangers to him. Suddenly, the

Vocabulary

collapsed (v) *fell down suddenly*

heroic (adj) *showing great bravery or daring like a hero*

Vocabulary

gratitude (n) *feeling of being grateful for something; appreciation*

elevator paused, then dropped several floors, coming to a stop between floors. Using the intercom, the occupants of the elevator learned of a problem above the 90th floor—the floors the airliner crashed into. Smoke began filling the elevator, and the air grew hotter as they searched for a way to escape. No longer able to reach anyone on the intercom, they knew they had to save themselves.

Forcing the elevator doors open and breaking through the wall seemed the only way to escape. But, without tools, breaking through the wall could be impossible. Demczur began using the end of his window-cleaning squeegee to dig into the wall. Alfred Smith, one of the other men in the elevator, said "It was like he was meant to do that . . . like he had a willpower that we are going to get out of here." Eventually, the men kicked through into a 50th-floor restroom, raced down the stairs, and exited the building about five minutes before it collapsed. Running from showers of falling debris, Demczur was fortunate to remain safe. He felt **gratitude** for his lucky escape. Demczur's quick thinking and determination saved his own life and the lives of the others in the elevator.

A squeegee handle used by Jan Demczur to escape with five others from an elevator in One World Trade Center is part of an exhibit at the Smithsonian's National Museum of American History.

Rose Riso
Office Worker

Rose Riso took her responsibility as fire warden of her office on the 86th floor of the south tower of the World Trade Center very seriously.

When the first airliner crashed into the north tower, workers in the south tower had no idea how serious the situation was. Her coworkers, thinking it was another fire drill, wondered why Riso wasn't wearing her cute fireman's hat and whistle. Fortunately for them, Riso immediately began ordering people to evacuate the building as fast as possible. When she began yelling for them to get out, they knew something serious had happened.

Many of Riso's coworkers boarded the elevator to exit seconds before the second plane crashed into their tower. Riso remained in the office, hurrying people out. What happened to Riso is unknown; she remains one of 24 people missing after the collapse of the towers. Only her identification badge was discovered in the wreckage. The story of her actions to help others

1 Inference

What in this paragraph tells you the men's escape from the elevator was heroic?

during this attack is told by the coworkers she saved. Those coworkers feel a sense of gratitude for Riso's selfless courage, and they consider her a hero. **2**

2 **Summarize**
What did Riso do to get people to safety?

Two Unnamed Firefighters
To Certain Death

Among the firefighters and police officials who participated in rescue attempts at the World Trade Center, most who survived said they were not heroes—they were doing their jobs. However, from the viewpoint of the fortunate people whose lives they saved, they were heroes, and they deserve gratitude.

Survivors tell of two unnamed firefighters who were climbing up the stairs of the north tower after the plane hit. People trying to leave the building jammed the stairwells and had begun to panic. These firemen walked past, calmly telling people to keep walking down, and assuring them they would get out safely if they remained calm. Then people walked down and out of the building in a more orderly way. No one is certain of their names, but these two firefighters almost certainly sacrificed their own lives to help others. **End**

Firefighter Mike Kehoe holds a copy of a photograph taken as he heads up the stairwell in the World Trade Center. John Labriola, who had an office on the 71st floor of the building, snapped the picture as he passed Kehoe. The photo, seen all over the world, is a symbolic image of that tragic day. Kehoe doesn't want to be called a "hero," but recognizes that for some, he holds an iconic place in the story of September 11.

Flight 93

81 Minutes to Doom

On September 11, 2001, Flight 93 lifted off at 8:42 a.m. (about 40 minutes late) from New Jersey heading for California. Each of the 44 people on board had a personal story for being on that horrific and historic flight, but fate would soon draw them together into a tale of **anguish**, terror, and unexpected **valor**.

Upon takeoff, the crew didn't notice anything unusual. They didn't know that minutes after their takeoff, Flight 11 from Massachusetts to California had been piloted by terrorist hijackers and flown into the north tower of the World Trade Center. Eighteen minutes later, another airliner, Flight 175, had slammed into the second tower. **1**

At 8:37 a.m., the Federal Aviation Administration (FAA) notified the North American Aerospace Defense Command (NORAD) that Flight 11 had been hijacked. F-15 jet fighters scrambled from Otis Air Force Base, but no one knew where to send them. Confusion mounted on the ground as air traffic personnel tried to evaluate the situation in the skies. Meanwhile, Flight 77, having also

1 Make Connections
How does this information compare with the information you read in "9/11: Terror from the Sky"?

been hijacked, crashed into the Pentagon. At 9:42 a.m., the FAA issued a nationwide order: "clear the skies." This meant all aircraft had to land immediately. Across the country, 4,500 commercial and general aviation aircraft landed without incident. It would not be so for Flight 93.

Hijackers Take Over

In the cockpit of Flight 93, Jason Dahl was the pilot, and Leroy Homer Jr. was the copilot. At 9:24 a.m., a notice from an airline controller

Jason Dahl

appeared on the flight monitor; the message warned "Beware any cockpit intrusion: two aircraft hit World Trade Center." Dahl asked for confirmation of this message that warned of attack.

Meanwhile in the cabin, three passengers rose from their seats and tied red bandannas to their heads; one claimed to have a bomb. A fourth hijacker was somewhere else in the airliner. Armed with knives, two of the hijackers stormed the cockpit to seize control. Ground control officials heard sounds of a very noisy **confrontation** and the phrase, "Hey, get out of here."

At 9:32, one of the hijackers in the cockpit announced to the passengers—on a microphone that also transmitted to controllers on the ground—"Ladies and Gentlemen; here the captain. Please sit down keep remaining seating.

We have a bomb on board. So sit." The poor English did not go unnoticed; obviously, the hijackers had taken over. At 9:35, the aircraft turned east.

At 9:41, ground control lost radar contact with Flight 93, and signals that normally confirm the aircraft and its location stopped. **2**

Anguished Communications

Most captive passengers had been herded into the rear of the plane by the hijackers, and many used cell phones and Airfones to reach families, friends, and officials. Relatives and friends listened with anguish to their loved ones, fearing the worst.

Passenger Tom Burnett called his wife Deena four times. Deena told him at 9:34 about the attack on the World

Tom Burnett

Trade Center, then she listened with anguish as Tom said, "They're talking about crashing this plane. Oh my God, it's a suicide mission." At 9:45, Tom called again, and told his wife that a group of passengers was putting a plan together. The last she heard from Tom was at 9:54, when he told her, "Don't worry. We're going to do something."

Todd Beamer was on an Airfone talking with an operator for

Todd Beamer

2 Visualize

Think about the description of the action in the plane. What do you see? How does it make you feel?

13 minutes, asking her to inform the authorities, to pray, and to take messages for his wife, Lisa. He told the operator they planned to jump the guy who they believed had the bomb, and before he hung up, he said, "Let's roll."

By 9:58, cell phone communication ended, probably because the passengers started to try to break into the cockpit to regain control. The flight recorder captured noise and confusion, with the hijackers discussing if they should "pull it down."

The Final Moment

At 10:03, the airliner crashed near Shanksville, Pennsylvania, killing everyone on board. **3** The passenger revolt had prevented the aircraft from reaching its planned destination, and the valor of those passengers may have saved hundreds or thousands of innocent lives.

Victims' relatives have received certificates praising the patriotic valor of those on Flight 93. The incident has been called the first victory of the War on Terrorism, but it cost 40 innocent lives. End

Lisa Beamer and son David, 4, unveil a decal on the nose of an F-16 fighter jet in 2002. The decal memorializes the famous fighting words of Lisa's husband, Flight 93 victim Todd Beamer. The Air Force announced that the decal would be applied to select aircraft throughout the Air Force and Air National Guard.

3 Inference

If everyone on board was killed, how do we know details about the hijackers' actions? Support your inference with evidence from the story.

Glossary

abyss	(n) a very deep hole that seems to have no bottom
academic	(adj) having to do with schools, colleges, or teaching
accumulation	(n) the process of piling up, collecting, or gathering over a period of time
accurate	(adj) correct; without mistakes or errors
achieve	(v) succeed in doing; accomplish
acknowledge	(v) admit to be real or true
activities	(n) things you do
acute	(adj) sharp
adhere	(v) stick with an idea, plan, or rules
adorn	(v) decorate
advanced	(adj) not simple or easy
affect	(v) bring about a change
alter	(v) change
alternative	(adj) allowing a choice between two or more things
amended	(v) changed
amplifies	(v) makes louder or stronger
analysis	(n) a careful study or examination of something
anguish	(n) great suffering caused by worry, grief, or pain; agony
antidote	(n) a substance that works against something that has caused bad effects
appropriate	(adj) suitable or right
approximately	(adj) almost exactly
assembled	(v) gathered together in one place
assert	(v) behave in a strong, confident way so that people notice you
assess	(v) determine the importance, size, or value of something
associate	(v) connect together
attributes	(n) qualities or characteristics that describe a person or thing
authority	(n) power
avoid	(v) keep away from

B

background	(n) a person's training and experience
bear	(v) put up with something
behavior	(n) the way someone acts
benefit	(v) get an advantage from something; be helped by something
bias	(v) cause someone's way of thinking to change to be in favor of or against
blunders	(n) ideas, answers, or acts that are wrong; mistakes

C

captured	(v) emphasized, represented, or preserved (as in a mood) in a permanent form
catalyst	(n) a substance that makes a chemical reaction happen at a faster rate
categorized	(v) grouped things based on similarities
cautious	(adj) tries to avoid mistakes or danger
characterized	(v) marked or identified with certain qualities
chemicals	(n) substances formed when two or more other substances act upon one another
civilians	(n) people who are not in the military
coincidence	(n) when things happen by accident and are not connected to each other
collapsed	(v) fell down suddenly
commerce	(n) the buying and selling of goods; trade
commotion	(n) a lot of noisy, excited activity
community	(n) all the people who live in a particular area
compelled	(v) made someone do something by giving him or her orders or using force
compete	(v) try hard to outdo others in a contest
competent	(adj) having the skill or ability to do something well
complex	(adj) very complicated; not simple
concept	(n) thought; general idea
concludes	(v) forms an opinion after thinking
conditioned	(adj) learned
conform	(v) act in an expected way

confrontation	(n) an open conflict or clashing of forces
conservative	(adj) traditional or modest
consumers	(n) people who buy products or services; customers
contain	(v) hold within itself; include
contemporary	(adj) at the present time
contributes	(v) has a part in bringing about
contrived	(v) formed or created in a specific way
control	(v) be in charge of; direct
controversy	(n) a discussion or argument over an issue
convenience	(n) something that is useful and easy to use
convert	(v) make a thing into something else
convey	(v) tell or communicate
coordinate	(v) work well together
correspond	(v) write to someone
crisis	(n) a time of great danger or difficulty; anxiety about the future
critical	(adj) especially important
crucial	(adj) important
culture	(n) a way of life, ideas, customs, and traditions specific to a group of people
current	(adj) of the present time; most recent
customs	(n) ways of doing things that have been done for a long time and are widely accepted or have become traditions

D

debate	(v) discuss something
deceived	(v) fooled or tricked; misled
defend	(v) protect something or someone from harm
deliberate	(adj) planned or intended
depend	(v) rely on someone or something
depicted	(v) showed something in a picture or by using words
depleted	(v) reduced in number or quantity so as to endanger the ability to function
design	(n) the particular plan that is followed to make something work
desperate	(adj) very serious with little or no hope

determine	(v) reach a decision about something after thinking about it
develop	(v) work out the possibilities of something
developed	(v) created or produced over time
devices	(n) pieces of equipment that serve a special purpose
devoted	(adj) loyal and loving
differentiate	(v) show a difference between two things
diluted	(adj) thinned out or weakened by adding water
disabilities	(n) physical or mental handicaps
disapproval	(n) a negative or bad thought about something
disastrous	(adj) causing great distress or injury
discern	(v) recognize or identify
discriminate	(v) make a difference in treatment on a basis other than individual merit
distinct	(adj) clearly different
diverged	(v) branched out; split apart
diverse	(adj) varied or assorted
domestic	(adj) to do with the home; not wild
dominated	(v) controlled

E

ecology	(n) the balance between people's lifestyles and the living things on Earth
effects	(n) the results or consequences of something
efficient	(adj) bringing about the wanted result using the least amount of time, materials, or effort
elaborate	(adj) very detailed
eliminated	(v) left out or got rid of
emphasize	(v) give special attention to; put stress upon
employment	(n) a person's work; job
encourage	(v) attempt to persuade
endeavors	(v) tries very hard to do something
energy	(n) the power of certain forces in nature to do work
enforced	(v) made to obey
enhance	(v) make greater or better
enrich	(v) make better by adding something

environment	(n) all the conditions surrounding plants, animals, and people that affect the health, growth, and development of those living things
established	(v) brought about; made firm or stable
ethnic	(adj) to do with a group of people sharing the same national origins, language, or culture
evaluate	(v) decide the condition or value of someone or something after thinking carefully about it
exact	(adj) perfectly correct
except	(prep) apart from; not included in the general rule
exchange	(v) give one thing and receive another
excretes	(v) passes waste matter out of the body
exhibited	(v) showed
expanding	(adj) growing bigger or wider
experience	(n) something a person has done or lived through
expert	(adj) very skilled at something
explore	(v) discuss or think about carefully
express	(v) show what you feel or think by saying, doing, or writing something

F

factors	(n) things that help produce a result
fashion	(n) the popular or up-to-date way of dressing, speaking, or behaving; the style
fathom	(v) understand
ferocious	(adj) fierce; savage
fiends	(n) evil or cruel people
financial	(adj) having to do with money matters
focus	(v) fix attention on something
foreign	(adj) having to do with another country
forfeit	(v) have to give up or lose something because of a failure to do something
founders	(n) people who start or establish something
frail	(adj) weak
fraud	(n) an act of deceiving or misrepresenting; a trick
frequently	(adv) often
fundamental	(adj) basic or main; serving as the basis

generated	(v) produced; created
genuine	(adj) real; not fake
globe	(n) Earth
goods	(n) things that can be bought or sold; products
government	(n) those people in control of a nation, state, or city
gratitude	(n) feeling of being grateful for something; appreciation
grave	(adj) significantly serious
gruesome	(adj) causing fear and disgust; horrible

H

habitat	(n) place where an animal or plant is normally found
heroic	(adj) showing great bravery or daring like a hero
hybrid	(n) something that has two different parts performing essentially the same function

I

ideal	(adj) perfect; very suitable
identity	(n) who you are
image	(n) a picture or other likeness of a person or thing
impact	(n) the power of something such as an event or idea to cause changes or strong feelings
impair	(v) weaken or damage
imported	(adj) from another country
impose	(v) set as something that has to be paid, obeyed, or fulfilled
incorporate	(v) make a part of something else
incorrigible	(adj) difficult or impossible to control
indeed	(adv) certainly
individual	(n) a single being or thing
infinitely	(adv) endlessly; in a never-ending fashion
influence	(v) have power over something or someone
ingredient	(n) one of the items that something is made from
initial	(adj) first; at the beginning
innocent	(adj) not guilty; did not do something wrong
inquiry	(n) examination of the facts; investigation
inspiring	(adj) stimulating or exalting to the spirit

instances	(n) occurrences or things that happen
instinct	(n) behavior that is natural, not learned
instruct	(v) teach
instruments	(n) objects used to make music
intense	(adj) involving or showing extreme effort
interacted	(v) acted between each other
intricate	(adj) detailed and complicated
involve	(v) include

J

judgment	(n) a conclusion or opinion

K

keenly	(adv) being sharp and quick

L

labyrinth	(n) a place full of intricate passageways
loyal	(adj) faithful to someone or something

M

majority	(n) the greater part or number of something; more than half
manage	(v) succeed in getting something done
maneuvers	(n) difficult movements that require planning and skill
manifest	(v) show or demonstrate plainly
manufacture	(v) make products in large amounts
media	(n) the system or people through which information is communicated to society
merchant	(n) a person who buys and sells things to make money
merely	(adv) only; no more than
modern	(adj) having to do with the latest styles, methods, or ideas; up-to-date
morphing	(v) transforming
motion	(n) movement
motive	(n) reason that makes a person do something
mutual	(adj) shared or joint

nature	(n) everything in the physical world that is not made by human beings
negligent	(adj) being careless
nominal	(adj) trifling; insignificant
nominated	(v) named as a candidate for election
nuzzled	(v) put close to something

officials	(n) people who hold important positions in an organization
opinionated	(adj) sticking to one's thoughts, feelings, or beliefs in an excessive way
opposed	(v) went against something; competed
order	(n) a request for something that someone wants to buy or receive
organic	(adj) made using only natural products
organizations	(n) groups of people joined for particular purposes
originated	(v) began from somewhere or something

participate	(v) take part in something with other people
particles	(n) extremely small pieces of something
patterns	(n) repeated sets of actions
peculiar	(adj) strange or odd
perceptibly	(adv) clearly or noticeably
perhaps	(adv) maybe or possibly
persecuted	(v) treated someone cruelly and unfairly because of his or her ideas or beliefs
personal	(adj) one's own; private or individual
phase	(n) a stage in growth or development
physical	(adj) of or relating to the body
politics	(n) the activities of government officials
population	(n) all the people living in a certain place
portray	(v) make a picture or mental image of
positions	(n) jobs
poverty	(n) condition of being poor; lack of money

practical	(adj) useful and sensible
predict	(v) declare that something is going to happen in the future
prejudices	(n) opinions formed by people without knowing the facts or by ignoring the facts
prescribe	(v) advise to take a certain medicine or treatment
preserve	(v) protect from harm or damage; keep in a certain condition
presume	(v) take for granted; assume
prevalent	(adj) common or usual
primary	(adj) most important
probable	(adj) likely to happen or be true
produce	(v) make or manufacture
profiles	(n) brief accounts of people's lives
prohibit	(v) forbid by law or by an order
project	(v) cause to be seen on a surface
prominent	(adj) important or famous
protest	(v) object to something strongly and publicly
proverbial	(adj) relating to a proverb, or old familiar saying
purpose	(n) an aim or goal; reason for doing something

Q

qualified	(adj) fit for a given purpose

R

range	(n) between limits; from one extreme to another
rational	(adj) reasonable and sensible
react	(v) act in response to something
reaction	(n) a response to something
recipes	(n) instructions for preparing something
reform	(n) correction of faults or evils
register	(v) make a record of
regulates	(v) controls or manages
reject	(v) refuse to accept or take
remote	(adj) far away, isolated, or distant
renders	(v) makes or causes to become
replicate	(v) make a copy of; duplicate

represent	(v) show or picture something
residential	(adj) characterized by residences, whether houses or apartment buildings
resources	(n) things that are available to take care of a need
response	(n) something that is said or done in answer; a reply
reveal	(v) make known
revolting	(adj) disgusting
risk	(n) the chance of losing, failing, or getting hurt; danger
roots	(n) the source, origin, or cause of something; where it came from

S

seldom	(adv) rarely; not often
selection	(n) a collection of things to choose from
severe	(adj) hard to bear or deal with
severed	(v) cut off or apart
shabby	(adj) run-down; falling apart
significant	(adj) very important
situation	(n) condition or state of affairs
social	(adj) having to do with people coming together in a friendly group
society	(n) people living together as a group with the same way of life
solitude	(n) being alone
soluble	(adj) can be dissolved in liquid
spectacle	(n) a remarkable and dramatic sight
spectrum	(n) a continuous sequence or range
speculate	(v) wonder or guess about something without knowing all the facts
stagnant	(adj) not active
standards	(n) rules or models used to judge how good something is
status	(n) a person's rank or position in a group, organization, or society
stimulus	(n) anything that causes an action
submit	(v) agree to obey something
substance	(n) something that has weight and takes up space; matter

survive	(v) stay alive through or after a dangerous event
suspicion	(n) thought or feeling that something is wrong or bad
symbol	(n) an object that represents something else
synthesized	(v) produced a substance by a chemical or biological process
synthetic	(adj) something man-made or artificial; not found in nature
system	(n) a group of things or parts working together or connected in such a way as to form a whole

T

techniques	(n) ways of doing something that require skill
tenacity	(n) the quality of holding on firmly to something
tenants	(n) people who pay rent to live in a building or apartment
terminate	(v) bring to an end; stop
texture	(n) the look and feel of something
theory	(n) an explanation of how or why something happens
tolerance	(n) acceptance and respect of others and their beliefs
tolerate	(v) put up with; bear
tradition	(n) a custom, idea, or belief that is handed down from one generation to the next
transaction	(n) an exchange of goods, services, or money
transition	(n) a change from one way to another
transport	(v) move from one place to another
treatment	(n) medical method to try to cure or heal
trek	(v) make a slow, difficult journey
tribute	(n) something done, given, or said to show thanks or respect
typically	(adv) how things usually are; generally

U

unique	(adj) out of the ordinary; one of a kind
united	(v) brought together
universal	(adj) found everywhere; shared by everyone and everything
urban	(adj) to do with the city

V

vainly	(adv) unsuccessfully; futilely
valor	(n) courage or bravery
various	(adj) of differing kinds; representing a variety
vary	(v) be different
vast	(adj) huge in area or extent
venture	(v) put oneself at risk by doing something daring or dangerous
vicious	(adj) meant to harm; cruel
viewpoint	(n) a way of thinking about something; attitude; point of view
vile	(adj) low in worth; unpleasant
visible	(adj) able to be seen or noticed
visual	(adj) having to do with sight or used in seeing
vital	(adj) very important
volume	(n) loudness

W

wedged	(v) forced your way into or through

LITERATURE CREDITS

PHOTO AND ART CREDITS

©iStockphoto.com/blaneyphoto, ©iStockphoto.com/Shawn Gearhart; 190, ©iStockphoto.com/Shawn Gearhart; 191, Getty Images, ©iStockphoto.com/Shawn Gearhart; 192, ©iStockphoto.com/Shawn Gearhart; 193, ©iStockphoto.com/René Mansi, ©iStockphoto.com/Andrey Armyagov; 195, ©iStockphoto.com/Alexander Hafemann, ©iStockphoto.com/Andrey Armyagov, ©iStockphoto.com/pidjoe; 196, ©iStockphoto.com/parema; 197, ©iStockphoto.com/Alex Nikada; 198, Jack Hollingsworth/Getty Images

Expedition 11: 199, Ryan McVay/Stone/Getty Images, ©iStockphoto.com/Nina Matyszcak, Rui Vieira/AP, Chris Johns/National Geographic/Getty Images, ©iStockphoto.com/Steven Allan, ©iStockphoto.com/suemack, Peter Förster/epa/Corbis; 200, David Surowiecki/Getty Images News/Getty Images, ©iStockphoto.com/Dale Taylor; 201, AP Photo/Hidajet Delic, ©iStockphoto.com/Erik Lam; 202, AP Photo/FEMA, Andrea Booher, ©iStockphoto.com/Mel Stoutsenberger; 203, ©iStockphoto.com/Abel Leâo, ©iStockphoto.com/Boris Katsman; 204, Bettmann/Corbis, Manoj Shah/The Image Bank/Getty Images; 205, Behavioural Ecology Research Group -or- BERG, Oxford, Rick Friedman/Corbis; 206, ©iStockphoto.com/CostinT; 207, ©iStockphoto.com/Eric Isselée, Melanie Stetson Freeman/Christian Science Monitor/Getty Images; 208, AP Photo/Xinhua, Zhou Que, altrendo images/Getty Images; 219, ©iStockphoto.com/bojan fatur, ©iStockphoto.com/Mark Hayes; 220, ©iStockphoto.com/Dave Raboin

Expedition 12: 221, EyesWideOpen/Getty Images News/Getty Images; 222, ©iStockphoto.com/Chad Anderson, ©iStockphoto.com/Richard Scherzinger; 223, ©iStockphoto.com/ryan burke, ©iStockphoto.com/Stefan Redel, AFP/Getty Images; 224, Steve Smith/Getty Images, Stockbyte/Getty Images; 225, ©iStockphoto.com/Wojtek Kryczka, ©iStockphoto.com/Shawn Gearhart, 2009 © jojojojo. Image from BigStockPhoto.com; 226, ©iStockphoto.com/Mark Atkins, ©iStockphoto.com/Shawn Gearhart; 227, ©iStockphoto.com/Jim Jurica, Jyrki Komulainen/Getty Images, ©iStockphoto.com/Shawn Gearhart; 228, Paul Burns/Getty Images, Victoria Firmston/Getty Images, ©iStockphoto.com/Shawn Gearhart; 229, ©iStockphoto.com/Michael Krinke; 230, ©iStockphoto.com/Gautier Willaume, ©iStockphoto.com/Dieter Hawlan, ©iStockphoto.com/Nathan Gleave; 231, ©iStockphoto.com/Jan Rysavy; 232, *Adapted and reproduced with permission from Hansen, J, et al. Global temperature change. PNAS 103(39), September 26, 2006. Copyright 2006 National Academy of Sciences, U.S.A.*; 233, ©iStockphoto.com/James Richey; 235, ©iStockphoto.com/Pali Rao, ©iStockphoto.com/

Terrance Emerson, ©iStockphoto.com/Daniel Halvorson, ©iStockphoto.com/zentilia; 236, ©iStockphoto.com/Patricia Schmidt, ©iStockphoto.com/Pali Rao; 237, ©iStockphoto.com/Andreas Weber, ©iStockphoto.com/Jon Helgason, ©iStockphoto.com/Pali Rao; 238, ©iStockphoto.com/Björn Kindler, ©iStockphoto.com/Pali Rao; 239, ©iStockphoto.com/Daniel Tero, ©iStockphoto.com/Pali Rao; 240, ©iStockphoto.com/Gene Chutka, AFP/Getty Images, ©iStockphoto.com/Pali Rao; 241, ©iStockphoto.com/Jason Lugo, ©iStockphoto.com/Alistair Scott, ©iStockphoto.com/Loic Bernard, ©iStockphoto.com/Sandeep Subba; 42, ©iStockphoto.com/David Kay, ©iStockphoto.com/emholk

Expedition 13: 243, Joe Picciolo/AFP/Getty Images; 244, Olympic rings courtesy USOC, Michael Steele/Getty Images Sport/Getty Images; 245, CORR/AFP/Getty Images/Getty Images, Photo courtesy Waseda University Archives; 246, Associated Press, Sandra Behne/Bongarts/Getty Images; 247, HP_photo, Bettmann/Corbis; 248, Chicago Historical Society, Gary Paul Lewis; 249, NBAE/Getty Images; 250, ©iStockphoto.com/John Franco, Stanley Lumax; 251, ©iStockphoto.com/Ana Abejon; 252, DKP/Getty Images, fStop Images/Getty Images; 253, ©iStockphoto.com/tracy tucker, AFP/Getty Images; 254, Scott Camazine/Getty Images, ©iStockphoto.com/geopaul; 255, Visuals Unlimited/Corbis, NFL/Getty Images; 256, AFP/Getty Images; 257, Tasos Katopodis/Getty Images Sport/Getty Images; 258, ©iStockphoto.com/Mario Hornik, ©iStockphoto.com/Piotr Sikora; 259, Al Bello/Getty Images Sport/Getty Images; 260, AFP/Getty Images; 261, ©iStockphoto.com/Nikada, ©iStockphoto.com/DNY59; 262, ©iStockphoto.com/iofoto

Expedition 14: 263, AP Photo/Frans Dellian; 264, ©iStockphoto.com/Peeter Viisimaa, ©iStockphoto.com/Peeter Viisimaa; 265, MedicalRF.com/Getty Images, ©iStockphoto.com/Sergey Kashkin, DEA Picture Library/Getty Images; 266, ©iStockphoto.com/David T Gomez, ©iStockphoto.com/microgen; 267, AP Photo/Las Vegas Sun, Steve Marcus, Jose Jimenez/Primera Hora/Getty Images News/Getty Images; 268, ©iStockphoto.com/Anatoly Tiplyashin, Russ Dixon/Photo courtesy of values.com; 269, Team Hoyt; 270, Team Hoyt, ©iStockphoto.com/Yuriy Panyukov; 271, ©iStockphoto.com/Gino Crescoli, Photo courtesy of DePauw University; 272, ©iStockphoto.com/Heidi Kristensen, ©iStockphoto.com/Arman Zhenikeyev; 273, Photo courtesy of Harvard University, AP Photo/Bebeto Matthews; 274, Lisa Blumenfeld/Getty Images Sport/Getty Images, ©iStockphoto.com/itographer; 275, ©iStockphoto.com/Ernesto Solla Dominguez, Jason Szenes/epa/Corbis; 276, From BEYOND BELIEF:Finding the Strength